alternative media

alternative media

chris atton

SAGE Publications
London • Thousand Oaks • New Delhi

First published 2002

Apart from any fair dealing for the purposes of research or
private study, or criticism or review, as permitted under
the Copyright, Designs and Patents Act, 1988, this publication
may be reproduced, stored or transmitted in any form, or by
any means, only with the prior permission in writing of the
publishers, or in the case of reprographic reproduction, in
accordance with the terms of licences issued by the Copyright
Licensing Agency. Inquiries concerning reproduction outside
those terms should be sent to the publishers.

SAGE Publications Ltd
6 Bonhill Street
London EC2A 4PU

SAGE Publications Inc
2455 Teller Road
Thousand Oaks, California 91320

SAGE Publications India Pvt Ltd
32, M-Block Market
Greater Kailash - I
New Delhi 110 048

British Library Cataloguing in Publication data

A catalogue record for this book is available
from the British Library

ISBN 0 7619 6770 2
ISBN 0 7619 6771 0 (pbk)

Library of Congress Control Number available

Typeset by SIVA Math Setters, Chennai, India
Printed and bound in Great Britain by Athenaeum Press, Gateshead

contents

illustrations

acknowledgements

I would like to thank my colleagues in alternative media studies, Jay Hamilton and Nick Couldry, who were generous enough to read and comment on various draft chapters of this book. John Downing read the entire first draft and offered much pertinent criticism: I am in his debt. Their encouragement kept me going at dark moments. Natalie Fenton, Simon Frith, Peter Golding and Tony Harcup provided much welcome enthusiasm, support and criticism for this project. Sharif Gemie and Jon Purkis at *Anarchist Studies* trusted me: had they not, much of this work would be undone. Parts of the book began life as my PhD thesis: I thank my supervisors David Finkelstein, Alistair McCleery and Desmond Bell for their support and criticism, also my examiners George McKay and Ian Welsh. Numerous colleagues in the Popular Culture Association and the Media Studies, Communication and Cultural Studies Association provided much opportunity for discussion of the main themes of this work. I must also thank those editors, writers and readers who so generously and patiently answered my questions. Lucy Green at *Popular Music* cheered me up at an important moment. Thanks to Earache Records, Cyclops Records and Champagne Lake Productions for sonic refreshment in the final stages. Julia Hall, my editor at Sage, placed much faith in me – I hope it is repaid here. As is customary, I end by thanking those who had to endure this project out of hours: Kate, Daniel and Jacob. And Godzilla.

An earlier version of Chapter 2 appeared as 'A Re-assessment of the Alternative Press', *Media, Culture and Society*, 21(1), January 1999, 51–76. Parts of Chapter 6 appeared in earlier forms as parts of 'Are There Alternative Media after CMC?', *M/C Reviews*, 12 April 2000. <http://www.uq.edu.au/mc/reviews/features/politics/altmedia.html> and 'Anarchy on the Internet: Obstacles and Opportunities for Alternative Electronic Publishing', *Anarchist Studies*, 4(2), October 1996, 115–132. The material on *Green Anarchist* in Chapters 4 and 5 first appeared as part of '*Green Anarchist*: A Case Study in Radical Media', *Anarchist Studies*, 7(1), March 1999, 25–49.

introduction

In his fine book *Why Study the Media?* Roger Silverstone (1999: 103) affirms that alternative media 'have created new spaces for alternative voices that provide the focus both for specific community interests as well as for the contrary and the subversive'. It is all of these – the community, the contrary and the subversive – that are the subject of my book. Silverstone talks of the employment of mass media techniques 'to pursue a critical or alternative agenda, from the margins, as it were, or from the underbelly of social life'. How this is done and what it means to people who do it are similarly my concerns. To decide what alternative media are and how they may be considered alternative are tasks not easily achieved (indeed, a large part of this book wrestles with these fundamentals). In discussing my work with colleagues and friends I am most often asked two questions. The first is: Do alternative media still exist? For these questioners alternative media mean the underground press of the 1960s (such as *Village Voice* and *The Rat* in the US, *Oz* and *IT* in the UK). The question fixes these media historically as counter-cultural emanations – it also considers them as enterprises of the past. If their aims had not been achieved, they had at least been abandoned when their editors, writers and readers moved on to more mature activities (steady jobs, families, mortgages). The simple answer is: Of course they do. Examples abound. Far from disappearing in the early 1970s alternative media have burgeoned. The rise of the fanzine as an integral part of the punk subculture of the late 1970s was instrumental in generating a second wave of underground-like publications that dealt as much with the politics of liberation, direct action and anarchism as they did with popular music. This takes us to our second question: What are alternative media? For whilst the underground press of the 1960s, the punk fanzines of the 1970s and the direct-action papers of the 1990s offer examples that are more or less culturally and politically congruent (despite their apparent differences – at the time, the worst thing you could say about a punk fanzine was that it took its influence from the hippie press) – it is unlikely that these exhaust the list of candidates for inclusion as 'alternative media'.

Do we use 'alternative' as a catch-all for anything that isn't available at our local newsagents? Is it a synonym for 'underground', 'radical', 'oppositional' – even 'samizdat'? We might look beyond paper formats to video (such as the work of the Videofreex of the early 1970s or of the video activists of the 1990s); television (the radical Deep Dish satellite network in the US or the local community TV stations in the UK); radio (pirates or local micro-broadcasters); and inevitably the hybrid forms of communication and media that the Internet and the World Wide Web have enabled. Nor need the 1960s be our historical reference point. The radical wing of the English underground at that time took their cue from the English radical newspapers of the late eighteenth and early nineteenth centuries. Some, such as *Black Dwarf*, took both their revolutionary politics and their titles from such ancestors. Might we not even consider the inflammatory pamphlets of Abiezer Coppe, writing during the English Revolution, as alternative media? On both sides of the Atlantic, working-class organizations and communities have been producing their own media for at least the past two centuries. Now firmly separate, the traditions of socialism and anarchism were at one time more closely concerned with developing media of political value to both: such projects flourished during the late eighteenth and early nineteenth centuries (Quail, 1978). To these we can add the publications of new social movements, the political and the sexual, environmentalism, the gay and lesbian movement and feminism. Nor need we stop there. Any comprehensive audit of alternative media activity is almost impossible (which is not to say that such attempts are not without value: Atton, 1996a and Noyce, 1979 present useful guides to the literature, though both are very much products of their time). Many titles circulate in small numbers to specialist or elite groups; most never appear in newsagents or bookshops. Many cease publishing after a handful of issues (if that). In Edinburgh, Scotland, where I work and live, I wonder what happened to *Auld Reekie's New Tattoo? The Stockbridge and Newtown Rocket? Scottish Anarchist?* Perhaps they came to a close, their work done, their ambition achieved. Perhaps the money dried up or no one would distribute them. Perhaps no one cared enough.

This book does not attempt to be a comprehensive survey of alternative media, neither culturally, politically nor historically. This is not to ignore history: indeed, much of my argument rests on, if not historical continuity, at least on historical 'congruence' at one level or another. The study is, I hope, grounded in the histories of alternative media from the past two centuries. Rather than attempt a history that runs roughshod over political and cultural contingencies and that flattens out economic and social differences in its haste to construct a narrative of alternative media *avant la lettre*, I ground my study historically at appropriate junctures where contemporary study and historical record can illuminate one another. I have no wish to rewrite (at least) 200 years of popular struggle and radical democratic projects as though all they told us was the story of 'alternative media'. My study then begins with the alternative media of the 1990s, for two reasons. First, this is the period I know best; my own research has to date concentrated on that decade. Second, though most studies of alternative media could be far more detailed for any period, the 1990s are especially poorly represented. This is unfortunate, given the rise in independent and small-scale publishing the decade has seen, particularly the explosion of fanzines and zines since the 1980s. The new social movements centred on environmentalism and anarchism, and the attendant prominence of direct action and grassroots organizing and protests have also proved fertile ground for alternative media production. Whilst there is no shortage of writing on the movements themselves, their media are largely untouched. Lastly there is the use of electronic media, in particular the array of computer-mediated communication strategies available across the Internet. Although there is a vast range of media practices in current use I draw primarily on examples from the UK and the US in printed and computer-mediated media (despite what many pundits will have us believe, the printed page is far from moribund – nowhere does it appear more vigorous than in its alternative manifestations).[1] I make no apology for the detail of many of these examples: in a subject that is still developing and for which in some circles a case still needs to be made, I think it important to provide case studies that at times approach ethnography and at others offer close textual and organizational readings. This relates especially to the studies of new social movement media of Chapters 4 and 5 where my arguments proceed from detailed analyses of organization, writing and knowledge production. These arguments are then applied to a wider range of alternative media production, such as community media.

First I will work through some of the definitional problems that beset the study of alternative media, going on to propose ways of examining instances of a set of media practices which, whilst in need of a name, are hardly explained at all simply by being called 'alternative media'. It is with definitions that I begin in Chapter 1. Rather than attempt to define alternative media solely by content I propose a theoretical and a methodological framework that incorporates content as one element in an alternative media culture that is equally interested in the processes and relations that form around alternative media production. That is, I define alternative as much by their capacity to generate non-standard, often infractory, ods of creation, production and distribution as I do by their content. course, the two can hardly be separated at times. The radical deployment of collage in a punk fanzine is as much a process as a product. Similarly the practice of anti-copyright encourages readers to make their own copies of another's publication, as well as providing raw material for new titles. I am also concerned here with Benjamin's (1934/1982) notion of position and attitude in propaganda. Rather than merely reproducing an argument as content in a publication Benjamin held that, for the propaganda to be effective, the medium itself required transformation: the position of the work in relation to the means of production had to be critically realigned, not merely the argument on the page. This requires not only the radicalizing of methods of production but a rethinking of what it means to be a media producer. Alternative media, I argue, are crucially about offering the means for democratic communication to people who are normally excluded from media production. They are to do with organizing media along lines that enable participation and reflexivity. Raymond Williams (1980) highlighted three aspects of democratic communication which we might consider as foci for this realignment: decapitalization, deprofessionalization and deinstitutionalization. The following chapters include detailed instances of how the framework presented in Chapter 1 can be applied to the study of contemporary alternative media.

Chapter 2 examines decapitalization as a function of the economics of production. It is particularly interested in the circulation and distribution of the alternative press, both within its 'alternative public sphere' and in its attempts to break out of its ghetto and reach a wider audience. At its heart is an examination of the alternative press as an economic enterprise, albeit one which has sought to find alternatives to mainstream ways of doing business, just as it has sought to find alternative organizational methods. It also explores the reprographic technologies employed by the alternative press since the 1960s and its circulation and its distribution, in order to gauge how it is influenced by low finance. Finally it examines forms of distribution peculiar to the alternative press, such as anti-copyright and 'open distribution' which not only impact upon economics but also offer creative and productive models for readers to become media producers.

Chapter 3 develops this interest in economics to examine how the zine (and the fanzine before it) provides cheap methods of promoting and sustaining identity and community. Here we also begin an examination of deprofessionalization. The zine offers arguably the most vivid exemplar of the do-it-yourself ethic of alternative media production. A zine may be simply handwritten, photocopied cheaply and stapled by its editor, requiring no professional skills at all. Further, what in mass media enterprises are discrete roles, in zine culture become collapsed into one: an editor is often the sole writer, designer, paste-up artist, finisher and distributor. Despite this, zine culture has tended towards elitism. This chapter goes to examine how the use of the Internet to produce zine-like communication transforms this type of alternative media production and opens it up to a far wider range of people.

When media are used by new social movements the simplicity of the single-person publication is left behind and problems of organizing a medium to encourage a large group of deinstitutionalized activists appear. Chapter 4 focuses on these problems in organization, in particular those of the collective. Within alternative media practices, this notion is mostly concerned with collective approaches to policy-making and consensual decision-making. This chapter examines how appropriate collective models are for such organizations, and the opportunities and threats they present. Is the collective merely a utopian model, whereas the everyday activity is undertaken by a small elite? Many media privilege small-scale 'affinity groups' that work together with almost no hierarchical formation and an absence of bureaucracy. Those involved in the production of the media might be as interested in their prefigurative political roles as they are in what they are writing – once again, there is an interest in position, not simply in attitude. Such media open themselves up to continual democratization as more people see the potential for working from such positions. Radically participatory methods of organization may well form the seedbed for transforming readers into writers. This is the central topic of Chapter 5. More broadly, this chapter also asks: Who contributes to the alternative media? and identifies the extent to which 'experts' and professional writers contribute to new social movement media. It introduces the notion of 'native reporters' – activist-writers who write from a position of marginalization in order to attract power to the social movement to which they belong. Finally, this chapter addresses the production and reception of knowledge in alternative media. What types of knowledge are presented there and for whom? Who reads the media? For what purpose? We must note that the opportunity for all readers to become writers is no guarantor of a comprehensive set of discourses; even less does it guarantee coherence.

My final chapter examines some of the ways in which computer-mediated communication has been employed by new social movements to create new media forms. Choices about which types of media to employ are often as bound up with economic and ideological decisions as they are with notions of 'penetration' and effectiveness (there is, for instance, a significant 'Luddite' tendency amongst the anarchist media). Where Chapter 3 showed Internet-based media opening up alternative media forms to a wider range of participants, here I argue that Internet technology has the capacity to erode the binarism of alternative and mainstream media and the polarities of powerful and powerless, dominance and resistance. Whilst I do not think that this argument upsets my opening definitional and theoretical claims for the distinctiveness of alternative media, it does attest to the difficulty of defining alternative media and to the dangers of over-hasty categorization.

This book approaches the study of alternative media as a process. Perhaps even more than the mass media, which are Roger Silverstone's (1999: 78) concern, they 'are central to experience' because they are 'media that inform, reflect, express experience, our experience, on a daily basis' – if not more than the mass media, then at least in a significantly different manner, in that for those involved in their production, the very creation of such media becomes part of daily life, of quotidian experience. Silverstone argues that the political strength of the media comes from the struggle over cultural forces such as access and participation, ownership and representation. I believe that the study of alternative media – and of their organization, production and dissemination – opens up politically liberating approaches to these 'media on the margins'.

Note

1. This emphasis means that I do not address alternative radio and television in equivalent detail, though Chapters 5 and 6 do deal with alternative video and television projects as part of wider discussions about community media, and information and communication technologies. For a survey of global grassroots and community television initiatives I recommend Tony Dowmunt's (1993) *Channels of Resistance*. Deirdre Boyle (1997) offers a useful study of the pioneers of video and TV activism in the US. For radio I especially admire Jankowski, Prehn and Stappers's (1992) *The People's Voice,* and Amanda Hopkinson's and Jo Tacchi's (2000) edited volume of the *International Journal of Cultural Studies*.

©📖📄💾💾📑📹®

1

approaching alternative media: theory and methodology

Preliminaries

In this chapter I propose a theory of alternative and radical media that is not limited to political and 'resistance' media but which may also account for newer cultural forms such as zines and hybrid forms of electronic communication. It draws principally on the theoretical 'sketches' of Downing (1984), Dickinson (1997) and Duncombe (1997) and expands their work to propose a model that privileges the transformatory potential of the media as reflexive instruments of communication practices in social networks: there is a focus on process and relation.

Alternative and radical media hardly appear in the dominant theoretical traditions of media research. This is surprising, since some theoretical accounts seem to have space for them. The classic Marxist analysis of the media contains within it the seeds of such a space, in that alternative media may be considered as offering radical, anti-capitalist relations of production often coupled to projects of ideological disturbance and rupture. The Gramscian notion of counter-hegemony is discernible through a range of radical media projects (and not only in the obvious places such as the working-class newspapers (Allen, 1985; Sparks, 1985) and radical socialist publications (Downing, 1984)). Attempts to theorize and develop conceptual frameworks for alternative and radical media alone are even sparser. The Frankfurt School appear to have supported an alternative press through Adorno's assertion that the culture industry was best combated by 'a policy of retreatism in relation to the media which, it was argued, were so compromised that they could not be used by oppositional social forces' (cited in Bennett, 1982: 46). Adorno found the mimeograph 'the only fitting ... unobtrusive means of dissemination' to be preferred over the bourgeois-tainted printing press (ibid.).

Enzensberger (1976) has proposed a politically emancipatory use of media that is characterized by (1) interactivity between audiences and creators, (2) collective production and (3) a concern with everyday life and the ordinary needs of people. Denis McQuail has configured this as an extreme of the liberal-pluralist scale, but doubts whether the model is able to withstand such a radical reconception:

> we are now speaking of a version of relationships yet another step further from the notion of dominant media, in which people using small-scale media prevail and large media institutions and undifferentiated content can no longer be found. (McQuail, 1987: 88)

The range, number and diversity of alternative media in all their forms (printed and electronic) and perspectives (single-person zines, large-scale working-class newspapers, radical community newspapers, magazines of sexual politics, anarchist samizdats) suggest the theory of liberal pluralism pushed to its limits. A model of the media where 'people using small-scale media prevail' need not be the product of idealism or entail the overthrow of large-scale media; we may find spaces in which small-scale media already prevail (I shall explore these conceptually later). In a revised edition of McQuail (1987) we find a 'democratic-participant' model (again based on Enzensberger) that is founded on the use of communications media 'for interaction and communication in small-scale settings of community, interest group and subculture' that favour 'horizontal patterns of interaction' where 'participation and interaction are key concepts' (McQuail, 1994: 132). This theory is only superficially limned: nowhere (not even in Enzensberger) is it fully developed. From McQuail (1987) we may also take a warning that perhaps it is more useful to find theoretical purchase for alternative and radical media not in existing accounts of dominant media, but in accounts of the media that oppose such domination. Here I propose a theory of alternative and radical media that proceeds from these accounts. The theory will not be limited to political and 'resistance' media: the intention is to develop a model that will also be applicable to artistic and literary media (video, music, mail art, creative writing), as well as to the newer cultural forms such as zines and hybrid forms of electronic communication (ICTs). Even within a single area of alternative media there is much heterogeneity (of styles, of contributions, of perspectives).

We might consider this range of production as a Foucauldian 'insurrection of subjugated knowledges' (Foucault, 1980: 81). The range of voices that is able to speak directly about these 'subjugated knowledges' moves closer to a situation where 'the Other' is able to represent itself, where analogues of Spivak's (1988) 'native informants' can speak with their own 'irreducibly heterogeneous' voices. Alternative and radical media might then be considered a 'heteroglossic (multiple-voiced) text' (Buckingham and Sefton-Green, cited in Gauntlett, 1996: 91, and drawing on the dialogism of Mikhail Bakhtin) that gives full, heterogeneous voice to all those Others. The model presented here goes further than the textual, however, finding heterogeneity, experimentation and transformation in the principles of organization, production and social relations within and across these media by considering the means of communication as socially and materially produced (Williams, 1980). This approaches Raymond Williams's earlier notion of democratic communication, the origins of which are 'genuinely multiple ... [where] all the sources have access to the common channels ... [and where those involved are able] to communicate, to achieve ... [a]ctive reception and living response' (Williams, 1963: 304).

In his study of zines in the US, Duncombe (1997: 15) talks of his attempts to 'discipline undisciplined subjects'. How well a single theoretical model may 'contain' such diversity will be one of its tests, along with an examination of its explanatory power. I will draw principally on the theoretical 'sketches' presented by three key studies: the politically radical media of the US and Europe in the 1970s and early 1980s (Downing, 1984), a study of British 'cultural alternatives' (Dickinson, 1997) and Duncombe's (1997) study of American zines. I will also use aspects of cultural theory (Bourdieu, 1984, 1993 and 1997).

Defining 'Alternative' and 'Radical'

The apparent looseness in defining terms in this field has led some critics to argue that there can be no meaningful definition of the term 'alternative media' (Abel, 1997). Whilst 'radical' encourages a definition that is primarily concerned with (often revolutionary) social change (and 'Radical' the same for a specific period of English history), 'alternative' is of more general application. Custom and practice within alternative media of the past decade appear to have settled on 'alternative' as the preferred word. As a blanket term its strength lies in the fact that it can encompass far more than radical, or 'social change publishing' can; it can also include alternative lifestyle magazines, an extremely diverse range of zine publishing and the small presses of poetry and fiction publishers. To deploy 'alternative' as an analytical term, however, might afford us little more specificity than saying 'non-mainstream'. Some commentators appear to confuse the two terms.

I think it valuable to look in some detail at the competing definitions of the alternative media. The most conspicuous arguments put forward by both proponents and antagonists of the alternative media are inadequate, since neither offers a sophisticated understanding of the phenomena. In their place I propose a model of the alternative media that is as much concerned with how it is organized within its sociocultural context as with its subject matter. I shall begin, though, with that subject matter.

There is no shortage of studies to show how the mass media characterizes and represents specific social groups in ways suggesting that those groups are blameworthy for particular economic or social conditions, or that they hold extreme political or cultural views. Such groups rarely comprise the powerful and influential elites that routinely have access to such media. By contrast, other groups are marginalized and disempowered by their treatment in the mass media, treatment against which they generally have no redress. The Glasgow University Media Group (1976, 1982, 1985, for example) have shown how trade unions, striking workers and the depiction of industrial relations are portrayed largely from the position of the powerful: the politicians, the company owners and their managers; workers and their representatives, on the other hand, are portrayed at best as irritants, at worst as saboteurs operating outside the bounds of logic and common sense. David Miller's (1994) study of the mainland reporting of Northern Ireland, Todd Gitlin's (1980) examination of the American media's characterizing of the American New Left in the 1960s and Marguerite J. Moritz's (1992) study of the American media's representation of gays and lesbians all point to extremely selective and prejudiced news reporting. I am less interested here in exploring the reasons for the social construction of mass media news (based on a complex of newsroom routines and rituals, conditions of production, notions of professionalism and objectivity, rehearsed standards of writing and editing, as well as accident and opportunity); rather I wish to emphasize the alternative press's responses to such construction as demonstrated not simply by critiques of those media but by their own construction of news, based on alternative values and frameworks of news-gathering and access. In short, these values proceed from a wish to present other interpretations of stories – and to present stories not normally considered as news – which challenge the prevailing 'hierarchy of access' (Glasgow

University Media Group, 1976: 245) normally found in the media. An élite of experts and pundits tends to have easier and more substantial access to a platform for their ideas than do dissidents, protesters, minority groups and even 'ordinary people': 'powerful groups and individuals have privileged and routine entry into the news itself and to the manner and the means of its production' (Glasgow University Media Group, 1980: 114). The aim of that part of the alternative media interested in news remains simple: to provide access to the media for these groups on those groups' terms. This means developing media to encourage and normalize such access, where working people, sexual minorities, trade unions, protest groups – people of low status in terms of their relationship to elite groups of owners, managers and senior professionals – could make their own news, whether by appearing in it as significant actors or by creating news relevant to their situation.

John Fiske (1992d) has pointed out differences between the mainstream media and the alternative media in their selection of news and in the way that selection is made, particularly how the alternative media politicize the 'repression of events' (though Fiske is severely sceptical of the relevance of the alternative press to the quotidian concerns of ordinary people). This remains a continuing, defining characteristic of how much alternative media view their approach to their content. The US pressure group Project Censored produces an annual publication that contains the US's 'top censored stories'. Of the 25 stories presented as 'the news that didn't make the news' in its 1999 volume, only four had been covered by the American mainstream media. Since its founding in 1976, Project Censored has consistently proved the assumption that the alternative media is the home to stories that, for whatever reasons (government advice, commercial pressure from advertisers or cross-media ownership, an innate conservatism in news reporting, news priorities) do not appear in the mainstream media. Whilst no such project exists in the UK, it is possible to find similar examples here too. *Lobster*, the British journal of parapolitics, was the first to break the story about Colin Wallace and 'Operation Clockwork Orange', the MI5 plot to destabilize the Wilson Government. Well before *The Sunday Times* and *Nature* locked horns over the topic, the occasional alternative investigative magazine *Open Eye* published an annotated feature on Peter Duesberg and the AIDS/HIV controversy, which also included notes on where to find more on 'unconventional viewpoints' regarding AIDS. News on some British topics is only to be found abroad: the US journal *Covert Action Quarterly* has published an extensive feature on the targeting of Republican teenagers in Northern Ireland by the British military. In a media culture that appears less and less interested in in-depth investigative reporting, alternative media provide information about and interpretations of the world which we might not otherwise see and information about the world that we simply will not find anywhere else. Alternative publications are at bottom more interested in the free flow of ideas than in profit.

Two American studies demonstrate the significance of alternative media for radical or unconventional content. Patricia Glass Schuman (1982: 3) argues that 'the alternative press – in whatever format – is our modern pamphleteer'. The alternative media employ methods of production and distribution, allied to an activist philosophy of creating 'information for action' timeously and rapidly. As such, they can deal with emerging issues. It is in the nature of such media to have these emerging issues at their very heart, since it is in the nature of activism to respond to social issues as they emerge. Schuman shows how rape as a social issue was first constructed as a 'sex crime' by an alternative press publication – a full year before the *New York Times* identified it as such, and four years before a major book publisher tackled the subject. In the second essay, Terri A. Kettering (1982) examines the issue of rape in more detail, comparing its coverage in the US alternative media and in mainstream publications, along with a similar study of the Iranian revolution of 1970s. In both cases she presents compelling evidence to confirm her thesis that 'in both timeliness and content, the alternative press can be shown to be a more dependable information resource' (1982: 7). Subsequently my own work (for example Atton, 1996a: Ch. 3) has presented further confirmation from a British perspective.

Such arguments bear out the second and third elements of a definition of the alternative press proposed by the Royal Commission on the Press (1977):

1 An alternative publication deals with the opinions of small minorities.
2 It expresses attitudes 'hostile to widely-held beliefs'.
3 It 'espouses views or deals with subjects not given regular coverage by publications generally available at newsagents'.

The Commission went on to emphasize the potential value of '[a] multiplicity of alternative publications [that] suggest satisfaction with an insufficiently diverse established media, and an unwillingness or inability on the part of major publications to provide space for the opinions of small minorities' (1977: 40). It also recognized the marginality of many of the presses, their small print runs and virtual invisibility in the marketplace.

For the most part this assessment rings true. However, the first element of the Commission's definition is contentious: the size of minority audiences is debatable (the alternative media have published and continue to publish for some large minorities: the gay and lesbian media are one example). In the light of mass protest movements, it is arguable whether such views as are propounded in the alternative media are not in fact 'widely-held'. Similarly, John Fiske's (1992a: 47) assertion that much of the alternative media 'circulates among a fraction of the same educated middle classes as does official news' is also contentious. In the light of the accounts of contemporary alternative news production (for example, Dickinson, 1997; Minority Press Group, 1980a; Whitaker, 1981), his further assertion that this represents 'a struggle between more central and more marginalised allegiances within the power-bloc, rather than between the power-bloc and the people' is less credible. Indeed, this would be flatly contradicted by those whose aim in setting up an alternative news publication was to regain power over their lives, since they consider themselves emphatically not of the power bloc.

The editors of *Alternatives in Print* (the major current bibliographical reference work in this field) present three apparently simple criteria against which to test the publishers that appear in their pages. They hold that a publisher can be thought of as alternative if it meets at least one of the following:

1 The publisher has to be non-commercial, demonstrating that 'a basic concern for ideas, not the concern for profit, is the motivation for publication'.
2 The subject matter of their publications should focus on 'social responsibility or creative expression, or usually a combination of both'.
3 Finally, it is enough for publishers to define themselves as alternative publishers. (*Alternatives in Print*, 1980: vii)

Such apparently simple criteria present problems. Whilst non-commerciality is rare enough in mainstream publishing, no indication is given as to how a concern for ideas might be demonstrated. Non-profit-making publishers can easily include charities, some of whose aims might well conflict with what our authors have in mind in their second criterion. Although they do not provide examples of 'social responsibility' the authors are writing from a perspective where we would expect three issues to be prominent: the promotion of sustainable economics, of local communities and of local democracy, all in the face of the increasing globalization and concentration of commercial and political power into a nexus of national government and corporate interests. Unfortunately, the addition in this second criterion of 'creative expression, or usually a combination of both' first of all widens the definition of alternative media to include any type of artistic publication, then apparently narrows it to a category that is, in my experience, rarely encountered in this field: the combination of creative expression and social responsibility. In my survey of British and American alternative presses, I was able to identify many examples of these two categories as separate, but none that combined them. Though the diversity of features that typify the zine might well include both in one cover, this is not to say that there is any articulation between them (Atton, 1996a). The third criterion, that it is 'enough for publishers to define themselves as alternative publishers' hardly needs comment. Since the rise of the zine in the 1980s, many mainstream publishers (mostly newspapers) have tried to capitalize on their attraction to a young readership largely disaffected with the mainstream media by issuing their own ersatz zines (as I shall show in Chapter 3). This last criterion makes no allowance for such deceit.

Finally, these three criteria – and we must bear in mind that they are meant to be separate criteria, for which a publication need only fulfil any one to be considered 'alternative' – ultimately lead us nowhere more precise than does the more common negative definition best summarized by Comedia: 'it is not the established order; it is not the capitalist system; it is not the mainstream view of a subject ...; or it is simply not the conventional way of doing something' (Comedia, 1984: 95).

Such vagueness of nature and intent leaves proponents of the alternative media and the presses themselves open, on occasion, to fierce criticism that questions their very existence. If they cannot even define what they do, why should they be considered as the special cases they so clearly see themselves to be? Richard Abel has argued that, 'what we are left with is a term so elastic as to be devoid of virtually any signification' (Abel, 1997: 79). He claims that the alternative media fail to offer any convincing display of uniqueness in any of three areas: on the grounds of content, on the championing of social change and on the grounds of economic freedom. A constructive definition of alternative media can begin with the presence of radical content, most often allied to the promotion of social change. Some would argue that the availability of Noam Chomsky's political writings at any branch of Waterstone's (when they were once the mainstay of the small press and the anarchist journal) proves that we simply do not need alternative media for the transmission of radical ideas. However, there remains much opportunity for radical content outside the mainstream: the British and American mass media are supremely uninterested in the radical politics of anarchism (in all its hues). Witness the demonization of the term 'anarchist' in mainstream media coverage of the May Day 2000 protests in London or in the coverage of the previous year's protests in Seattle against the World Trade Organization. The equation of anarchism with thuggery (at worst with terrorism) is perennial (Atton, 1996b). By contrast the mass of anarchist journals, magazines, newsletters and web sites offer accounts of working-class resistance and struggles against global capitalism that, whilst highly personalized and explicitly biased, present stories from under the police baton. The electronic archive Spunk Press (examined in more detail in Chapter 6) offers a rare blend of populist rhetoric, activist information and intellectual substance. We may choose not to subscribe to their views, yet they are available in such 'alternative' publications in the absence of case-making elsewhere. And is not the content of most football fanzines radical to some degree? They are certainly oppositional in large part. At their heart is a critique of corporatism as thoroughgoing as any we might find in an anarchist magazine. An editorial in *Not the View*, the Celtic supporters' fanzine, demonstrates this well enough: 'The problem with having the club run by financial investors is that when they look at Celtic they only see a bunch of assets which make money.... When we as fans see Celtic, however, we see something unique and magical.' However idealized the latter statement might be (and however contentious it might be to, say, a Rangers supporter), to redress the former would require a radical programme of social change. *Not the View* may not be setting out a five-year plan, but it is certainly critiquing the causes of the malaise. It is no surprise that the roots of many football fanzines have been seen to lie in the punk fanzine and that such fanzines have exhibited a similar oppositional stance. Some editors of punk fanzines have gone on to edit football fanzines. This argument sees homologies between two groups of fanzines based on their identity as sites of cultural contestation. *Not the View* demonstrates how popular culture can be politicized to social advantage. It is perhaps not too fanciful to see in the football fanzine a way of creating the kind of counter-hegemonic power bloc of which Stuart Hall has talked.

Tim O'Sullivan (1994: 10) introduces the notion of 'radical' social change as a primary aim of 'alternative' media, in that they 'avowedly reject or challenge established and institutionalised politics, in the sense that they all advocate change in society, or at least a critical reassessment of traditional values'. Elsewhere, in defining independent production (which itself can be construed as a part of alternative media) he notes a further two characteristics that set alternative media practice apart from the mainstream:

1. a democratic/collectivist process of production; and
2. a commitment to innovation or experimentation in form and/or content.
   (O'Sullivan et al., 1994: 205)

For O'Sullivan, alternative media argue for social change, seek to involve people (citizens, not elites) in their processes and are committed to innovation in form and content. This set of aims takes into account not only content, but presentation and organizational procedures. It defines alternative media positively and usefully. With these considerations in mind, we can consider Michael Traber's notion of alternative media where:

> the aim is to change towards a more equitable social, cultural and economic whole *in which the individual is not reduced to an object (of the media* or the political powers) but is able to find fulfilment as a total human being. (Traber, 1985: 3; emphasis added)

Traber argues that the conventions of the mass media marginalize the role of the 'simple man and woman', foregrounding instead the rich, the powerful and the glamorous. The former are regarded only as observers or marginal commentators on events (as in the 'vox pop' interview); they achieve prominence only when they are the actors in a situation that is bounded by values based on, for instance, conflict or the bizarre. He divides alternative media into two sectors: advocacy media and grass-roots media.[1] The alternative advocacy media adopt very different news values from the mass media, introducing 'alternative social actors [such as] the poor, the oppressed, the marginalised and indeed the ordinary manual labourer, woman, youth and child as the main subjects of [their] news and features' (Traber, 1985: 2).

It is the grassroots media, Traber argues, that offer the most thorough version of alternative news values. They are produced by the same people whose concerns they represent, from a position of engagement and direct participation. This need not preclude the involvement of professionals, but they will be firmly in the role of advisers, their presence intended to enable 'ordinary people' to produce their own work, independent of professional journalists and editors. Traber is arguing from his experience as a journalist and journalism tutor in India, Zambia and Zimbabwe. His primary concerns are with the production of news and information in areas of these countries where the mass media (if it exists) does not penetrate, but also to provide a counter to the often state-run media or very limited channels for the dissemination of news. This counter, Traber argues, is best provided by local people, often working with a small number of professional journalists. These are not there to set agendas or even to insist on specific working practices; they are there to assist local people in developing their own networks of news-gathering, offer support and instil confidence in them as reporters, writers and editors. Traber is arguing that when media production is placed in the hands of ordinary people the types of news and the style in which it is presented will be more relevant, more 'useful' and more appropriate to the communities in which such news is produced and distributed. Traber presents a set of alternative news values bound up not just with what is considered as news, but also with approaches to news-gathering and with who writes such news and how such news is presented.

This model can be seen as a form of community media. Similar concerns were at the heart of the alternative community newspapers that sprang up in the early 1970s throughout Britain. Community media have at their heart the concepts of access and participation:

> a conviction that the means of communication and expression should be placed in the hands of those people who clearly need to exercise greater control over their immediate environment.... Once this happens, a process of internal dialogue in the community can take place, providing opportunities for developing alternative strategies. (Nigg and Wade, 1980: 7)

A leaflet distributed to publicize the launch of the *Liverpool Free Press* in 1971 proclaimed its difference from mainstream newspapers:

> it's not part of a big newspaper chain and it's not trying to make money. The Free Press believes that as long as newspapers are run by businessmen for profit, there will be news that is not reported. The Free Press aims to report this news. In addition, it tries to provide information which community groups, factory workers, tenants and others will not only find interesting – but useful. The Free Press does not represent the views of any political party or organisation. The paper has no editor or owner – it is controlled by the people who work for it (a group of unpaid volunteers). The Free Press really is a different kind of newspaper. (Whitaker, 1981: 103)

This was certainly a different approach from that taken by the mass media, but the *Liverpool Free Press* was also one in a long historical line of newspapers that sought to be free from commercial considerations and to provide 'ordinary people' with news and information that was directly useful to them in their daily lives. The publicity material for the *Liverpool Free Press* identified three prime elements that it shared with many alternative media ventures: commercial independence (anti-commerciality, even) and the journalistic freedom this was felt to bring; editorial independence from political parties and other organizations; and the empowerment of specific communities of interest (which in the case of the *Liverpool Free Press* and many other similar papers is also a local community).

As an unnamed participant in a seminar led by Noam Chomsky put it: 'by alternative I'm referring to media that are or could be citizen-controlled as opposed to state- or corporate-controlled' (quoted in Achbar, 1994: 197). By such control not only freedom from corporate influence may be obtained, but also the freedom to publish on subjects directly *useful* to citizens and to involve those same citizens in their production.

Whilst the content of such media is clearly important, my concern here is to examine theories of alternative media that privilege the processes by which people are empowered through their direct involvement in alternative media production. Stephen Duncombe has said that 'the culture of consumption can neutralise all dissenting voices' by 'assimilating their content' (1997: 127). In other words, it is not the simple content of a text that is evidence of its radical nature; Duncombe is arguing what many alternative publishers would also argue: that it is the *position* of the work with respect to the relations of production that gives it its power and enables it to avoid recuperation by the mere duplication of its ideas. This is not to deny the significance of content, rather it is to present it within a productive context that can be the radical equal of content in the pursuit of social change. Here I follow Duncombe in his argument that 'the medium of zines is not just a message to be received, but a model of participatory cultural production and organisation to be acted upon' (Duncombe, 1997: 129).

In arguing for social change alternative media may then not only be understood as producing instrumental discourses (theoretical, expository, organizational) to provoke change: following Duncombe, they are able to enact social change through their own means of production, which are themselves positioned in relation to the dominant means of production. Position and attitude both may argue for social change at a number of levels. The change that is looked for need not be structural on a national or supra-national level; it may be local, even individual: for Duncombe even the personal act of becoming a zine editor is a social transformation, regardless of how few copies of the zine are sold (or even made). If the personal may be political, the personal may be of social consequence.

At this stage it is useful to develop a set of characteristics that proceed from the above definitions and place these, rather than definitional competition, at the heart of a theoretical framework. Definitions, in any case, have historical and cultural contingencies. 'Alternative' in West Coast counter-cultural terms invokes 'alternative therapies' and 'New Age' thinking. 'Radical' for some can be as much to do with avant-garde artistic activity as with politics. For zine writers, neither term may be preferable: the even looser 'DIY publishing' might replace both. Does 'radical' always entail 'opposition'? Downing talks of 'radical media' (1984), an 'alternative public realm' (1988), 'alternative media' (1995) and 'radical alternative media' (2001), but he also refers to 'counter-information' and 'popular oppositional culture'. His discussion of Negt and Kluge's (1972/1983) work raises Gramsci's notion of 'counter-hegemony' which, Downing implies, is also a driving force behind the contemporary media he is examining. We might consider the entire range of alternative and radical media as representing challenges to hegemony, whether on an explicitly political platform, or employing the kinds of indirect challenges through experimentation and the transformation of existing roles, routines, emblems and signs that Hebdige (1979) locates at the heart of counter-hegemonic subcultural style. Jakubowicz (1991) finds in 'alternative' a wider meaning: not simply sects or narrow special interests, but a wide-ranging and influential sphere that may include all manner of reformist groups and institutions. Yet its influence is significantly mitigated by state censorship (since its publications are very visible) and its own policy (an interest in long-term survival) prevents it from advocating widespread social change. This last is reserved for an 'oppositional', revolutionary public sphere.

From a sociological point of view, there is a discrepancy between what 'alternative' signifies and what 'oppositional' (and what we might consider its cognates: 'counter-information' and 'counter-hegemony') signifies. It is instructive here to refer to Raymond Williams's interpretation of them:

> Williams made a vital distinction between alternative and oppositional practices. Alternative culture seeks a place to coexist within the existing hegemony, whereas oppositional culture aims to replace it. For instance, there is a world of difference between a minority 'back-to-nature' cult and the ecology movement's global reach. (McGuigan, 1992: 25)

Culturally and politically, then, such media as defined by Downing as 'alternative' and by Jakubowicz as 'oppositional' are perhaps best considered as oppositional in intent, having social change at their heart. This accords with Williams's hope that the culture of the new social movements, although termed an 'alternative' culture, was 'at its best ... always an oppositional culture' (Williams, 1983: 250). In his study of radical media in the US and mainland Europe, Downing (1984) offers one of the few detailed essays into a theory of the media of these oppositional cultures.

Downing's Theory of Radical Media

Downing proposes a set of 'alternatives in principle' that draw on anarchist philosophy, though they do not presuppose any explicit anarchist tendency within any particular publication (indeed, none of Downing's case studies are of anarchist publications; most might be broadly characterized as radical socialist). Instead, he presents these principles in contrast to 'transmission belt socialism', which, he argues, rather than liberating media, constrains them by demanding unquestioning allegiance to the Party, its intelligentsia and the institutions of the State. Revolutionary socialist media, Downing holds, whatever their totalizing claims against the monopolies of the capitalist mass media, are hardly exemplars of media democracy in action: they are as hierarchical, limiting and bound by authority as are the mass media of capitalism. Whilst interested primarily in political media, he is not prescriptive about content: rather he privileges process over product, organization and engagement over words on the page and circulation figures. He argues:

1 the importance of encouraging contributions from as many interested parties as possible, in order to emphasise the 'multiple realities' of social life (oppression, political cultures, economic situations);
2 that radical media, while they may be partisan, should never become a tool of a party or intelligentsia;
3 that radical media at their most creative and socially significant privilege movements over institutions;
4 that within the organisation of radical media there appears an emphasis on prefigurative politics. (Downing, 1984: 17)

Downing was writing before the radical transformation of the Communist countries after 1989 and his arguments against the Party and the State are less urgent today. Neither does Downing offer an historical perspective that stretches back further than the 1960s: the anarchist presses of the US and Europe and the varieties of radical (and Radical) newspapers before them remain untouched, their 'alternatives in principle' unconsidered. Downing also ignores zine culture and the Party newspaper. In his extensively revised edition of this work, Downing (2001) ranges much more widely through history and culture, drawing richly for example on eighteenth- and nineteenth-century political cartoons in Britain, German labour songs of the nineteenth and early twentieth centuries, and nineteenth-century African American public festivals. There is not space here to engage with all these manifestations of radical media that take us well beyond the print and radio media which were Downing's earlier concerns. It is worth, however, examining Downing's updated theoretical perspectives as they proceed from and inform his historical instances. Downing stresses features of his earlier model, particularly the emphasis on multiple realities of oppression (once more he draws on anarchist philosophy, an approach I also find valuable and to which I return throughout this book); organizational models that suggest prefigurative politics; and the privileging of movements over institutions. This last informs his entire approach to the extent that he considers radical media as the media of social movements. As in his 1984 work, this means that single-person or small-group ventures such as fanzines and zines are ignored, as are what some (Downing, amongst them?) might term 'weaker' forms of alternative media such as the personal web page. His approach is reflected in his choice of terminology: he prefers 'radical alternative media' which, he argues, is a more precise term than 'alternative media' ('alternative media is almost oxymoronic. Everything is, at some point, alternative to something else': Downing, 2001: ix). For me his designation signals an interest in considering media as radical to the extent that they explicitly shape political consciousness through collective endeavour (after all, 'rebellious communication and social movements' is the subtitle of his revised work). As we have seen, Downing is now open to a far wider range of media than he was in his 1984 edition, yet his model remains limited by his emphasis on social movements. His nuanced arguments draw on a richer, more subtly layered account of radical media than his earlier work. He brings together considerations of an alternative public sphere, counter-hegemony and resistance, the place of the Gramscian organic intellectual in such media, the role and nature of audiences – all of which I also examine here for the same reason: to move away from the futile 'hunt for sole [social] agents' (Downing, 2001: 98) and to place radical and alternative media as complex 'agents of developmental power, not simply as counterinformation institutions, and certainly not as a vapid cluster of passing gnats' (2001: 45). Downing acknowledges that his earlier binarism (between radical and mainstream media) and 'antibinarism' (seeing in radical media a way forward beyond the then dominant opposition between Western capitalist media and the Soviet model) prevented him from seeing more finely gradated positions, such as the possibility of democratizing mass media or the occasional, radical deployment of mass media. Yet his striving for a more 'impure', hybridized version of radical media is left unfulfilled by his focus on social movements. Hybridity and purity as problematics of alternative media are certainly accessible through an examination of new social movement media, but they can also be approached through media that accommodate themselves rather more cosily with mass media and mass consumption (as in my examination of Jody LaFerriere's personal web site, *The Big DumpTruck!*, in Chapter 3), where a celebration of the banal and the mundane replace political consciousness-raising. The limits of Downing's approach also extend to his coverage of artistic production as an instance of radical alternative media: he considers street theatre and performance art only as media practices of social movements. This leaves no space for the performance art of, say, the Vienna actionists (Green, 1999), or the 'demotic avant-garde' that characterizes the work of British artist Stewart Home (as presented for example in Home, 1995). (Though Downing does make an important point when he reminds us that by considering art, media and communication together we 'do not fall into the trap of segregating information, reasoning and cognition from feeling, imagination, and fantasy' 2001: 52.)

There are resonances with Downing's principles of 'rebellious communication' in the Radical reformist papers that flourished in England from the late eighteenth to the mid-nineteenth century. Amongst these we find a redrawing of technical and professional roles and responsibilities, and social and cultural transformations, such as: (1) clandestine, underground distribution networks; (2) 'pauper management'; (3) journalists seeing themselves 'as activists rather than as professionals'; (4) an interest in 'expos[ing] the dynamics of power and inequality rather than report[ing] "hard news"' (Curran and Seaton, 1997: 15); (5) developing a close relationship with readers – to the extent where many papers were supplied with reports written by readers (such as those by 'worker correspondents' – *Workers' Life*, 1928/1983 and 'reader-writers' – Atton, 1999a); (6) close links with radical organizations, highlighting the value of 'combination' and organized action; and (7) the key role of radical media in a working-class public sphere (Eley, 1992). At this time 'the militant press sustained a radical sub-culture' (Curran and Seaton, 1997: 20). Similar parallels may be found in the anarchist presses of the turn of the century (Hopkin, 1978; Quail, 1978) and of the 1990s (Atton, 1999a), where they also resonate with a larger, non-aligned network of social movement publications centred on radical environmentalism (Carey, 1998; Searle, 1997). This is not to ignore the historical and cultural contingencies of these practices, nor to homogenize their political content or their aims. Alternative media – like any forms of cultural production – and their creators are positioned, 'enunciated': 'we all write and speak from a particular place and time, from a history and a culture which is specific' (Hall, 1990: 222). Social relations, forms of technology and styles of discourse (for example) and their combination are likely to be 'available' for transformation within alternative media at particular places and times. Whilst the bracketing-off of processes (and even content) might afford us conceptual clarity, the better to look closely at what we mean by 'alternative media', we must not forget to recouple them with history and culture when dealing empirically.

Downing's principles also have relevance to the products of 'zine culture' (Duncombe, 1997). This invites further theoretical consideration regarding the radicality of process over content, a consideration which encourages us to account for alternative and radical media with content that is not explicitly political or that has an avowedly non-political content, where the processes of production enable the 'position' of the media and its producers to be radicalized.

Beyond the Political: attitude versus position in alternative and radical media

The separation of attitude and position has been explored by Stephen Duncombe in his work on American zines. For him, it is not the simple content of a text that is evidence of the radical nature of a zine. The content of many zines is hardly politically or socially transforming in itself. Their value proceeds not simply from their content – that is, not from the work's 'attitude toward the oppressive relations of production that mark our society, but [from] the work's position within these relations' (Duncombe, 1996: 315). This draws on Walter Benjamin's idea of 'the author as producer' (Benjamin,1934/1982) which Duncombe goes on to apply to the production of zines. He finds three characteristics that distinguish the production of zines from that of mainstream magazines and that exemplify their position within 'the oppressive relations of production' rather than simply their attitude towards them. First, zine producers are amateurs; second, their product is cheaply produced and promoted by multiple-copying at no profit; third, the distinction between producer and consumer is increasingly blurred.

In his original text, however, Benjamin's analysis goes further than Duncombe takes it. Benjamin argues that an author's works must have 'an organizing function, and in no way must their organizational usefulness be confined to their value as propaganda' (Benjamin, 1934/1982: 216). The development of the zine has encouraged many readers to produce their own publications. Zines developed as vehicles of personal expression; a network of zines arose where horizontal communication between editors and readers became perhaps as important as the production of the zine itself. The very format of the zine – with design and production values that owed more to the copy shop than the printing press – encouraged readers to become editors themselves. As Duncombe notes, 'emulation – turning your readers into writers – is elemental to the zine world' (1996: 123). He draws on Benjamin for support: culture 'is better the more consumers it is able to turn into producers – that is, readers

rs into collaborators' (quoted in Duncombe, 1997: 127).
we can find resonances beyond the immediate genre. An
nple of this may be found not in the zines of the 1980s
ncombe's focus) but from the counter-culture of the 1960s:
⌐uc of the New York underground paper *Other Scenes* once offered
an entirely blank set of pages for readers as a do-it-yourself publishing
project (Lewis, 1972).

Zine culture indicates how radicality can be further located within production values and cultural values. Hebdige extended Kristeva's understanding of 'radical' to account for the punk fanzine's interest in 'the
destruction of existing codes and the formulation of new ones' (see
Hebdige, 1979: 119). Here is an artefact expressive of a subculture (some
argue it is constitutive of a subculture: 'Zines *are* punk,' declared an
anonymous editor of *Hippycore* – Rutherford, 1992: 3). The punk
fanzine stands for much more than an aesthetic preference; the radical
bricolage that characterizes the visual language of punk fanzines (Triggs,
1995), its graphics and typography can be seen as 'homologous with
punk's subterranean and anarchic style' (Hebdige, 1979: 112). Its use of
the photocopier as a liberating agent for the tyro editor became central
to the 'copy culture' that grew out of punk over the next two decades
(*New Observations*, 1994).

Towards a Model of Alternative and Radical Media

Any model must consider not simply the differences in content and
medium/carrier (and its dissemination and delivery) but how communication as a social (rather than simply an informational) process is construed. The question: What is radical about radical media? then becomes
two questions: What is radical about the ways in which the vehicle (the
medium) is transformed? and: What is radical about the communication
processes (as instances of social relations) employed by that media?
Dahlgren (1997) has observed that the focus of media research continues
to move away from the 'classic steps of the communication chain', that
is: (1) the sender and the circumstances of production; (2) the form and
content of the message; (3) the processes and impact of reception and
consumption. This is in significant part due to the 'awkward fit' of such
steps with questions surrounding the production of meaning by media
audiences. A model of alternative and radical media must account not

only for active audiences in the Fiskean sense of creating 'oppositional readings' of mainstream media products (Fiske, 1992a) but also for 'mobilized audiences' – as well as notions of horizontal linkage, reader-writers and extremely democratic organizational structures. Here the fit with dominant communication models becomes even more awkward.

A communications perspective on alternative media is useful as long as we are able to keep in mind that its value will, as Dahlgren argues, be best realized by cultural interrogation. As a set of communication processes within (sub)cultural formations, alternative media privilege the involved audience over the merely informed (Lievrouw, 1994); that audience partakes of the media from a social point of view, not merely as a 'public'. What we are calling 'alternative media' can be thought of as being organized along similar lines to Benjamin's desideratum. They typically go beyond simply providing a platform for radical or alternative points of view: they emphasize the organization of media to enable wider social participation in their creation, production and dissemination than is possible in the mass media. Raymond Williams (1980: 54) highlighted three aspects of communication as foci for this realignment: 'skills, capitalization and controls'. In an explicit echo of Williams, James Hamilton (2001a) has argued that to distinguish alternative media from the mass media the former must be deprofessionalized, decapitalized and deinstitutionalized. In short, they must be available to ordinary people without the necessity of professional training, without excessive capital outlay and they must take place in settings other than media institutions or similar systems.

The model I propose here deals with similar concerns: social relations stand to be transformed through radical communications processes at the same time as the media (the vehicles) themselves stand to be transformed (visually, aurally, distributively). In this model, roles and responsibilities are no longer discrete; there is much overlap and transformation of notions such as professionalism, competence and expertise. No existing communication model offers an easy fit with such transformations. Robert Darnton's (1990) reconfiguration of the communication chain as a circuit gets closer than does the classical communication chain to the features and relations that might illuminate the social processes at work in radical media production and reception. His model at least acknowledges technical and professional roles such as those of publishers, printers and distributors.

Perhaps Darnton's circuit is over-utilitarian: its focus is on roles and responsibilities rather than on processes, with cultural and social determinants given the status of mere influences. His model emphasizes the dominant and discrete roles of, for example, writers, publishers,

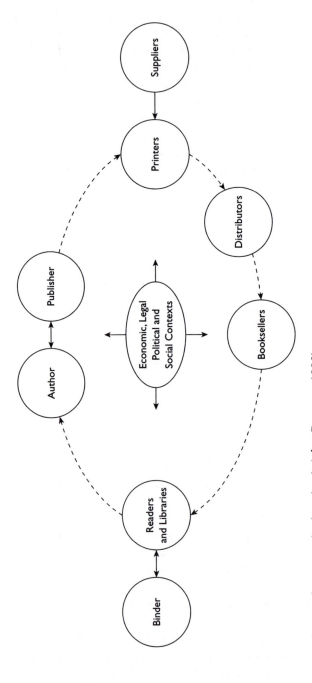

Figure 1 Darnton's communication circuit (after Darnton, 1990)

distributors and readers. In radical and alternative media these roles are often confused and conflated, at times to an extreme degree: in the case of a zine, the writer and publisher is typically the same person, as well as being its designer, printer and distributor. In the case of a collectively organized paper, all such duties might be undertaken at different times by every member of the collective. Darnton's roles provide a poor fit with the transformed roles and social relations (often experimental and shifting) that radical media invoke and promote (perhaps most remarkably in the reappearance throughout history of the notion of the reader-writer).

Box 1 A typology of alternative and radical media

1. Content (politically radical, socially/culturally radical); news values
2. Form – graphics, visual language; varieties of presentation and binding; aesthetics
3. Reprographic innovations/adaptations – use of mimeographs, IBM typesetting, offset litho, photocopiers
4. 'Distributive use' (Atton, 1999b) – alternative sites for distribution, clandestine/invisible distribution networks, anti-copyright
5. Transformed social relations, roles and responsibilities – reader-writers, collective organization, de-professionalization of e.g., journalism, printing, publishing
6. Transformed communication processes – horizontal linkages, networks

---

Box 1 presents a typology that draws on the preceding analysis of existing definitions and theory. In it, elements 1–3 indicate products and 4–6 processes. It is these six elements that form the basis of the model presented here. The broad division into products and processes does imply independence, however. The social processes will activate and inform the development of the products to the extent that each position in a communications circuit such as Darnton's will be amenable to radicalization in terms of products and processes, resources and relations. Using the model it becomes possible to consider each point on such a circuit as a dimension of communication, of social process ('writing', 'printing', distributing', etc.). 'Positions' becomes too fixed a term for them, since there may be overlap; for example, between the roles of writer, editor, publisher and distributor of a zine. As dimensions, roles and responsibilities can comprise a constellation of activities and relationships. An alternative publication might then be interrogated as to its radicality in terms of its multi-dimensional character, a perspective that privileges the overlap and intersection of dimensions. Here are two examples.

First, a radical approach to distribution can entail making use of skills and sites belonging to groups and communities normally excluded from mainstream modes of distribution in an alternative public sphere (Downing, 1988), as well as making use of transformed notions of intellectual property (such as 'anti-copyright': Atton, 1999b). These in turn suggest forms of reprography that facilitate further production by 'readers' (such as the *Open Pamphlet* series from the US, printed so as to open out to A4 to facilitate photocopying) who themselves become hybrid printers, finishers and distributors.

Second, the position of a solitary agent who is writer, editor and printer should be explained not simply as the outcome of a dilettante interest in trying out new jobs or as a result of lack of resources (though it may be these as well), but from a perspective that transforms these positions in relation to established notions and standards of professionalism, competence and 'possibility'. At the same time the roles have the power to transform one another by their coming together (whether by mutual abrasion or a more 'liquid' interpenetration). Each dimension need not be limited to activities and relationships; it can also include the products of activities and technological transformations that lead to those products (aesthetics, reprographic technologies, innovations in distribution). Dimensions that intersect can generate counter-hegemonic strategies of ownership (ownership of capital and intellectual property), power relations within the media and its audience. Here we locate Downing's notions of lateral linkages and the empowerment of active audiences through those linkages (Downing, 1984, 2001) and those relations which engage with prevalent forces, especially regarding the status of creators and producers in comparison with equivalent roles in prevalent culture (the dominant public sphere versus the alternative public sphere).

Is it possible to make any comparative assessment of radicality across various instances of alternative and radical media? How do we construe a publication that tends to radicality in differing degrees in differing dimensions? What is our scale for measuring those degrees? For instance, a publication may be radical in its organization, but conservative in respect of those who write for it – one that employs only professional journalists yet in a collective decision-making organization. Within each dimension there is complexity: within a reprographic ('printing') dimension a radical use of reprographic technology (the photocopier by zine producers, for instance) may be present along with a new social relation (an amateur writer working also as a printer): this presents a transformed power relation in contrast to the prevailing professional culture of printing.

We need also to be alert to historical or geographical contingency: the absence of radicality in any dimension may not limit a medium's revolutionary potential: the dimension may not be 'available' for radicalization at that time or place, or in that culture. The authorship need not be concerned solely with political radicality, but equally or instead with cultural content. This encourages us to approach these media from the perspective of 'mixed radicalism', once again paying attention to hybridity rather than expecting consistent adherence to a 'pure', fixed set of criteria: '[i]f ... radical alternative media have one thing in common, it is that they break somebody's rules, although rarely all of them in every respect' (Downing, 2001: xi). Despite these difficulties, I hope that my model avoids homogenizing alternative and radical media as the media of radical politics, of publications with minority audiences, of amateur writing and production. It suggests an area of cultural production that – whilst it lacks the explanatory power of a totalizing concept – enables us to consider its various manifestations and activations as part of an autonomous field (in the Bourdieusian sense) that is constituted by its own rules.

Alternative Media as a Field of Production

How appropriate is it to consider alternative and radical media as a field? Bourdieu's (1993) field of cultural production does recognize a space for avant-garde artistic activities, which may comprise some aspects of alternative and radical media practice (independent record labels, mail art, artists' books). Fiske has suggested that the systems of production and of distribution within fan culture comprise a 'shadow cultural economy' (Fiske, 1992b: 33). For all that it may admit, the cultural field is perhaps too limited: it is after all concerned with literary and artistic values of production. This is despite the ability of Bourdieu's field of cultural production to encompass 'extremes' of creative activity. For Bourdieu, though, these take place within the sector of the field concerned with restricted production, to be distinguished from an opposing sector of large-scale production. One purpose in positing an entire 'oppositional field' – rather than attempting to accommodate contestation within any existing formulation – is that Bourdieu's field seems inhospitable to certain notions of radicality. Within alternative media production are numerous avant-gardes that confound the dichotomy of restricted/large-scale sectors. Mail art (Held, 1991) might be thought of as a democratized version of restricted artistic production, where elite art practices (such as the limited edition and invitations to group exhibitions) are opened up to as many as wish to contribute (*Global Mail* is a zine devoted to calls to such 'open' exhibitions). In this arena at least, the value of the limited edition work of art is seriously eroded by its being opened up to producers/agents that are typically drawn from the public for large-scale cultural production. Restricted field practices are radically repositioned by being transformed under demotic conditions more usually associated with large-scale production strategies and techniques. We might also consider even the radicalization of plagiarism in such a 'demotic restricted field'. Bourdieu (1993: 128) sees plagiarism in large-scale production as an indicator of 'indifference or conservatism': in the hands of an avowedly working-class autodidact such as Stewart Home (a further example of the composite artist-author-editor-publisher) plagiarism is radicalized as a demotic avant-garde (for example Home, 1995). A demotic avant-garde appropriates and repositions capital and authority directly from high culture, radically re-legitimizing an artistic practice from that legitimate culture.

More recently, Bourdieu (1997) has proposed a journalistic field. It is difficult to see how alternative and radical media could fit into this formulation: as Marliere (1998: 223) has shown, the field itself is too undifferentiated, too monolithic 'to provide a realistic account of a plural and heterogeneous reality' of dominant journalistic practices, let alone alternatives to them. There may be some value in considering it as a field in its own right, as an oppositional counterpart to Bourdieu's dominant journalistic field. Again, though, the multi-dimensionality of the model suggests a conceptual space wider than journalism *tout court* – are zines journalism? What is the relationship of anarchist web sites and Internet discussion lists to journalism? The range of media products and activities available to the present model encourages a hybridized field that comprises cultural (artistic, literary) practices and journalistic practices and that admits of extremes of transformation in products, processes and relations between the two. In this chapter I have proposed definitional and theoretical models that privilege the transformatory potential of the media as reflexive instruments of communication practices in social networks: there is a focus on process and relation. The model does at least encourage interrogation across the range of production in this field, the better to place its constellations of products, activities, institutions, movements, moments and cultures in structured, explanatory settings. In what follows I shall examine in more detail those transformations, particularly those in the processes and relations that create the popular practices of what I am calling 'alternative media'. I shall begin by addressing alternative media approaches to the economics of production and the cultural products and formations that have arisen to realize them.

Note

1. Traber's terminology reflects his background in development and alternative journalism in the South; 'advocacy' and 'grassroots' are terms little used in British media studies, for instance. This twin role of the alternative press has also been noted by Elizabeth Fox (1997) in her survey of media and culture in Latin America, where she highlights the organizational and educational value of such media. The term 'grassroots' is more commonly used to define such media as are described in Tomaselli and Louw's (1991) studies of the alternative media in South Africa. These terms are used in the present study simply to clarify two trends in alternative media, the better to analyse one; there is no intention to imply sociopolitical similarities between the conditions of production in the South and those in Britain.

2

the economics of production

This chapter focuses on the circulation and distribution of alternative
media within its alternative public sphere. At its heart is an examination of the alternative press as an economic enterprise which has
sought to find alternatives to mainstream ways of doing business. It will
explore the reprographic technologies employed by the alternative press
in order to gauge how they are influenced by low finance. Finally, it will
examine the economics of production in relation to an alternative public
sphere, in particular exploring the articulation of economic factors with
prefigurative methods of political organization. I shall look at the dominant trends in the economic history of alternative publishing since the
1960s and apply this examination to a comparison of two key print titles
in the British alternative media of the 1990s, *The Big Issue* and the lesser-
known *Squall*. *The Big Issue* was founded in 1991 and has four separate
fortnightly editions in London, Scotland, Wales and the North of
England. Its aim, as is well known, is to 'help the homeless help themselves', by selling them copies of the paper that they then sell on the street
(making 45 pence per copy sold). Its unusual (though not unique) distribution technique and the undoubted impact it has had on both its vendors and the public should not, however, distract us from the differences
between it and the alternative grassroots press. As a member of the advocacy press, *The Big Issue* speaks on behalf of the homeless and undoubtedly provides a lifeline to many. But it is emphatically not the direct voice
of the homeless. Only two pages in a 48-page issue are typically given
over to contributions by the homeless ('Street lights', a forum that is
mostly taken up with poetry, and offers no space for articles); the rest of
the paper is written mostly by young journalists. Nevertheless, we should

not ignore its presence on Britain's streets, not least because it offers comparison in all the areas of this study. (All the British editions of *The Big Issue* are at least more interested in the homeless than is the Los Angeles edition which, according to Chris Dodge (1999: 61), 'doesn't even pretend to be a voice for homeless people'.) Moreover, its aims are generally similar to those of some grassroots titles, most obviously *Squall*, which was launched in the year after *The Big Issue* to provide information for the homeless, for squatters and travellers. *Squall* is more convincingly the voice of the homeless, since it is largely written by activists, many of whom are active in the squatting movement and have experiences of being homeless themselves. It has also featured lengthy articles by homeless people. It is edited entirely by activists, not by professional journalists. From 1992 until 1997 it appeared quarterly in tabloid format after which it ceased publication in print. It has since moved to on-line publication. This chapter deals with its print history. (The economics of on-line publishing and the transformation of notions such as circulation and distribution are examined in Chapter 6.)

The Alternative Press in its 'Ghetto'

In the previous chapter I highlighted Michael Traber's argument that a grassroots alternative press offered the truest, most thorough version of alternative media values. Against it he set the advocacy press, one that tended to commerciality and 'distance' from the subjects of its news. This view has not been accepted uncritically by some commentators on alternative media. The most forthright critique has been the Comedia's (1984) pessimistic assessment which, though over fifteen years old, has not been significantly added to (nor argued against) in the ensuing decade. The failure of grassroots media, the group argued, was caused by the inability or unwillingness of the alternative press to adopt methods of financial planning and organizational efficiency that would enable it to survive in the marketplace. Comedia's solution for this 'underdeveloped' section of alternative press was mainstream economic and organizational planning (that is, using conventional managerial means) and a shift of content in order to increase circulation by moving more into the mainstream. Comedia was certainly accurate in that a cavalier approach to finances, coupled with non-hierarchical forms of organization, has characterized the history of the alternative press. Where there is scope for argument is regarding the extent to which such attitudes inevitably lead to 'failure'.[1]

The alternative press still espouses such anti-commercial methods today, as a deliberate demonstration by such publications of their practical commitment to their political strategy, one that is against capitalism and managerialism. According to Comedia, this choice dooms the alternative press to 'an existence so marginal as to be irrelevant': it will never break out of its 'alternative ghetto'. The only alternative publications that can be considered successful are those that have broken out of the ghetto and have attracted significant parts of the mainstream audience by adopting values more reminiscent of Traber's advocacy press (Comedia cited *New Internationalist* and *New Socialist* in this regard).

Comedia held that such non-hierarchical, collective methods can only disadvantage the alternative press, because they are always adopted for political, never for economic, ends. Success can only be judged against increased circulation and increased market penetration. The very subtitle of its paper ('The Development of Underdevelopment') implied that the alternative press is by its very nature in a subordinate position to that of the mainstream press. This analysis is similar to that found in studies of earlier periods of the British alternative press (Fountain, 1988; Nelson, 1989). In his study of the British underground press, Nigel Fountain (1988: 198) called finance and distribution 'those two great rocks of the underground' and notes that even by the time of *The Leveller* (founded in 1976), the alternative press had not solved these problems. (*The Leveller*'s problems are examined in detail by Landry et al., 1985.) Summarizing the dominant problems of the underground and alternative press from the late 1960s to the early 1970s, Fountain identified them as 'internal organisation, distribution and sales' (p. 198). Similar conclusions were reached by the Comedia group's predecessor, the Minority Press Group, in their series of reports (especially Minority Press Group, 1980a, 1980b; Whitaker, 1981). All have in common their accounts of the low-waged, underfunded editors and workers of the alternative press; all emphasize how marginal and precarious an existence many papers had. From such literature a picture emerges of an alternative press that has wrestled with the problems of democratic participation in the production of its titles and that has found itself repeatedly in financial crisis. In addition, it has suffered from low visibility in the marketplace through its problems with distribution, which has further increased its financial problems. Circulation, and therefore finance, has remained low.

Comedia offer us only an 'alternative ghetto', but there is another, powerful context available in the notion of the alternative public sphere. John Downing posited this concept in his study of West German anti-nuclear media (Downing, 1988) as 'a culturally embedded social practice' (Boyd-Barrett, 1995: 230). He identifies in the German anti-nuclear movement an 'alternative public realm' of debate, itself the 'seedbed of many alternative media'. Downing convincingly replaces Habermas's twin historical foundations – the coffee-houses and salons, and the small-scale bourgeois media – with more contemporary manifestations: he presents 'the alternative scene' of 'bookstores, bars, coffee-shops, restaurants, food-stores...' that provide the fora in which discussion and debate of the issues presented by the periodicals of the anti-nuclear movement take place. Such an 'oppositional political culture' Downing found to be 'much better nourished in West Germany than in Britain', not simply because of the amount of alternative information circulating, but because of that crucial other, 'the experience of exchange inside a flourishing alternative public realm', in other words, strong horizontal channels of communication, with an emphasis on 'activity, movement and exchange ... an autonomous sphere in which experiences, critiques and alternatives could be freely developed' (1988: 168).[2] An alternative public sphere would seem an appropriate theoretical foundation for such phenomena in its formulation of a nexus of institutions that work together without parliamentary influence, to enable the public to address and debate political and social issues independently of the state. This nexus of institutions inevitably includes the media; the alternative public sphere treats its media and the constituencies they serve and inform (and are in turn informed by) as inseparable. It is thus an appropriate model for contextualizing a theory of the alternative press, given the vital relationship between the alternative press and the grassroots movements that it supports and reports. Indeed, the emergence of many alternative media is inseparable from their social and political actualization (as movements).

Finance

Comedia's critique of the economic and organizational weaknesses of the alternative press proceeds from the sector's failure to take seriously the necessity of financial planning (Comedia, 1984). It notes that the bulk of the alternative press of the 1960s and 1970s was heavily subsidized, and that survival was only possible as long as such subsidies continued. There were two major forms of subsidy: the music business and 'self-exploited labour'. Whilst the former, in the shape of benefit concerts from the rock groups of the time, was largely limited to the underground press titles of *Oz* and *IT*, the latter is a recurring feature of these as well as of the working-class press of the *Morning Star* and *The Newsline*. People work for the paper for little or no wages as volunteers, a phenomenon encouraged by, as Comedia has it, 'their commitment to squatting and claiming as a way of life' (1984: 97).

These primary subsidies were clearly still at work in the grassroots press of the 1990s. *Squall* continued to get part of its funding from benefit concerts. It was run by volunteers, and Comedia's note on 'squatting and claiming' still holds good: *Squall* promoted squatting as a way of life. Given that capital investment is minimal, and that the producers of these titles are already working for no wages, there is not only little margin for expansion, there is hardly space in which to survive. The subscription is a common method of obtaining capital funding. The ratio of subscriptions to other sales of *Squall* during its life as a print publication was roughly 1: 9 (800 of a circulation of 7,000). Despite its low level, the subscription at least offered a little financial security, providing the opportunity for forward planning, however limited. *Squall* also regularly appealed for donations (and still does in its electronic form). In the absence of such funds, a publication can only rely on sales and advertising. Yet even these common commercial strategies are problematized by the economic situation of the alternative press. Against such problems we should compare the financial buoyancy of *The Big Issue*, made possible by a subsidy for its first two years. This was provided by businesses, most conspicuously by the Body Shop, whose Gordon Roddick provided £500,000 to launch the paper. No such subsidy would be forthcoming for a title such as *Squall*. Funding – when it does not come from readers or explicit supporters of the alternative press – is looked upon with some suspicion. The editors of *Squall* summarized their attitude as 'cautious ... we do not [want to] become a marketing bucket' (from an interview conducted by the author). Nowhere is this a more vexed issue than in attitudes to advertising. We must note, however, that, from a combination of fund-raising activities, sales and advertising *Squall* was able to meet 'the in excess of £16,000 sum [*sic*] it takes to run and produce *Squall* for a year' ('The State We're In: a Notice to Readers', *Squall*, 14, Autumn 1996: 12). Not that this was without difficulty: '[w]e've had, and still do have, a lot of financial trouble holding the project together' (personal correspondence with *Squall*, June 1998). Compared to *The Big Issue* (which takes a wide range of advertising but, it appears, none for expensive consumer products, nor for cigarettes and alcohol), advertising in *Squall* was scarce. It never ran more than a handful of advertisements in each issue. These were invariably small in size (never more than a sixteenth of a page) and tended to advertise books, pamphlets and periodicals produced by other alternative presses; *Squall* reassured its readers that it would not carry advertising 'for multinationals or cultural hijackers' ('The State We're In', p. 12).

Such a policy has its roots in both the mainstream analyses of press freedom and more radical commentaries upon it. Curran and Seaton argue that increased dependence on advertising has given the advertisers themselves 'a *de facto* licensing authority' since, without their support, many newspapers would cease to be economically viable (Curran and Seaton, 1997: 34). A more radical view is that of Herman and Chomsky (1994), who hold that the reliance on advertising as a primary source of income inevitably leads to business interests (both internal and external) directly controlling the content of the media. They cite it as their second 'news filter' in their propaganda model of the mass media. As if in support of this view, no grassroots titles are willing to carry advertising that could interfere with their freedom as a result of advertisers seeking to dictate the content of the rest of the publication.

But we should also consider the possibility that advertising, even if it were welcome, is simply not attractive enough to advertisers outside the alternative public sphere and thus the revenue available from it is small. This contradicts Comedia's claim that 'the relatively privileged economic position of [the] readers' of the alternative press makes such titles attractive to advertisers wanting to target 'ABC1 consumers'. We have already noted that the producers of the titles under discussion are far from 'ABC1 consumers' themselves.

For all that, there is thus far little challenge to Comedia's main thesis, that financial exigency will ensure that the alternative press remains in its own 'ghetto'. But do all alternative publishers wish to break out of the alternative ghetto? If in the place of 'ghetto' we posit 'alternative public sphere', a very different picture emerges, one where the social and cultural apparatus is every bit as diverse as that in the dominant public sphere; where discussion, debate and the promulgation of ideas and opinions take place within a complex articulated structure of economics, organization and social action. These come together most conspicuously in what John Downing describes as 'prefigurative politics, the attempt to practice socialist principles in the present, not merely to imagine them for the future' (Downing, 1984: 23). It is the methods employed to achieve such aims that Comedia dismisses as idealistic and as displaying an ignorance of business practices in 'the real world'. Yet it can be shown that such methods mesh with alternative fora for discussion and channels for distribution in far more sophisticated ways than Comedia found. In the 1990s, these were most conspicuous in the use of reprographic technologies and distribution channels.

Reprographic Technologies

'Offset was exciting. Offset was freedom ... the copy could be pasted on to the boards and, with no need for hot metal, or skilled printers, was camera-ready' (Fountain, 1988: 24). What offset litho was to the publishers of *Oz* and *IT*, the photocopier was to the punk movement of the late 1970s. Despite the fact that the alternative publisher was still dependent on the printer, the offset process meant that, in Fountain's words, 'around five stages on conventional newspapers were leapfrogged' (p. 112). On the other hand, the photocopier enabled editors to paste up and print their own publications, which they did in their hundreds. The photocopier opened up a new avenue for cheap, quick reproduction; it was fast, clean and mostly reliable. The punk explosion of 1976 saw for the first time dozens of music magazines published in photocopied formats, using a variety of typewritten and hand-written formats, often illustrated with plagiarized graphics and photographs from the music press and record sleeves:

> Fanzines are the perfect expression – cheaper, more instant than records. Maybe THE medium. A democratisation too – if the most committed 'new wave' is about social change then the best fanzines express this. (Savage, 1991: 401; emphasis in original)

The fanzine (and, after it, the zine) offers a relatively cheap means of communicating. Bob Bellerue, editor of the American zine *Basura*, in his survey of zine publishing in the US proposes that '[t]he photocopier revolution alone may be the central feature of the current zine explosion' (Bellerue, 1995), and it is noteworthy that during the 1970s and the 1980s alternative publishers increasingly made use of reprographic technologies that made them, if not financially independent, at least technically independent. The arrival of the self-service photocopier, the exploitation of workplace copiers and their provision in local community centres have all enabled alternative publishers to reproduce titles quickly and cheaply. (We must exclude *The Big Issue* from this analysis since, despite its use of cheap newsprint, it has employed offset and extensive colour throughout since its inception. Once again, this is a direct result of the heavy subsidy from its earliest days.)

Some titles begin as photocopies, considering it progress to move to offset when finance allows (if it ever does). *Squall* began as a cheaply printed magazine with a mix of typewritten and hand-written copy originated and pasted up by the editors. As it became established and its circulation and its funding increased (however marginally), it moved quickly from a cheaply produced, cut-and-paste A5 magazine of a couple of dozen pages to a thick, professionally typeset tabloid of some 70-odd pages. This is explained in significant part by its aim to reach further than its immediate, activist audience. A further experiment with format has taken place amongst grassroots titles that have used the Internet to raise their profile. *Squall* began by using its web site to advertise the printed version, presenting a small selection of articles, illustrations and subscription information as part of a wider site of related links to other protests, campaigns and information sources. Since the cessation of the printed version in 1997, the web site (www.squall.co.uk) has developed into a full-blown on-line magazine. A hard copy version of the articles and photographs on the site has been promised (when funds permit).

Circulation

No product of the alternative press can ever hope to reach circulation figures comparable with its mainstream counterparts. This can be achieved only by extending circulation beyond the alternative public sphere. The majority of the publications surveyed in the Royal Commission on the Press's (1977) report on the alternative press had circulations of 2,000 or less, yet this was nowhere considered a failure. Comedia focuses on the economic success of two 'exceptions' in the alternative press, *New Socialist* and *New Internationalist*, which, it says, have broken out of the 'alternative ghetto' due to their sales of around 25,000 each. Data on the circulation of the contemporary alternative press are not systematically collected; none of its titles are audited for circulation, the only attempt at data collection being that by the magazine *Radical Bookseller* in the early 1990s.[3] The circulation of *Squall* was small, yet between 1992 and 1997 (when it published in print) its circulation rose consistently. Though data for early issues are not available, with no. 6 circulation had reached 1,500. This had doubled by the next issue (Autumn 1994), whilst the circulation of *Squall*, 9 (its first tabloid edition, appearing a little over a year later) was 5,000 (Malyon, 1995). Circulation continued to improve: no. 14 (Autumn 1996, its penultimate issue) had a circulation of 7,000, according to its editors (from an interview conducted by the author).[4]

The Big Issue, by contrast, has a circulation significantly higher than even many mainstream magazines. The combined circulation of its four editions is estimated at almost half a million (Swithinbank, 1996); the most recent audited circulation for its London edition is 132,787. By mainstream standards, this is extremely successful. By alternative standards it is unimaginable. But is it possible to judge the success of an alternative title by its circulation alone? Is low circulation a necessary indicator of 'failure'? For Aubrey (1981), it is. Given a choice between high circulation of a handful of titles and smaller circulation across a diverse and wider range, he promotes the former. Drawing on the experiences of the underground press in the early 1970s, he argues that in that era the impact of such consolidated (and influential) titles as *Oz* and *IT* was diluted by the appearance of dozens of magazines ranging across all manner of topics: 'the women's movement, ecology, education, fringe theatre, anarchism, scientific developments, fascism' (1981: 172). It was this 'mass of magazines concerned with the fragments, and major slices, of the non-aligned left opposition' that had in the late 1970s replaced 'at a national level the underground press of cultural rebellion' (p. 167).

We should also take note of a more recent counter-argument from the 'younger generation' of zine publishers. The editors of the alternative review zine *Bypass* have argued that hundreds of small circulation titles not only encourage diversity of information and opinions but ensure the survival of the alternative press: '[d]ecentralization not only gives people a voice.... It may prove a key strategy for the survival of dissent, or even just plain old independent thinking in a society that seems to be getting more and more authoritarian every year' (cited by Atton, 1996a: 101). The micro-press 'Oxford Institute of Social Disengineering' similarly considers the proliferation of titles as a democratic strength: '[o]ne hundred publications with a circulation of one thousand are one hundred times better than one publication with a circulation of one hundred thousand' (cited by Atton, 1996a: 133). In this both publishers are in agreement with the Royal Commission on the Press, which also recognized multiplicity as a strength. This declaration appears to imitate that in an unnamed advertising handbook of 1851:

> a journal that circulates a thousand among the upper or middle classes is a better medium than would be one circulating a hundred thousand among the lower classes. (cited by Curran and Seaton, 1997: 35)

In any event, it certainly subverts the intention of the latter by privileging diversity of titles – and, implicitly, the involvement of many hands – over more elitist publications. Mark Pawson and Jason Skeet, two inveterate self-publishers and mail artists, have similarly subverted other notions of the media industry, coining the term 'narrow casting in fibre space' in conscious imitation of the phrase 'broadcasting in cyberspace'. This useful conceit brings together two notions that are disruptive of mainstream media conceptions of communication. The first 'is intended to counter the term broadcasting, the idea that the aim of all media production is to reach as large an audience as possible' (Pawson and Skeet, 1995: 78); the second argues that multiplicity of production is best achieved through paper-based media which are diversely available throughout the alternative public sphere. Downing has also argued for the impact that even a small-circulation paper can have (Downing, 1995). He employs as an analogy the Boston Tea Party, an insignificant enough event in itself that nevertheless sparked off a revolution: 'size alone was no index of the impact … [a]nd that is the beginning of wisdom in thinking about radical alternative media' (1995: 240). And although he is silent on the matter 11 years earlier in his study of self-managed media (Downing, 1984), the range of titles he chooses to examine – and the range of circulation and audiences they exhibit – implies that he is accepting of plurality, in the sense of a multiplicity of relatively small circulation papers.

The argument is perhaps best settled by an appeal to historical contingency; the period that most interests Aubrey (and Comedia/Minority Press Group, of which he was a member) is the 1970s, a time when many of the social and political ideas of feminism, environmentalism and socialism were being developed by a largely youthful movement. In such circumstances, it was important to build large memberships in order to ensure a presence on demonstrations, in the mass media, in local elections. A handful of large-circulation titles would raise the profile and the understanding of such new ideas better than numerous smaller and marginal publications. What Aubrey would now consider fragmentation is the result of what many activist environmentalist campaigners see as an unwelcome development in those radical organizations that have their roots in the 1970s, such as Friends of the Earth and Greenpeace, where organizational size and its attendant bureaucracy has minimized the opportunity for grassroots participation and local, independent, small-scale activist campaigning. It is the rise of such campaigning in the present decade that has brought with it a range of publications, often intended initially as local newsletters, but often (as in the case of *Squall*) growing into nationally read and distributed publications. Furthermore, strategies peculiar to the alternative press of the 1990s have been developed to enable a wider circulation of ideas than might be expected from such a multiplicity of publications. These can be brought together under the heading 'distributive use' to signify innovations in distribution that confound simple calculations of circulation and their attendant analyses of 'failure'.

Distributive Use in the Alternative Public Sphere

Here we must turn to other grassroots titles for evidence, since *Squall* exemplifies distributive use in only one way. 'Distributive use' here refers to two strategies of production and distribution that have been uniquely developed within the alternative public sphere, and that are concerned with the deliberate decentralization and relinquishment of control of the processes of reproduction and distribution of alternative publications by their original publishers. The two strategies are, in the language of the alternative publishers of the 1990s, 'anti-copyright' (sometimes 'open copyright') and 'open distribution'.

Anti-Copyright

In the alternative press of the 1990s there developed a radical view of copyright with a strong movement against intellectual property rights. Because the ethos of much alternative publishing is concerned with the widest possible dissemination of unorthodox, dissident ideas using the smallest amount of resources, many authors and publishers encourage the free circulation of their material. Many books and journals will have 'anti-copyright' or 'open copyright' statements, indicating that the reader or purchaser is free to copy as much of the document as they wish, provided that it is not for commercial purposes. It is expected that those doing so might wish to make a charge to cover their duplicating costs, but this is not expected to include a profit margin. Some titles explicitly encourage the copying and distribution of the work in its entirety, only asking that the original publisher is informed, so that they are kept aware of the number of editions circulating. (After all, a small publisher on a tight budget might decide that, due to the number and extent of pirate editions in existence, there is no need for a reprint of the original edition. It can then channel its energies into new titles.)

Although it has made no explicit statement regarding the copyright status of its own content, the extremist environmental newspaper *Green Anarchist* has itself benefited from anti-copyright publications. In common with many other publications, it has reprinted articles by Bob Black and Hakim Bey, two prolific and controversial writers in the alternative milieu. In the 'zero-work' issue (no. 39, Autumn, 1995) there appeared a lengthy article by Black ('Primitive Affluence: a Postscript to Sahlins'); his article 'Technophilia: an Infantile Disorder' might be considered the keynote article of the 'anti-technology issue' (no. 42, Summer, 1996). Hakim Bey (a pseudonym for the writer Peter Lamborn Wilson) is best known for his formulation of the Temporary Autonomous Zone (Bey, 1991, itself an 'anti-copyright' work), which has quickly become a significant theoretical tool for many commentators within the alternative public sphere (see McKay, 1996). 'Lascaux', a chapter from *Radio Sermonettes*, also appears under Bey's name in the 'zero-work' issue of *Green Anarchist*.

The value of having such work in a publication is twofold. First and expediently, it fills a space. There will always be an anti-copyright piece available that can be slotted into an issue, without the need to worry about an author missing a deadline, or negotiating payment or other conditions of publication. Second, prestige will attach to any publication that features such 'movement intellectuals' as Black and Bey; their names will help to sell the publication. The writing style of such an experienced polemicist as Black or of such a theorist as Bey can raise the status of the publication, lending a welcome 'professionalism' (or at least, a variety in tone and rhetoric) to what might otherwise be a monotonous voice. *Green Anarchist*'s house style, for example, is typically colloquial, confrontational and militant. The inclusion of more 'intellectual' writers might lead the 'floating' reader to suppose that these writers support *Green Anarchist*'s editorial viewpoint, leading such a reader to approach the rest of the publication with more interest than they might otherwise do.

Squall, on the other hand, rather than reprinting the anti-copyright work of others, assigned an 'open copyright' status to its own articles that allowed copies to made for non-profit-making purposes. This waiving of copyright is an extension of the concept of 'fair dealing' in copyright law or of the licence given to educational institutions for the production of multiple copies. *Squall* encouraged both individuals and groups or organizations to copy any number of articles, in any quantity, not only for private study (the limits of fair dealing and copyright permissions in educational institutions), but for distribution through channels apart from the paper's own (this includes republication as pamphlets and booklets). We should also note here the pirating of photographs and other graphic materials in zines and in particular their 'détournement' to subvert the original meaning of such items. Détournement is a strategy borrowed from the situationists that involves 'taking elements from a social stereotype and, through their mutation and reversal, turning them against it... [to produce] a parodic destabilization of the commodity-image' (Bonnett, 1991/1996: 193). It was most famously employed by the situationists in their addition of revolutionary captions to strip cartoons. These practices of 'guerrilla semiotics' seek to unmask hypocrisy and the corporate ideology behind advertisements. *Adbusters Quarterly* specializes in designing and publishing parodies of current major advertising campaigns. It is especially well known for its versions of Calvin Klein's Obsession and Absolut Vodka, at the same time as it reports on the encroachment of advertising into such areas as public education. This subversion has led to the portmanteau term 'subvertising' to describe advertisements altered or redesigned to make a social or political point, usually highlighting the activities of the business or product being advertised. Such 'culture jamming' is examined briefly yet authoritatively by Mark Dery (1993). James Hamilton (2001a) offers valuable insights into these practices and their similarity with the history of photomontage, in particular with the work of John Heartfield. The work of the American avant-garde music group Negativland (1995) uses samples of radio and television programmes – as well as music – to create sonic collages that function as commentaries, critiques and satires on aspects of the mass media.

Open Distribution

Whilst anti-copyright as a common practice within the alternative public sphere was a phenomenon of the 1990s, almost a decade before *Squall* formulated its 'open copyright' statement the first issue of the class-struggle anarchist news-sheet *Counter Information* (22 September 1984) encouraged its readers to make free use of its contents 'as required, or for reprinting'. To assist in the latter, it offered 'electrostencils or duplicate printing plates'. This early version of what has come to be known as 'open distribution' we must consider as purely experimental – moreover an experiment that failed, since the offer has never been repeated. *Squall* did not favour open distribution, preferring to retain control over all the copies it published. However, the notion was taken up by *Do or Die*, the magazine for the UK 'section' of the radical environmental movement Earth First!. It, too, in its first issue, recommended open distribution as its primary form of distribution: 'if you've got access to cheap photocopying facilities, print up copies of this yourself, we don't mind, we are not capitalists'. Its choice of format for this issue seems to have been made with open distribution in mind; copies are A4 folded to A5 and unsewn, making it easy for the 'reader-distributor' to dismantle the publication for copying. Unfortunately, a steady increase in the size of subsequent issues (the first issue had 20 pages; its eighth issue, in 1999, had 344) has worked against such wholesale reproduction, although it still declares itself '@nti-copywrite – Copy and Distribute at will. Share information'. With regret, the editors have now abandoned open distribution in the UK, finding that improved sales through more professional production have made this irrelevant. However, it is a method they still adopt to distribute cheaply overseas. The printing plates of issue no. 6 were sent to an Earth First! group in the Czech Republic, enabling them to print copies for their own distribution.

If *Do or Die*'s desire to expand its pagination has eroded its ability to participate in open distribution, the shorter *SchNEWS*, an activist newsletter based in Brighton (normally two pages of A4) lends itself to quick and cheap recopying and reprinting. Although it began life as a centrally produced and distributed publication, within five months it was offering its contents – in part or as a whole – to anyone who wished to use it: 'Strictly @nticopyright – customise ... photocopy ... distribute' (22 April 1995). As with *Counter Information* and *Do or Die*, it offered 'originals' to anyone who plans to copy it for further distribution (18 August 1995). Around 70 originals were sent out in this way in 1998 and, whilst the editors do not track the number of all subsequent copies made by the groups and individuals that receive it, CAMFIN (Cambridge Free Information Network) regularly prints and distributes 200 copies from its original. The *SchNEWS* web site also presents the paper in Portable Document Format (PDF) files (which replicates the printed version) to further encourage copying by readers. It has been estimated that the readership of *SchNEWS* could be as high as 20,000, from a combination of copying and visits to its web site (compared with a print run of between 2,500 and 5,000 per issue) (Searle, 1997: 125). It has remained resolutely anti-copyright and pro-open distribution, and even encourages others to establish their own version of *SchNEWS*, using as much of its content as they wish. Edinburgh's *Auld Reekie's New Tattoo* and Glasgow's *Solidarity* are two such publications modelled on *SchNEWS*. By emulating the processes of the source publication (collectively written and edited, anti-copyright and employing open distribution), further publications retain a radical power that avoids recuperation.

Alternative Fora as Methods of Distribution

So far *The Big Issue*, representing the contemporary advocacy press in Britain, has been notable for the great differences between it and the grassroots titles under discussion. Benefiting from strong financial backing from a millionaire philanthropist, as well as from much advertising revenue. Enjoying a circulation unimaginably higher than those of its grassroots counterparts; it has achieved this not through high-street retailers and newsagents but through street-selling. This is not a new technique; working-class papers such as *The Morning Star* and *Socialist Worker* have used street-selling for many years. Of the other titles mentioned in this chapter, *SchNEWS* is handed out free on the streets of Brighton, where it is produced. *Green Anarchist* has a more extensive street-selling network, but only 600 copies from its present circulation of 2,500 are sold in this way. What is startling about *The Big Issue* is its success with this method. This is in part due to the large numbers of vendors the system has attracted by providing work that raises their self-esteem and makes them money (Berens, 1997). In Scotland the paper has 1,000 vendors; in London it has almost 6,000. But it is also due to the rigorous organization behind the street-selling; whereas *Green Anarchist* is sold on the street on an *ad hoc* basis by anyone who wishes to do so, *The Big Issue*'s system is tightly controlled: vendors receive training, sign a 'code of conduct' and wear identity badges. In Scotland, for instance, the network is co-ordinated by 60 full-time workers in five offices throughout the country.[5]

The Royal Commission on the Press (1977) found that the ability of the alternative press to take advantage of mainstream distribution and retail networks was very poor and that of all economic considerations in the alternative press, 'distribution is the most difficult problem to be overcome' (1977: 63). The failure of the alternative Publications Distribution Co-operative in the 1980s was due to its inability to compete with mainstream distributors. For, despite what Phil Kelly (1989) calls the 'collective commercial strength' acquired by the titles that made up the Collective, it was still dependent on the major distribution chains (John Menzies and WH Smith) for its penetration into newsagents'. Higher circulation, more advertising, 'a more professional product' and 'repping' directly to newsagents by the publishers – only when these requirements were met would John Menzies and WH Smith be willing to take the Collective's titles (Minority Press Group, 1980a).[6] Alternative publications are not always better off with alternative distributors for other reasons. The editor of the American anarchist magazine *The Match!* has recounted his chronic problems with the alternative distributor Fine Print which, he alleges, consistently refused to pay him for copies of his publication that they were distributing (Woodworth, 1995). His criticism goes beyond non-payment: he is also concerned with control over the market, creating monopolies the equal of any mainstream enterprise. He notes that in 1995, Fine Print were distributing to 323 bookshops in the

US – '323 bookstores that the magazine you are holding cannot get into, because they haven't had contracts with Fine Print and aren't about to order from a single unrepresented publisher such as ourselves. Yes, I call that control' (1995: 55). Since then Fine Print has gone bankrupt, leaving many titles unpaid. It may well be that the alternative distributor that fails does not simply fail to get the alternative media into bookshops and newsagents; it may be responsible for their demise.

Not all publications find their way barred to direct distribution to shops. Many publications in the UK deal directly with alternative book-shops and other fora within the alternative public sphere. The first might be considered analogous to mainstream channels. These are the alternative bookshops such as Compendium and Housmans in London, Mushroom in Nottingham and alternative distributors such as AK, Counter Productions and Turnaround. As primary methods of distribution and retail they have remained largely unchanged since the 1960s, though the 1990s saw the rise of a number of specifically anarchist distributors such as DS4A, Slab-o-Concrete and the largest, AK. Second are channels whose primary func-tion is not the distribution or retail of alternative press titles, but which are nevertheless primary constituents of the alternative public sphere – amongst them vegetarian cafés, independent record shops and the latest manifestations of the 1960s 'head shops', selling jewellery, clothes and paraphernalia for the dope-smoker. All of these provide fora for the discussion of alternative and radical ideas and opinions.

In the 1990s, a third category was added. To view it as a composite of the first two is to only partially describe its interrelated, multi-functional significance within the alternative public sphere. This is the 'infoshop', a phenomenon that grew out of the squatted anarchist centres of the 1980s, such as the 121 Centre in Brixton, London. As the term suggests, central to the function of an infoshop is the dissemination of informa-tion, for example by acting as an alternative Citizens Advice Bureau to claimants and squatters. It might offer a reading room of alternative pub-lications, perhaps even a small library. It acts as a distribution point for free publications, and as a retail outlet for priced publications. Importantly, it provides cheap do-it-yourself design and reprographic services to alter-native publishers. (At its most basic, this might be a table and a photo-copier. Some infoshops will have professional DTP facilities, however.) It can act as a 'mail-drop' for alternative publishers and local activist groups (an important function when the publisher or group contact is living in squatted premises, unsure of their future and unable to afford a PO box). Finally, it might offer space for discussions, meetings, concerts and exhi-bitions.[7] The rise of activist video in the 1990s and in particular the alter-native news video *Undercurrents* (founded in 1993) prompted many infoshops to present public screenings and discussions of such features. Not only are these able to act as spurs to action and debate, their purchase by the infoshop displaces the cost of purchase by individual viewers. In sum, the infoshop provides a forum for alternative cultural, economic, political and social activities. Its typical range is described in a flyer circulated by the Autonomous Centre of Edinburgh (ACE) to announce its founding in 1996:

- Advice and solidarity against dole harassment
- A meeting place for community-political groups
- Radical books, 'zines, and information
- A low-cost vegan cafe and drop-in centre
- Local arts and crafts
- Underground records, demos, t-shirts, badges
- People's food co-operative
- Socializing in an *anti*-sexist, -racist, or -homophobic environment
- An epicenter of alternative/DIY kulture (Spelling and emphasis in original.)

Whilst ACE has not yet achieved all these (it has not, for instance, established a food co-op), its aims are common to all such centres. It also exemplifies the close relationship the alternative press can have with an infoshop. ACE and *Counter Information* have in common a number of workers; editorial meetings for the paper are held at ACE; computing equipment there is used to lay out the paper and organize its web site. In return, the information network of which *Counter Information* is a part, and through which it keeps up to date with events of interest to it and its readers, supplies ACE with its publications; after they have been used to inform stories in the paper or to make contact with activists, the alternative press titles received by *Counter Information* are used to establish the infoshop at ACE: an archive of newspapers, magazines, newsletters, flyers and posters on topics relevant to ACE's users. Since *Counter Information* is part of national and international networks for such exchanges of information, ACE is itself able to contribute to infoshops across the country – and, indeed, the world – through contacts made by *Counter Information* and the other publications produced by groups that use ACE. The activist unemployed group Edinburgh Claimants, for example, produces its own newsletter, *Dole Harassment Exposed!*. Moreover, Edinburgh Claimants is part of a wider network of anarchist unemployed groups in the UK, known as Groundswell (see Shore, 1997 for an overview). Once again, the value of the network as a central communications strategy is highlighted.[8]

This network is in continual flux: publications come and go; infoshops come and go. Following its eviction from premises owned by Edinburgh City Council in 1994, ACE spent two years as a 'virtual' centre, with no physical location, yet continuing its function as a disseminator of information. As a point of contact and a mail drop it used the address of another node (so to speak) on the alternative network, Edinburgh's Peace and Justice Centre. Though it is now established with its own premises, the future of ACE is uncertain: it occupies a rented shop front with no long-term lease and must regularly find the money to pay the rent and bills from a very low income. Such a marginal existence is common amongst the alternative press; it is also common amongst institutions of the alternative public sphere. Yet this is not necessarily a cause for worry amongst those involved: Hakim Bey's (1991) formulation of the Temporary Autonomous Zone (TAZ) emphasizes the transient nature of such institutions; he argues that this will aid their invisibility and prevent 'the State' from identifying and thereby neutralizing their activities. George McKay warns against highlighting the transient nature of *all* such institutions, however. Whilst transience might be an appropriate enough mode for travelling people or for occasional parties and festivals, he stresses the 'possibility or desirability of permanent effectiveness, of transformation rather than simply transgression' (McKay, 1996: 156). McKay looks for 'transgressive constancy' in such actions, expecting history to show that there was more consistency and permanence in the ideas and actions that filled these spaces, despite the temporary nature of their existence.

Amongst those in the alternative public sphere, however, the notion of the TAZ is still an attractive one, if only because it acts as a leveller, preventing any one institution or publication from gaining authority over the rest. An article in *Green Anarchist* by Alder Valley Anarchists enthused about the notion of the TAZ, seeing it in many manifestations of the alternative institutions: 'our own space, whether a co-op or squat or anarchist desert island, anywhere where we can create an organic, Green, natural, wild commune' (Alder Valley Anarchists, 'Temporary Autonomous Zone', *GA* 49/50, Autumn, 1997: 16). In the same issue, an anonymous article celebrates the impermanence of *Green Anarchist*. Under threat as a result of conspiracy charges against four of its editors, the article insists: '[i]n the end, it doesn't matter what happens to *GA*. There will be other publications, better theories, better analysis. A zine is just a zine but the revolution is for keeps' ('Gandalf in Court', ibid.: 11).

The Limits and Freedom of 'Alternative Economics'

That the alternative press cannot compete with the mainstream press in terms of finance, circulation or distribution is, for Comedia, due to the alternative press's over-reliance on prefigurative politics as a determinant of its economic and organizational activities. (I follow Downing in defining prefigurative politics as 'the attempt to practice socialist principles in the present, not merely to imagine them for the future', Downing, 1984: 23). This argument persists to the present, and the experience of *The Big Issue* can be used to show how 'success' can be assured only if strong leadership is in place, along with substantial financial backing (there has been much interest in the mass media on the ebullient personality of John Bird, editor of *The Big Issue*). The press that ignores the 'reality' of economic life under capitalism will always fail in its project (and, on Comedia's reasoning, will deserve to fail).

Such an argument, however, is based on a narrow view of the alternative press as an economic rival to its mainstream counterpart; a view that it is merely in competition with the mainstream in terms of products and 'market penetration', but no more. Yet far from being in competition, the alternative press actively rejects the economic conditions of the mainstream, even to the extent of developing innovative forms of distribution. Its recurrent financial crises are due less to the unwillingness to adopt strategies of financial planning and more to do with the integration of the activities of economic production into the lives of its participants and the integration of the press itself into the alternative public sphere. We have seen how the infoshop describes this in microcosm, where an alternative economic strategy (what has been called a 'black and green economy', recalling the colours representing anarchism and environmentalism) is integrated with other social, cultural and political activities.

Rather than prefigurative methods of economics and organization being barriers to the development of the alternative press, we might consider them essential components of media that seek to integrate themselves with the movements they are supporting, reporting and, indeed, developing. This argument is supported by Downing (1984) in his study of 'self-managed media'. Such a designation is useful in that it reminds us that the alternative press can be considered as quite inseparable from the alternative public sphere. The relationship is mutual and synergetic; the alternative public sphere provides opportunities and outlets for the production and consumption of the alternative press, at the same time as the press itself provides material that sustains the sphere's function as a place for the formulation, discussion and debate of radical and dissenting ideas. *The Big Issue* fits uneasily into this model; its economic strategy is drawn from the media of the dominant public sphere, yet its method of distribution is a hybrid. Whilst its sites of distribution are public spaces and emphatically not those of an alternative culture, its approach is radical enough to have opened up an alternative space of sorts within those public spaces, where regular acts of dialogue and discussion now accompany a commercial transaction; it has been estimated that a quarter of a million people talk to the vendors about homelessness (Swithinbank, 1996). Such an opening up of dialogue in an arena hitherto unknown to such activity (before this, talk was more likely to be one-way, 'them and us', not dialogical) is surely an example of Downing's 'moments of transformation'.[9] When we turn to the grassroots press, that is, to the alternative press construed as an inseparable part of the alternative public sphere and as an enterprise managed by the same people who participate in opinion formation, then such moments also might very well entail 'inchoate organizational models for future political formations' (Duncombe, 1996: 313), that by their incompleteness are less efficient or effective than their mainstream counterparts. But such shortcomings need not be interpreted as failure. The value of such pre-figurative projects proceeds not simply from their content – from their attitude to the oppressive relations of production that mark our society – but from their position within those relations.

The overarching economic conditions in which the grassroots alternative press chooses to place itself are emphatically anti-commercial, more concerned with the creation of a 'black and green economy' than with direct competition with the mainstream press, whether in terms of markets or of production economics. Such a commitment brings with it a commitment to the decentralization and sharing of resources as well as to the educational and empowering potential of the methods employed to construct alternative media, in order to increase participation in their activities.

Alternative media are, or should be, interactive, concerned with everyday life and the ordinary needs of people, not simply with the economy and economic determinism. Collective organization then takes on a different aspect and becomes an attempt to include the readership in decision-making. Downing has briefly referred to how the 'active audiences' of much critical media studies research 'are but one step away from being media creators and producers themselves' (Downing, 1995: 241). In her account of alternative video production with AIDS patients, Alexandra Juhasz summarizes one aspect of this radical repositioning of the audience thus: 'to look is to see and know yourself, not the other' (Juhasz, 1995: 138). The vertical, top-down communication that is typical of most media is simply inappropriate here; horizontal communication between writers and readers (some people will be both, of course) and between different manifestations of alternative media will be crucial in furthering the primary aim of social change. Through Traber and Downing we can argue that such methods of communication and alternative forms of production and distribution are far from mere ideological fixities; instead they spring naturally from the nature of alternative media conceived as methods of achieving social and political action.

Notes

1. Gholam Khiabany (2000) has argued interestingly that even when Comedia's commercial strategy is followed it has led to failure and cites the monthly *Red Pepper* as evidence. By contrast the section of the alternative press that has proved successful (in attracting more readers and lasting longer) on Khiabany's somewhat uncritical terms is the working-class or socialist press (such as *Militant* and *Socialist Worker*).

2. Downing's is not the only formulation of an alternative public sphere, but his offers the best 'fit' for the present study. Negt and Kluge (1972/1983) had first posited such a sphere – strictly a working-class public sphere – in response to Habermas's bourgeois formulation. They make no mention of the place of media in this sphere, however. Apart from Downing, only Jakubowicz (1991) has adapted the concept of the public sphere to a more inclusive vision of communication and media. He identifies alternative public spheres in his study of Poland in the 1980s: an oppositional public sphere and an alternative one. But the historical and political contingencies of his study render his work of limited applicability to Britain in the twenty-first century. In particular this is because his definition of 'alternative' is reserved for the activities of the Polish Roman Catholic Church, its newspapers and periodicals, whilst 'oppositional' refers to the samizdat publications of the Solidarity movement.

3. A special issue of the magazine (no. 71, [March-April?] 1990 and *The Radical Bookseller Directory* (1992 – the only edition that appeared)) that updates it included circulation figures for some of the titles it listed. These data were however supplied by the publications themselves. Chan (1995: 67) provides more recent figures for a handful of anarchist journals.

4. Searle (1997: 125) flatly asserts that *Squall*'s readership 'is far higher' than its print run, though she offers no figure. Jim Carey, one of *Squall*'s editors, however, draws on the results of a questionnaire sent out to subscribers. From an analysis of the 400 replies (half of the total number of subscribers) he finds that: 'an average of 5.5 people read each single copy of *Squall*, with the majority of respondents tending to pass the publication around; an inspiring communal network' (Carey, 1998: 73).

Carey observes that these subscribers make up only a seventh of *Squall*'s readership (though my findings indicate a lower proportion) and are largely those with 'stable addresses'. Given *Squall*'s primary audience and subject matter ('sorted itinerants' with 'unstable addresses'), it is reasonable to expect that copies will be shared at least as much – probably more – in the communal settings in which such people live. Carey's extrapolated estimate of a readership of 35,000 may even be conservative, therefore. The 'free spaces' in which all five titles circulate (protest sites, infoshops, festivals, squats, communes) – all of which are typified in part by shared resources – will ensure that readerships are in general 'far higher' than circulation figures, though how much higher remains to be discovered.

5. The Scottish figures are taken from a talk given by Mel Young, director of *The Big Issue in Scotland*, at the Edinburgh Peace Forum, 28 October 1996. The number of vendors in London appears in Berens (1997).

6. In 1996 a further attempt to establish a periodicals distribution network that is capable of getting alternative titles onto newsagents' shelves was underway. INK, calling itself both the 'Independent News Collective' and 'The Association of Radical and Alternative Publishers', has indeed begun 'repping' directly with newsagents and has so far identified '150 newsagents willing to take INK titles' (*INK Update*, October 1996). Whilst this was undoubtedly an achievement, it represents only a tiny percentage of the newsagents in Britain. Counting only the 28,500 members of the National Federation of Retail Newsagents (Henderson and Henderson, 1996), 150 represents just over 0.5 per cent of the total. If 'multiple newsagents' and other retail outlets for periodicals are included, this figure could be as low as 0.25 per cent. Since its launch, there has been little evidence of INK's success.

7. Corollaries of the infoshop are to be found throughout the history of the alternative press, though none that precisely replicate it in its contemporary manifestation. Striking forerunners, however, appear in accounts of the radical press of previous centuries. Christopher Hill cites Giles Calvert's print shop which functioned during the English Revolution as both radical press and meeting-place and 'perhaps came nearest to uniting the radicals in spite of themselves' (Hill, 1975: 373). A century and a half later, John Doherty's 'Coffee and Newsroom', attached to his Manchester bookshop, was a haven for radicals, where no fewer than 96 newspapers were taken every week, including the illegal 'unstamped' (Thompson, 1963/1991: 789). More recent are the *centri sociali* in Italy which emerged around 1980 as centres 'where young people could work out their own tactics for living and develop their own cultural forms' (Downing, 2001: 294).

8. The network of infoshops in the UK is, for all its importance, not as highly developed as that in the US, which in the first half of the 1990s had its own organizational network, the Network of Anarchist Collectives, and its own networking zine *(Dis)Connection* (Munson, 1997; apparently the network and the zine are 'no longer active': Dodge, 1998: 63). By contrast, some of the most significant achievements of centres similar to ACE have been as a result of individual, local campaigning. Exemplary here is Bradford's 1 in 12 Club's campaign for a review of the city's public CCTV systems (documented in '1 in 12 Celebrates Success in Campaign against CCTV' and 'Class War 73', *Black Flag*, 212 (1997), p. 3 and p. 6 respectively).

9. It may be that such 'moments' also take place during street sales of *Green Anarchist*, though there is no evidence to confirm this. The relative failure of *Green Anarchist* to achieve large numbers of street sales is due not only to its looser organizational structure, but probably also to its selling an ideology rather than a charitable cause.

3

what use is a zine?
identity-building and
social signification in
zine culture

This chapter seeks to understand the production of zines and 'zine culture' in terms of the possibility they offer for building identity and community amongst their readers and writers. The term 'zine' was established in the 1980s to refer to a far wider range of amateur publications than could be encompassed by 'fanzine'. Fanzines are primarily concerned with the object of their attention (works of literature, music, films, or other cultural activities), though this is not to say that they are solely about consumption. John Fiske (1989/1991: 151) has argued that they are 'cultural producers, not cultural consumers'. In his exploration of the cultural practices of science fiction fans Henry Jenkins (1992) argues that 'fandom constitutes a particular Art World' that is based on the production of its own texts such as stories, pictures, videos and music-making (the latter known as 'filking'). He shows how fandom also constitutes 'an alternative social community' where cultural production is employed 'as a means of building and maintaining solidarity within the fan community' (p. 213). Clearly fanzines are major sites of this cultural production. Fanzines can also represent or stand in for, and activate or establish, a community. I want to argue that, in the case of zines, there is a movement away from the reception of primary texts (programmes, books, genres) and production as a consequence of that reception: in many cases those who produce zines ('zinesters') turn to themselves, to their own lives, their own experiences, and turn these into the subjects of their writing. At the heart of zine culture is not the study of the 'other' (celebrity, cultural object or activity) but the study of self, of personal expression, sociality and the building of community. Indeed, the zine may be chiefly construed as promoting sociality. It is dialogical in intent and offers itself as a token for social relations. In the second half of the chapter I shall explore the transformation of zines on the Internet, in particular how the notions of identity, sociality and community found in printed-zine culture are re-positioned through technical agents such as hyperlinking. There appears to be a rupture between two cultures: between the emerging, diffuse and inclusive e-zine culture and the more established, stable and (to a degree) exclusive nature of printed zine culture.

A Little History of Fanzines

The loss of the prefix 'fan' from 'fanzine' forces a re-examination of the zine as a site of 'marginal' cultural production and of its predecessor as the seedbed for such a change. What lies in the history of the fanzine to prepare for such a change? The fanzine is the quintessence of amateur, self-published journalism. It is typified for the most part by a single editor with a small pool of writers, though just as often entire issues are written by the editor. The editor will be responsible for the layout, design, typing, paste-up, and will arrange the printing and distribution and control the finances. It is almost superfluous to add that this editor will have the final say on everything that goes into the fanzine – as draconian a decision-maker as any tyrannical newspaper owner. This control stems from purity of expression: the fanzine is as much to do with expressing that editor's own desires, opinions and beliefs on a chosen topic as it is about informing or educating – or even communicating to – others. Inevitably, fanzines will express more than this: it is impossible to reduce the rationale behind establishing a fanzine to a single impetus. Michelle Rau (1994) argues that precursors of fanzine publishing are to be found in the amateur journalism of the second half of the 1800s, particularly with the establishment in the US of the amateur press associations beginning with the foundation of the first of these, the national Amateur Press Association in 1876. Rau traces the origin of fanzines as they are generally understood – as self-published magazines written and produced by fans of a specific cultural form or of an actor or creator within that form (a genre of fiction, of music, of film; an author, a musician, a film star) – back to the science fiction magazines of the late 1920s. Titles such as *Amazing Stories* not only presented short stories in the genre but also gave space to readers to discuss the science upon which the stories were premised. The first science fiction fan magazine – *The Comet* – appeared in 1930, published by the Science Correspondence Club. In the 1930s we see the appearance of 'comics fandom' in the US. Science fiction and comic fanzines were necessary to their writers and readers in order to validate genres of fiction that were generally ignored or reviled by the mainstream critics. They also functioned as virtual communities, bringing together fans geographically and socially distant from one another. As Martin Barker (1984) has shown in the case of horror comics, establishing a fanzine might also be to take a political stance against the enforced morality of elite groups in society. These three characteristics – the validation of a marginalized cultural activity, the formation of community, and publishing as political action – can also be found in subsequent generations of fanzine publishing, most visibly in the punk fanzines of the 1970s and the zines of the 1980s and 1990s.

Michelle Rau suggests that the stock market crash of 1929, the Depression and wartime rationing all contributed to a diminution in amateur publishing. The avant-garde art movements of the 1950s and 1960s she sees as engaging in 'fanzine-like activity' through their attempts to democratize artistic production such as mail art (Held, 1991). Though not an unreasonable claim, it seems to require a revision of the meaning and functions of publishing in previous artistic movements such as Dada and surrealism: whatever their revolutionary aims, the protagonists and their products in such movements were firmly located in the value discourses of high art. In these cases, publications were not 'amateur' they were 'privately published'. Print runs were not contingently limited (by finance, by the limits of a technology, by a small audience), they were 'limited' to promote their collectability. Similarly, whilst it is possible to see similar impulses to those of fanzine publishers at work in the underground newspapers and magazines of the 1960s (especially to do with the formation of alternative communities, political resistance and notions of freedom and liberation), there is anecdotal evidence to suggest that the fanzine continued throughout this period, if obscured by the impact and (perceived) significance of what Rau has termed the 'aboveground underground press' such as *Oz* and *IT* in the UK, *Village Voice* and *Rat* in the US. In the shadow of these papers flourished fanzines dealing with specialist musical genres (often overlooked by the underground press) such as early rock'n' roll, rhythm and blues, jazz and soul. Fanzines devoted to poetry, detective fiction and the perennial science fiction also continued. It is tempting to see these fanzines as a 'true' underground, their activities coming to wider public knowledge – and to the attention of academics – only when the underground press began to disappear or turn mainstream in the early 1970s.

For cultural commentators and academics alike, the punk movement of 1976–77 was the next watershed for the fanzine. Here we find the argument that the fanzine is not merely a medium for a marginalized cultural activity, it is definitively subcultural in its origins and intent. Taking as a given the contestable thesis that punk was essentially working-class in origin, Dick Hebdige argued that the radical bricolage that characterized the visual language of punk fanzines could be seen as 'homologous with punk's subterranean and anarchic style' (Hebdige, 1979: 112). Like the music it promoted, the punk fanzine's prime interest was in 'the destruction of existing codes and the formulation of new ones' (Hebdige, 1979: 119). The dominant sociological understanding of the fanzine is that the power of 'amateur' work lies in its subcultural location. Consequently, the defining moment of fanzine publishing identified as the symbolic product of troubled youth, of rebellion, of subcultural struggle, is the punk fanzine of the latter half of the 1970s. This argument dies hard: Teal Triggs's survey of British fanzines begins with punk: '[f]anzines are vehicles of subcultural communication' (Triggs, 1995: 74). The punk fanzine continues to be considered as constitutive of a subculture: 'Zines *are* punk', declared an anonymous editor of *Hippycore* (Rutherford, 1992: 3). By claiming that the fanzine is subcultural in origin, we run the risk of collapsing a range of class positions, social relations, political and cultural ends, and claims to solidarity and opposition into a social setting that is essentially structural.

Similarly, the roots of the British football fanzine have been seen to lie in the punk fanzine. Jary, Horne and Bucke (1991: 584) find in them 'the same orientation to contradiction, the oppositional stance, mentioned by Hebdige'; Shaw (1989) notes that some editors of punk fanzines went on to edit football fanzines. There are two arguments here: the first hopes to see homologies between two groups of fanzines based on their identity as sites of 'cultural contestation', the second is perhaps the weaker, structurally speaking, having more to do with the punk fanzine as a spur to continued publishing in different cultural fields. In some cases, the two converge, particularly where politically active punk fanzine editors established football fanzines that espoused similar causes, such as the anti-racist Leeds United fanzine *Marching Altogether*.[1] If we insist on remaking all football fanzines (and all other instances of fanzines and zines, as Triggs seems to want) as essentially subcultural, we end up remaking 'subculture' as little more than a label for marginal or out-of-the-way media production; shorn of its class distinction, it ceases to have any explanatory power. Angela McRobbie (1993/1994: 179) has already argued that '[t]here is certainly no longer a case to be made for the traditional argument that youth culture is produced somehow in conditions of working-class purity'. Andy Bennett (1999) has suggested Maffesoli's concept of *tribus* to replace 'subculture' as an analytic category to explain the more fluid nature of sociality that is a feature of late modern society, especially where notions of identity and sociality are less 'given' by structural conditions and are instead constructed by social actors in evolving, shifting 'communities'.

Zines and Sociality

It is from this position that I want to explore zine culture: from the perspective of social relations. To do this is to focus less on defining the zine in terms of unique, homogeneous content and more on exploring the processes, formations and significations that constitute zine culture (and that are themselves constituted by that culture). This is to go well beyond the over-generalizing and under-theorized definitions of the zine such as that offered by Cheryl Zobel (1999: 5): 'zines are self-edited, self-financed and self-published serials', a definition that can equally apply to little magazines dealing with poetry and fiction. We might consider the prefix 'self-' to refer to any publication that is not corporately financed. From this position it is tempting to include any independent serial publication published, edited or written by any number of people. Whilst we should not insist on the 'one editor, one writer' model in all cases, there is a danger that by accepting a definition as wide as Zobel's we admit as zines any non-corporate publication, regardless of its methods of production. Attempts to define zines in terms of their content are no more useful. In the introduction to his study of US zines in the 1990s, Stephen Duncombe (1997) presents a range of categories drawn from the American 'clearing-house zine', *Factsheet Five* – a 'zine taxonomy' that at the broadest level divides into: 'traditional' fanzines interested in cultural genres such as science fiction, popular music, sports, hobbies and pastimes; and (since the 1980s) 'zines' that go beyond fan writing to cover an extremely wide spread of subjects, including politics, the personal (perzines), 'fringe culture', and issues surrounding sexuality and sexual practices and life at work. At both levels of generality, almost any niche publication could be considered a zine. The use of the term in mainstream culture seems to expect this. Many large record shops now have a section devoted to zines in which it is possible to find examples that range from the intermittent, short-run, singly-edited punk zine to the glossy alternative music monthly that boasts staff writers, department editors and a photographic and graphic design team. Here the term is surely being used in much the same way that genre labels such as 'indie' and 'alternative' are employed by record companies, to, as Simon Frith (1996: 76) has it, 'defin[e] music in its market or, alternatively, the market in its music' in order to convert creative activity into a commodity.

A more fruitful route can be found by exploring Stephen Burt's argument that 'zines are always cheap, often bartered, and personal by definition' (Burt, 1999: 148). This is not to insist on the purity of the single-editor definition, though it is certainly to remain close to that model. First let us examine the economic claims of Burt's argument. Though not universal, the barter system is common within zine culture. Zines are traded between editors not necessarily according to a fixed monetary or exchange rate; a single copy of an extensive, highly professional zine may attract an exchange of a number of issues of another editor's smaller, more cheaply produced publication. Others are simply happy to swap one zine for another. Whilst it is an exaggeration to say that no money ever changes hands – many zines do ask for money, many offer subscriptions – this is usually only one method of payment. Stamps are a popular currency; many editors only ask for a stamped, addressed envelope in which to send the zine to the reader. With relatively few exceptions (such as the high-circulation, professionally produced zines, usually focusing on music and already inhabiting that grey area between zine and niche publication), zines are available in such a variety of economic methods as to make them almost universally available (banking charges between countries is not a problem, for instance, where there are other ways of 'purchase'); they are almost invariably cheap. Moreover, despite the inevitable cost of production, there is little interest amongst most zine producers in profit. Many zines run at a continual loss, the costs incurred being acceptable as the price of communication and self-valorization. The fluidity of the medium and expectations about layout and frequency mean that editors are able to publish when they are financially solvent; there is little pressure on them to maintain a regular schedule. This is not to ignore the periodicity of a zine, or the finiteness that publication can have: however irregular, there is a value in producing an item, not least because it stands for more than simply a product. Operating in this way at low or no cost, maintaining contacts and encouraging readerships, zine exchange can be considered a kind of gift relationship, where altruism plays no little part.

The zine as a medium here stands in for a social relationship: it is a token to be exchanged in all its forms. Even when the zine is used as a commodity transaction, it carries with it something of the obligation that a gift exchange carries: rather than being just a magazine bought from a vendor, the zine is almost invariably bought from an individual and is a product of that individual's labour, a sign of their individuality. Even when bought, then, the zine is the token in a gift relationship: 'gift economies are driven by social relations while commodity economies are driven by price' (Kollock, 1999: 222).[2] The acquisition of zines is surrounded by its own etiquette that expects readers to 'be patient – doing zines is rough and it takes time to answer mail and fill out orders' (Dyer, no date). Readers are encouraged to tell zine editors where they saw their zine listed, in order to maintain and monitor the most valuable parts of the zine network and they are reminded that 'zine editors ... love mail' (ibid.) – indeed, mail is surely at the heart of this amateur enterprise, where economic and cultural access are equalized towards an immense range of publications that, more or less, are the physical manifestation of a social relationship (or at least the tentative beginnings of one). Such is zine culture as it has developed.

I turn now to the second part of Burt's assertion, his emphasis on the zine as 'personal by definition'. I am concerned here with what Janice Radway (1999) has called 'the possibility of the social', rather than with the zine as a site for the promotion of instrumental ends.[3] We might consider two types of sociability: internal and external. Internal sociability privileges the transformation of formal and professional methods of organization, production, editing and writing. There can be something of the ludic, even the festive, in these activities. Where it involves more than one person, zine production is often the site for social gatherings (such as those that take place during the final stages of production: the 'mail-out party' might bring together editor and writers to collate, fold and staple copies of the zine, as well as address and stamp envelopes). Zines offer the possibility for creativity within a social setting and of production that is structured not as a separate occupational duty (and certainly not as a professional activity) but as part of the activities of everyday life.

External social relationships are based on a desire to establish relations (a community, even) through the medium of the zine. The zines I focus on below are generally inward-looking, whether on a personal level or from a small, community-of-interest perspective. It is not that the external world does not exist, but it is not an object for change. It is most often a source of negative influence, of constraint, from which the zine editor seeks refuge or solace within their own constructed community. If 'zine' is to hold any specific meaning beyond being an eroded catch-all term for any self-published or small-circulation periodical, it lies in an emphasis on the personal. This is not to say that the only zines that matter are 'perzines' – that is, those that deal exclusively with the editor's everyday life) – although I follow Duncombe in arguing that the personal is 'a central ethic of all zines' (Duncombe, 1997: 26). As predecessor of the zine, the fanzine also dealt with highly personal tastes and perspectives, yet was ultimately about cultural consumption. The zine offers a similar examination and presentation of matters beyond itself but appears more interested in the lived relationship of the individual zine writer to the world, from which position develops the possibility of the social. The cases that follow explore this movement – from the personal to the social – by considering a range of zines (and their editors) which show that the personal, the social (and the communal) may be realized in zine culture in differing ways.

Cases: *bamboo girl, cometbus, pilgrims* and MAXIMUMROCKNROLL

I begin with an unreservedly personal example, the US zine *Bamboo Girl* – written, designed and produced by one woman living in New York City. 'Sabrina Sandata' defines herself as being of 'mixed blood' ('Filipina ... Spanish and Irish/Scottish, with some Chinese'). She began her zine upon finding her identity and social position conflictual and uncomfortable as a lesbian punk within an Asian culture where heterosexuality, patriarchy and 'beauty' were the norms:

> punk and hardcore music/culture helped a lot with helping me [*sic*] to further form my issues, and also gave me the validation I need for not being the beautiful petite Asian flower all my friends were. (*Bamboo Girl*, 5, 1996, unpaginated)

She writes about her own experiences as she crosses from one social world to another, interviews other women in similar situations (such as the 'all-girl band' Super Junky Monkey from Japan and Julie Tolentino, the 'mixed-blood dyke' owner of New York City's Clit Club. She is as likely to review a slew of locally distributed punk singles as she is to critique the dominance of the beauty pageant in Filipin culture. Her graffitied reproduction of an advertisement for whitening cream détournes its text into neo-colonialist propaganda. She also seeks to retrieve aspects of her culture for feminist readings: her soubriquet 'Sandata' is a Tagalog word which carries the sense of weapon as a defensive tool and a harvesting tool: the domestic as martial; feminism arising from the everyday; militancy alongside the production of the daily bread. *Bamboo Girl* functions as a 'validation for myself' by discovering analogues of its editor's situation in other women, by appropriating repressive elements of her native culture and by providing her with a platform to develop her own identity alongside these and to proclaim it to whomever might wish to listen. It makes visible what in her native culture would remain invisible: 'This is my personal experience, but I know I'm not the only one who's had it. This is my chance to slap people back and say, "I'm not your fucking geisha!".' *Bamboo Girl*, like so many other labels of self-identified marginal groups ('queer'), appropriates a term of marginalization, of oppressive discourse, as power: the cover of the zine depicts a Filipina wielding a bamboo stick as a weapon.

Aaron Cometbus's self-titled zine *Cometbus* takes self-valorization further. He does not seek to affirm his own identity through the appropriation of cultural signs and relations, nor does he accumulate the life histories and struggles of other 'like-minded' individuals. Instead he presents narratives from his life written as self-contained short stories. They appear as fictional first-person narratives, not as diary entries. The immediacy of the narratives is reinforced by their presentation – the absence of illustrations save on the cover forces the reader to focus on the text alone, a text that is hand-written in neat capitals throughout. There are no page breaks between the stories: should one finish part-way down a page, the next continues directly under it. There is little sense of stories inhabiting a particular period of history; they might just as easily have taken place last week or a decade earlier. There is a feeling that they are all equally distant, yet all still active as parts of an index of Aaron's identity. Stories tumble one after the other: the storyteller cannot be stopped until his fund is exhausted. Readers have written to him questioning the factual nature of the stories: 'Stop asking me if the stories are true! Of course they are true' (*Cometbus*, 45, no date, unpaginated). The stories locate Aaron's self-identity in a social world that is picaresque; they recount his travels across America, in milieux both familiar and alien; at local 'hip' parties and in distant redneck bars. The stories are mundane: meaningless, eventless meetings and liaisons. Aaron appears to do nothing, yet his stories are vivid with his experiences and ideas. They speak of dislocation and not belonging, and seek those who are able to belong, though they may be as isolated as he:

> Beautiful girl at the stupid bar show in some other town, you could save me. You've got mystery and charm, style and form, a strength of character that says you know yourself well and don't notice me at all. You've got a certain something that stands out in a crowd. It says, 'I don't fit in,' while mine says 'I don't belong.' Girl, I need to know, how could you be so out of place at this place and still act like you own it? ('*BGATSBSISOT*', *Cometbus*, 45)

On occasion we get a sense of what it means to Aaron to 'fit in', however temporarily, and to feel comfortable with his own identity and his own ideas:

> Corey and I had stopped by on a whim, a chance to wind down after a stressful rehearsal. Much to my surprise, I was drawn in to a discussion of obsessive-compulsive disorders. Instead of hiding shyly in the corner or wasting time with small talk, I found myself speaking my mind about what's on it ninety-nine percent of the time. After all these years I'd finally come to the right party. ('Control,' *Cometbus*, 45)

It is such 'experiences and ideas which are "nothing at all" to the dominant society, whether because they are too regular, or too far outside what is regular, that zines report and communicate' (Duncombe, 1997: 25–26). Such stories appear as both diaries and reportage; eyewitness reports of a personal life, sharing a private life with strangers. As Burt finds, *Cometbus* – and hundreds of zines like it – is journalistic (that is, to do with private journals), yet it is hardly journalism.[4] Janice Radway observes how 'the shift to professional production [of novels] has reduced self-storytelling substantially' (Radway, 1984/1991: 45). This is in large part due to the cultural and social distance that has been placed between writers, publishers and readers. Zines have reduced this distance perhaps better than any other alternative media, since their focus is on the personal, and personal narrative above all. Zine culture collapses Radway's three categories of cultural activity into one and with it has re-emerged – albeit in a small-scale, artisanal, and 'anti-mass' field of production – self-storytelling. Unlike Radway's romance readers, who 'are *not* attending to stories they themselves have created to interpret their own experiences' (ibid.: 49; emphasis in original), Aaron is his own storyteller, publishing accounts that interpret his own experiences. He is also producing and distributing them in a search for identity and sociability, self-valorization and dialogue. His self-storytelling is not only about him creating stories from himself, he is creating them in order to (re)create and (re)present himself in them. He is his own narrator of his everyday life.

Zines such as *Cometbus* can be considered as instances of popular production rooted in the specificities of everyday life, whose authors – as active agents – (as McRobbie, 1992 argues) project their sense of self onto cultural practices. They represent their own quotidian experiences, producing their own lives as a work (Lefebvre, 1947/1991). Through this they produce difference and from that difference (as Stuart Hall, 1990 reminds us) come social identity and social relations. Production and sociation are together wrought from everyday experience through what

Fiske (1992c: 165) calls the 'bottom-up production of difference', created by the popular producer from the available technological resources of the dominant order, resources that tend to be used to create top-down media products that minimize or even discourage participation amongst their consumers. The dominant political economy that deploys these resources and that ensures their possession and control by media elites is here confronted by the development of a popular political economy of the media that opposes institutionalization, professionalization and capitalization. The zine is thus able to liberate its producer(s) from the controls and limits set by the dominant order by redeploying its resources in radical, infractory ways. In de Certeau's (1984) terms, the place that is the political economy and the site of production of the mass media is inhabited by those people normally outside such a place. As they practise media production within this place they establish their own spaces: the space that is the zine might be considered as an instance of de Certeau's 'practiced place', an exemplar of alternative media production as a set of practices embedded in everyday life.

The social world of *Cometbus*, despite its centrality for Aaron, is not a world which we as readers are invited to enter, to participate in, in which to locate our own identities. But the journal style is employed in some zines precisely to encourage readers to share in a social world from which they are distant. A sustained and complex account of this social world presents itself in *Pilgrims*, dedicated to the music of the progressive rock group Van Der Graaf Generator and its founder Peter Hammill. Though nominally a fanzine, editor Fred Tomsett's 'tour diaries' function in similar fashion to the perzine accounts of Aaron Cometbus. His diaries tell us much about a type of relationship between fan and musician in the contemporary progressive rock milieu. Tomsett is an inveterate touring fan who publishes accounts of all the tours (and single concerts) he attends. Here I will focus on one: Peter Hammill's 1998 European tour, recounted by Tomsett over 15 pages in *Pilgrims* 39 (representing two-thirds of that issue). He begins his account by situating himself in his own social world. A hired van, sharing the trip with a fellow English fan, breakdowns, bad weather, poor food at motorway service stations: all emphasize the banality of the situation. Such quotidian detail is present throughout the account: tales of one-way systems in European cities; difficulties in finding venues and hotels; traffic hold-ups and breakdowns. A sizeable chunk of the diary is taken up with pre- and post-gig events that have little bearing on the artist or the music, save perhaps to underscore the writer's dedication to his subject (though I doubt that this is done deliberately). Upon arriving at a venue Tomsett has expectations that speak to a sustained set of relationships with fans a continent apart: he names fans from other countries (sometimes not even the country in which he is) who he expects to turn up at the gig. He observes 'the same people you see at most of these Dutch shows' and sees 'more regulars here tonight: Adrian and Daniel from Switzerland'; the 'most notable absentee was our pal from Grenoble'; 'we hit the café for food and run into Dagmar'.

The two social worlds of the fanzine and the gig sustain each other and the relationships between fans. *Pilgrims* can be understood as maintaining those relationships during 'dead times' – as well as opening up the social experience to the (majority of) readers unable to make the gigs. These readers are also able to get close to Hammill himself: Tomsett has developed a close relationship with the musician over the years, in part due to his merchandize stall (the production and distribution of Hammill's work is resolutely artisanal), his promotional activity through *Pilgrims* and his almost-continuous presence at gigs. Readers participate in what Thompson (1995: 219) terms 'non-reciprocal intimacy at a distance', though in this instance they are enjoying the fruits of a more or less intimate relationship enjoyed by the editor of the fanzine with the musician. We might compare this non-reciprocity between reader and subject with the relationship between reader and subject of *Bamboo Girl* (i.e. its editor): 'Sabrina' projects her constructed self out to a potential readership and invites them to become intimate with her through the medium of the zine.

The American music zine *MAXIMUMROCKNROLL* is less interested in providing a vicarious social world centred on performers for its readers. One of its aims (*pace* Duncombe) is instrumental: to help create the conditions where marginal musics (in its case, hardcore punk) may flourish: 'helping to connect things internationally. Creating links all over the place' (Tim Yohannon, late editor of *MAXIMUMROCKNROLL*, cited in Turner, 1995: 191). It not only provides thorough coverage of the hundreds of tiny, group-owned independent labels as well as coverage of the groups' gigs and interviews with their members, it also seeks to encourage a network of self-sufficient fans and musicians (as with zine editors and readers, often the same people who will work together to put on gigs, arrange tours for one another and organize local distribution throughout the world). It has published a country-by-country directory of groups, venues, labels and individuals interested and willing to work with others to get their music heard, along with those willing to provide board and lodgings for travelling groups. It also lists sympathetic radio stations, record and book shops and zines. The title reflects its emphasis on self-organization and the urgency and power entailed by doing it yourself: *Book Your Own Fuckin' Life*. Yohannon attests to its success:

> For instance, there's a kid [who] [j]ust through pen-paling [*sic*] and whatever –
> I mean his band isn't even on a label, he's just put out his own releases, a cou-
> ple of singles and an LP – his band has gone to Japan twice, just left now for a
> tour of Australia, New Zealand, Thailand, Hong Kong, Japan again. (ibid.)

Instrumentality – at least in the sense of a search for personal contacts,
opportunities for travel and performance, for the acquisition of goods –
is not restricted to punk culture. In his extensive series of interviews with
other zine editors, Erik Farseth (editor of *Paper Scissors Clocks*) reveals
this again and again. Sarah Lorimer (editor of two zines: *Baby I Dig You*
and *Pinto*) suggests that her motives for publishing encompass both the
publicizing of the personal and a range of instrumental ends:

> Why do it? 'Exhibitionism, maybe. Doing zines has gotten me as much read-
> ing material as I can get through, many friends, a boyfriend or two, a place
> to live in a new city, and into graduate school.' (Farseth, 1998: 45)

'Yoonie' (another two-zine editor) trusts the zine community to provide
her with accommodation:

> The zine community IS very SAFE. I could just say 'I need someplace to stay
> in this city' and find a guy who does a zine there, through a friend or some-
> thing, and you know you have somewhere safe to stay. (Farseth, 1998: 55;
> emphasis in original)

> Like last summer I built up an entire summer vacation going up-and-down
> the East Coast based on meeting people who I'd written to for years, and
> read their zines, and really respected them and wanted to meet them. And
> that's different than just having a pen pal. (ibid.: 64)

Never do such achievements displace what appears to be the central feature of this personal odyssey: the need to communicate with others, however few, however distant. Not to meet people is to consider oneself a
social failure. For John Porcellino, editor of *King Cat Comics*, the social
failure came from social pressures during his schooldays; his zines
changed all that:

> when I did my own zines I found out that even though I was pathologically
> shy and mostly (I assumed) hated by my peers (i.e., Suburban H[igh] S[chool]
> kids) and an absolutely ill fitting freak – I found that, through zines, I could
> have friends – and that I could communicate and develop relationships with
> people just as frustrated, lonely and lost as me. It changed my whole life.
> (Farseth, 1998: 45)

'Paul', erstwhile editor of *Hippycore*, sums up this function well enough
when he talks of zines as 'prosthetics for these distant relationships' (cited
in Rutherford, 1992: 5).

Zines and Communication

The zine as a medium can be thought of as monological in practice yet dialogical in intent. Whilst its structure suggests other monological periodicals such as magazines and newspapers, it contains a powerful mechanism for enabling communication between individuals. Much zine writing might be construed as a kind of letter-writing. Whilst the producer does not require a direct and immediate response, the notion of zine culture will prompt dialogue far better than the daily newspaper or any mainstream magazine. The letter-writers (readers) of the latter are an elite in the pages of the periodical; their membership subject to criteria such as 'readability', concision and relevance. In zine culture, anyone may write letters to anyone; whether they are published is hardly the point; some may wish to present their letters as a zine of their own. Here perhaps is an example of a fusion of John B. Thompson's (1995: 82.ff) mediated interaction and mediated quasi-interaction.

Zines producers and readers do not simply use the object of their writing and reading as symbolic capital with which to communicate to others, as in Radway's romance reading groups. Zines are created precisely for people to communicate through them – they are multiple objects created by different producers to reflect and construct a complex of social realities. There is an emphasis on the act over the result, at least to the degree that success is not to be measured by quantity of responses or circulation. The British songwriter Momus recasts Andy Warhol's statement on fame for zines and other micro-cultural forms: 'In the future everyone will be famous for fifteen people' (cited in Burt, 1999: 171). For Radway's romance readers the possibility of the social lies outside the text; within zine culture sociality takes place primarily within and across texts – social performance is enacted within the pages of the zine. Acts of writing, acts of publication, acts of dialogue and exchange and intertextuality are essentially linked with sociality; the intersubjective is realized through the intertextual: ' "meeting people" ... is a key aspect of zines' (Duncombe, 1997: 17) – especially 'prosthetic' meetings.

Zine publishing stands in for meeting people: it can be explained as an instance of material culture that instantiates lived experience, a set of social relations. At the same time it presents an individual's declaration and construction of self-identity and invites others to engage in a dialogue about that identity. By embodying one's own history, experience and opinions within a publication (however narrowly published) one is 'authorizing' oneself to speak, validating one's life, making public one's voice – at least the parts of one's voice that otherwise would not get heard. We might think of these voices as constructing what Castells (1997: 8) has termed 'resistance identity', that is, identity constructed by social actors who find themselves marginalized, devalued or stigmatized by dominant forces in society and culture. These actors then produce 'communes, or communities' as expressions of 'the exclusion of the excluders by the excluded' (1997: 9). In the case of zine culture the remaking of the social world takes place primarily through symbolic production, not in spite of it or as an adjunct to other social activities; Thompson (1995: 35) argues that 'we feel ourselves to belong to groups and communities which are constituted in part through the media'. In the case of zines, it seems that for many those social formations are constituted wholly through the media. Earlier I found Cheryl Zobel's three-part definition ('self-edited, self-financed and self-published') too general. Perhaps her definition, with its mantric 'self' permeating all stages of the making of zine culture, comes closer than we first thought.

Zine Culture and E-zines

Is it possible to identify an e-zine culture as distinct as that surrounding the printed zine? There is evidence to suggest that the e-zine is not an equal replacement for its printed precursor. When the editor of *For the Clerisy* moved his zine to the Internet he found that he not only lost readers who lacked access to the Internet, but he lost readers who preferred the tactile and portable nature of the printed publication. The editor of the *Angry Thoreaun* concurred: 'having to sit at a desk and read it takes all the fun out of it'. After a few issues of the *Clerisy* e-zine, readership had dropped so low that it returned to print. Here we see the rehearsal of common arguments about portability and physicality familiar from any champion of the printed page. The Internet might well be a useful distribution mechanism for information, but it is ill-suited as a reading mechanism for discursive texts. Text can always be printed off, but this act results in a set of uniform pages, printed on one side only, that bear little similarity to the variety of formats that the printed zine can offer.[5] Further, if the zine is a physical token, an exchange mechanism for a social relationship, what precisely is being exchanged when it turns electronic? E-zines mostly appear as poor simulacra of the printed original. The imagination and experimentation in layout and design that are so common amongst printed zines are largely absent. What is also absent is the notion of zine etiquette, to be replaced by the generalities of 'netiquette'. Whilst this may not seem an irreparable loss, it removes at least one set of defining social relations from zine culture and moves the enterprise that bit closer to the mainstream. Its ways of 'doing business' (I use the term guardedly – hardly any zinester would consider their endeavours as a business) become less distinguishable from the dominant practices in cyberspace. What, apart from content, is there to set the e-zine apart from other forms of communication in cyberspace?

In his study of comic e-zines, Matthew J. Smith (1999) identifies two strategies for building communities in cyberspace: presentation and invitation. 'Presentation' has to do with demonstrating knowledge and expertize within the e-zine, valorizing the non-professionalized voices of editors and writers. 'Invitation' is founded on the principle of the active participation of these non-professionals in the writing, creation and production of the e-zine. Neither, as we know, is unique to the e-zine – printed zines, fanzines and most manifestations of alternative media beyond fandom display these two strategies. Though the technical manifestations of the strategies may have changed (the use of email, for instance, to 'publish' one's opinions on an e-zine's discussion list), the strategies are far from new or unique to the medium. In what follows I shall examine a sample of e-zines in more detail. First, though, we must identify such publications. To do so I have used the on-line equivalent of the paper-based networking and review zines. How are e-zines collected and organized by these 'meta-e-zines', and how do they compare with printed zines?[6]

Towards Cases: the etext archives and labowitz's e-zine list

The 240 e-zines collected (at January 2000) in *The Etext Archives* (http://www.etext.org/index.shtml) are all text-based; illustrative material is generated by the ASCII character set. These e-zines are so formatted since they are mailed out to subscribers. They seek to replicate a printed publication in terms of its movement from producer to reader and in terms of its form (though the ASCII e-zine is far more limited in its visual presentation than even the most 'primitive' hand-written zine will be; visually the collection is undifferentiated). When zines move to the Web and not only make use of more sophisticated graphics (through scanning or importing) but add audio and video files to pages, each e-zine becomes more distinctive. (Arguably these multimedia publications require a category separate from 'zine' to accommodate them. For the present purpose, however, I shall consider them all as zines since they continue to be centred on text. Furthermore, my argument in this chapter is interested in processes of communication, identity formation and sociality rather than in formats and features.)

John Labowitz's archive of web-based e-zines (http://www.meer. net/~johnl/e-zine-list/) is considered 'probably the most comprehensive list available on the Internet' by the editors of *The Etext Archives* (at January 2000 it contained 4,225 zines).[7] Of these, relatively few seem to accord with the principles and interests of the printed zines we have already encountered. By contrast, the majority are primarily interested in 'product' and promoting that product. Labowitz has exploded the notion of zine to encompass so many categories as to make the term meaningless: in his list we find career newsletters, advice bulletins for small businesses, web sites for regional and city radio stations in the US. The list can be searched by title or by keyword: of the 80 most-cited keywords, the 'top five' subject headings are poetry (with 460 occurrences), business (441), music (399), marketing (386) and humour (378). The poetry and music e-zines resemble their print analogues in all their diversity: the former focusing on amateur poetry, most often comprising e-zines written by a single poet; the latter ranging across the various genres and sub-genres of popular and classical music (mainstream and 'alternative'). In the world of the printed zine, we might expect those concerned with business and marketing to be critiques of dominant economic practices (such as *Adbusters, Corporate Watch* and any of the hundreds of radical environmental and anarchist zines). Labowitz's list exclusively comprises 'business-positive' publications, mostly guides for small (often one-person) businesses.

Yet Labowitz's definition of e-zine as presented on his web site contains elements familiar to us from the culture of printed zines. E-zines are 'generally produced by one person or a small group of people, done often for fun or personal reasons, and tend to be irreverent, bizarre and/or esoteric'. Of the e-zines searchable through his 'top five' keywords, very few fit all of these categories. He does admit that the term 'has been co-opted by the commercial world, and has come to mean nearly any type of publication distributed electronically', but nowhere does he suggest – as seems to be the case – that the majority of e-zines in his list fit better with this latter, co-opted definition. (A further attempt at defining the web zine, hardly fares better: 'a persistent online location for extended writing that is posted periodically'; Locke, no date.) An attempt to find e-perzines similar to those discussed earlier retrieves 74 titles indexed by the keyword 'personal'. These are remarkably diverse, including web sites on handwriting analysis, 'personal computing experiences' (!), personal taxation, health and beauty, and 'personal success' – examples of what Wilson (1999) has termed 'niche-casting'. Amongst them I was able to find only four titles that suggest an outlook and a rationale similar to their print analogues.[8]

E-zine Cases

The title page of Amy Funaro's *Starache* (http://www.geocities.com/Wellesley/Garden/2600/) gives her snail-mail postal address prominently, and other clues in her pages (such as information on the availability of back issues) suggest that her web site is primarily intended as publicity for her 'real' zine, which she continues to produce in printed form. What we have on-line appear to be textual extracts from that zine, within which we encounter a voice similar to the perzines we have already met:

> I can't stop doing zines. I'm addicted, I suppose. I guess maybe it's my way of still doing something. I don't want to change the world anymore. But I still want to do something, to let me know I'm still alive and this is it. ('An explanation of my past "riot grrrl" articles', *Starache* web site; http://www.geocities.com/Wellesley/Garden/2600/explain.html)

Amy presents essays on her shyness, on women and music, her 'riot grrrl past' and a selection of her poetry. Her site is supported by advertisements, a common feature of e-zines of all stripes. *Starache* on-line appears incomplete; knowing that there is a printed version available and seeing only text leaves us with an e-zine that is basically a signpost – there is little of the socially communicative force behind what is essentially an advertisement for a printed zine. Similarly, whilst the quiet, understated accounts of the editor's daily life that make up the e-perzine *Kickbright* (http://kickbright.com/) call for 'interaction', they hardly seem to need it. Existing only on the Web, the zine makes limited use of hypertext links, and seems satisfied in quietly proclaiming its editor's own interest (mostly US 'indie' bands).

Save for its first issue, which had a print run of one (and, according to its editor, was read by 'about seven people'), *Diba, Diva?* (http://www.geocities.com/ryaneza/) has existed since early 1996 as an e-zine, due to its editor's avowed enthusiasm for computers. It too is supported by advertisements and contains an archive of the e-zine as well as a separate daily journal called *Piglet*. Its editor (Richard Francis Yaneza) is unabashed about his e-zine's subject: 'You've probably noticed that I just like to

babble on and on. And that's precisely what "Diba, Diva?" is: me babbling'
(http://www.geocities.com/ryaneza/about.html).

Yaneza's e-zine does not behave like the ASCII e-zines of *The Etext Archives*: when it is updated ('every two weeks or so') readers can expect the entire site to change. Yaneza makes use of storage conventions now commonplace in cyberspace (the archive) at the same time as he takes advantage of the unfixedness, floating and multiple approaches to authoring that the Web can bring. Whilst the traditionalist zine editor might balk at an e-zine that dispenses with periodicity and becomes essentially unstable, is this anything more than extending the already fluid boundaries of zine publishing, where frequency is a moveable feast, and format and layout are the outcomes of a meeting between creative thought and available materials? Yanzena's apparently cavalier approach has at its heart an interest in exploring form and presentation no less drastic than numerous printed zines.

My last example takes us where the mundane becomes the raw material for cultural production by an 'ordinary person' to a significantly greater extent than even the personal stories of Aaron Cometbus (which, in the end, have a literary flair). For this reason I make no apology for examining it in some detail. What I now focus on is a personal web site that gives full flight to the banal as its subject matter. *The Big DumpTruck*! (www.bigdumptruck.com/, subtitled 'Throwing Little Thought Pebbles at Your Windshield') is produced by Jody LaFerriere, a suburban office worker, mother and resident of Massachusetts. The following gives some indication of the type and style of content found on Jody's site:

1   'My Favorite Xmas Music': this includes albums by the Carpenters, John Denver and the Muppets, Johnny Mathis and 'A Charlie Brown Christmas' ('These are the ones I listen to year after year'). She encourages visitors to her site to 'have fun with Amazon. Enter "Christmas" as your search term and see what you get!' (from http://www.bigdumptruck.com/xmas.htm at 1 November 2000).
2   Jody's list of 'Famous People Who Have a First Name for a Last Name' which at 1 November 2000 comprised around 400 entries, including Woody Allen, Klaus Barbie (!), Eric Carmen, Joseph Conrad, Martin Denny, Philip K. Dick, Dean Martin, Diana Ross and Mary Shelley (from http://www.bigdumptruck.com/lists/).
3   An account of her brief meeting with American TV Food Network chef Emeril Lagasse at a book signing: 'He made the spinach salad with potatoes, onions and bacon from the Christmas book. I wish I had been able to taste it, because it smelled unbelievable. He didn't really pass it around to anyone, and by the time he was done he went

to sign books so I didn't really see what happened to it' (from http://www.bigdumptruck.com/emeril/).

Jody uses the products of capitalism to create both her own mundane cultural forms and her means of communication – the decapitalization in the hand-written or photocopied fanzine is not to be found here; personal Internet connectivity, as we know, remains largely the province of the affluent, white middle class. In both her choice of cultural products and her choice of medium Jody is resolutely suburban. Doubly then, her activities will tend to be overlooked by academics who insist on or look for resistance and infraction in everyday cultural production (as does John Fiske) or who regard popular (civic) use of the Internet narrowly as a tool for political empowerment within marginalized communities (such as Mele, 1999). Yet, following de Certeau, may we not argue that 'marginality is becoming universal' (1984: xvii), at least in the sense that there is a majority of non-producers of culture? Jody is surely part of that silent majority who have become hidden from most studies of everyday cultural production by slipping through what we might think of as the standard 'grids of disempowerment' formed by the intersection of such essentializing categories as gender, age, class and race.

In part this might be because Jody's activities represent an uncomfortable accommodation with capitalism. Her consumption tends to the spectacular (her site contains many images of the products she adores: CD sleeves, Emeril Lagasse book covers), she unashamedly (and for her unproblematically) advertizes amazon.com on her site ('Please support *The Big DumpTruck!* by using this link when you purchase books, videos and popular music from amazon.com). Her site has been designed by a Massachusetts company, Aeropub Communications, which shares the copyright in the site and to whom requests to advertise on Jody's site must be addressed. Not only do we find the deployment of professional skills and reliance on an institution (in the employment of a web consultancy firm); capitalization is sought too. Much zine culture treats advertising with suspicion and scepticism, believing it to be a mechanism for the compromise, dilution and 'recuperation' of the radical. Jody has even had designed *Big DumpTruck!* mugs and mouse mats. Her activities force us to reassess the claims made by Jay Hamilton regarding deprofessionalization, decapitalization and deinstitutionalization as imperatives of alternative media. Such practices as Jody's alert us to the problematic of 'purity' in alternative media practices (Atton, 2000), a theme I return to in Chapter 6. Whilst these three features may be eroded, there remains much in Jody's web site that might be considered alternative: at the very least, that she is giving voice to her own cultural expression through a publishing medium over which she, and not an elite group, has control. She enacts a selection of texts rather than an interpretation of them – her choices are closer to 'top tens', there is little evidence of their being transformed into a new cultural form. What they do become, though, is communicated – and they themselves are the vehicles for communication. Jody does not just want to share her tastes with others, she wants others to use them to communicate with her – to embellish them, to embroider the mundane with more mundanity (how long does a list of people with a last name for a first name have to be? Answer: as long as Jody wants it to be.) What do the texts she selects signify? Do they not stand as tokens for sociality? They do not simply proclaim Jody's tastes, they reach out to seek others who share her tastes and who will valorize them by contributing similarly to her web site. What is at stake here is the power of these texts as socially centred signs for intersubjective communication – Jody's tastes are perhaps marginal after all, at least marginal in her neighbourhood. So she looks more widely for a community. The texts then become socially relevant (regardless of any qualitative value they may have to either Jody or her virtual community). Are Jody's activities perhaps 'therapeutics for deteriorating social relations' in suburban life (de Certeau, 1984: xxiv)?

Need this absence of interpretative significance in the site worry us? In the case of her favourite Christmas music Jody's texts are not there for appreciation, criticism or discussion – they are there as symbols of her taste. Unlike a fanzine, we are not taken into Jody's musical experience, what such experiences mean to her, how they explicitly contribute to her identity. What she does tell us, is how to purchase them – she links each item to its stock record at amazon.com. These are strong recommendations: we are urged to trust her and to buy them. Jody's version of 'networks in the everyday' constitutes readers and contributors but also reaches out to the commercial world – the immediacy and proximity enabled by the practice of hyperlinking compresses these two networks further. While the space produced by Jody is reappropriated from the dominant value system, her choices of texts are largely untransformed – the societal space she produces is organized to a significant degree according to the dominant value system. This is not to find in Jody's web site a resistive, Fiskean power of what we might call 'progressive consumption'. Instead we have the expression of the everyday as Andrew J. Weigert (1981: 36) has described it, as 'a taken-for-granted reality which provides the unquestioned background of meaning for each person's life'. From this expression proceeds her desire to share her mundane humour and the foci of her preferred popular culture (the Carpenters, Emeril Lagasse) with anyone with whom her mundane tastes, opinions and experiences resonate.

It is difficult to consider Jody's site as a zine on the principles we have already discussed. Jody appears as a consumer of mainstream culture. Castell's 'exclusion of the excluders by the excluded' is quite absent from this style of e-zine. Mainstream popular culture is embraced; not only that, Jody and her interests are more likely to be the objects of scorn and contempt within a zine such as *Bamboo Girl* than to be seen as a progression of zine values and culture. Is this the final co-optation of zine culture – its immersion and implementation by 'the majority'? Perhaps what Jody is achieving with her site is less a progression from the zine and more to do with the extension of the concept of the web site and the use of email. Jody's producerly, cultural activities are concerned with the commonplace, the trite, even the dull. Jody is 'breaking out' very differently from our zine editors – taking with her the desires and pleasures of the mainstream, of the unabashedly popular, simply hoping to embrace them in the virtual company of like-minded others. There is little radical here, nothing infractory or antagonistic. On the other hand we might find her 'liberation' in a valorization of the everyday that perhaps exceeds even that found in *Cometbus*. Jody's interests are in classification, in the ordering of the mundane. Her activities tend to the repetitious. Of course her self-publishing is far from revolutionary in content, but it might be that in re-presenting her massified tastes and quotidian humour as special, as particular to her, she is *producing herself differently*, constructing her everyday experience as her identity just as certainly as we have seen Sabrina and Aaron do in their zines.

Does it make sense to talk of zines in cyberspace? Whilst zines persist (and show no signs of disappearing) in printed form and continue to support a definable zine culture around them (however diffuse), in cyberspace it is difficult to separate e-zines 'proper' from other forms of 'personal publishing'. Shorn of their marginality in cyberspace, subject to the equalizing force of the search engine (whether to make them equally visible or equally invisible), the e-zine appears less distinct, its culture more amorphous. Of course, the printed zine was already a simulacrum for face-to-face communication, already a symbol for social relations. Yet the boundaries that such physical objects provide – with their limits on print runs, interactions with copy shops and printers (I mean the human version not the machine), the physical necessity of circulating them, the reliance on other physical publications such as review zines to help move them around – meant that their production and promotion took up measured space in the world. The various types of synchronous and asynchronous computer-mediated communication such as chat rooms, newsgroups, MUDs and MOOs, discussion lists, emails and web pages – and their multiple use at single sites – take away any notion of physicality.

Significantly, though, they offer new opportunities for sociality that are arguably more immediate than those found in printed zine culture.

Without wishing to go down the Baudrillardian road of hyperreality and the extreme fracturing of subjectivities and identities, cyberspace has clearly opened up combinations of communicative activity but with them the possibilities for fragmentation. Does original expression become lost as we construct our identity from the fragments of others' sites, continually rebuilding ourselves, reinventing our sociality, just as the Web is continually in flux? As we produce more and more 'text', and add more multimedia fragments to it, do we come to enunciate less and fall back into an interior monologue? The more we engage in 'performativity without consequence', Roger Silverstone (1999: 77) has argued, 'the more we may find ourselves alone' in cyberspace. More prosaically, a radical employment of hyperlinking can result in the editorial 'glue' of a publication becoming so weak that readers move away from a site so thoroughly that they forget their starting point. For a zine that hopes to call out to others from a fixed point, from a single individual's point of view, such fragmentation is anathema. This might explain the relatively conservative use of hyperlinking by e-zines such as *Starache* and *Diba, Diva?* – their links mostly keep the reader within the site, the better to emphasize the compactness and identity of the site with its author.

This is not to deny either medium the possibility for developing and maintaining relationships that are supportive and intimate: Wellman and Gulia (1999: 186) have argued convincingly that relationships in cyberspace 'are much like most of the ones [people] develop in their real life: intermittent, specialized and varying in strength' – the same appears to be true for those relationships developed through (printed) zine culture. Wellman and Gulia go further, claiming that relationships in cyberspace might even reverse the trend of the privatization of public spaces, promoting community and social trust amongst participants who lack these in their everyday, lived experience. In the first instance, though, what the printed zine and the e-zine have in common is that they are both 'prosthetics', substitutes for sociality. Most writing about the Internet considers distance as a spatial or temporal concept that can be reduced across electronic networks. In the case of the e-zine the reduction of social distance does not merely enable isolated or separated individuals to communicate with one another, it appears to reduce the barriers to sociality itself. It enables the personal, the intimate experiences and accounts to be collapsed into a form of sociation that structures on-line publishing as more than a simple alternative to the mass media and one that is determinedly not designed for mass appeal. The massification of most mainstream attempts at on-line publishing and more generally on-line transactions (such as e-commerce) relies on the Internet's power to diminish physical distance. Alternative on-line publishing employs technology to reduce social distance, to enable the personal and the interpersonal, even to erase the notion of audience or readership.

The zine (printed and electronic) and its productive context also have the capacity to reduce cultural distance: the everyday conditions of production and the everyday experiences from which the zine is created break down the classic aesthetic barriers we see erected in high-art value systems between cultural activity and everyday life. High cultural capital and educational capital, along with economic capital, are not required. Further, the zine *requires* the elision of cultural activity and everyday life: the stuff of the latter informs the content and the processes of the former. Anyone can produce a zine, anyone can read one, goes the philosophy of the zinester: there are few barriers to participation at any level. With the e-zine, cultural distance between the reader and the publication (and its author) is reduced further by erasure of the physical object. For some zine commentators the late 1990s saw the 'death of the zine' (Marr, 1999; Yorke, 2000). They argued that the distinctiveness of zine culture (as a print-based culture, centred on the non-professional, single-editor working within a community of other similar producers) was being eroded by bandwagon-jumpers, corporate co-optation and zinesters interested in publishing only as a fashion statement. They also acknowledge that zinesters (the majority of whom are, to judge from Stephen Duncombe's survey, in their teens or early twenties) grow up, take on new responsibilities (careers, families), find it more difficult to find time and money to devote to what might appear an increasingly futile activity (being famous for a mere 15 people). What such pessimism allows little room for is the erosion of the notion of 'zine culture' in a more positive direction: doing away with the elitism surrounding much zine activity. After all, the recent history of zine publishing is to be found in the 'copy culture' arising from punk, a set of cultural practices quite alien to people like Jody. Such practices were simply not available to her; they were those of an elite (however marginalized they deemed themselves to be, they were not without power). In his exploration of what it means to speak of a culture of everyday life, John Fiske refers to the

> weaving of one's own richly textured life within the constraints of economic deprivation and experience ... of controlling some of the conditions of social existence [and] of constructing, and therefore exerting some control over, social identities and social relations. (Fiske, 1992c: 160)

Fiske is interested not in people who through their actions and activities proclaim themselves to be part of a subculture (such as Aaron and

Sabrina); he does not even appear to be interested in people like Jody. Even though she is creating a personal media space woven into her everyday activities, this is hardly equivalent to the resistance that Fiske considers the result of incorporating capitalist resources into everyday culture. Jody creates her own texts through far more subdued means than the cultural 'guerrillas' whom Fiske champions: 'evading hegemonic capture' (Fiske, 1989/1991: 137) could not be further from her agenda. Jody is perhaps erasing the vestiges of cultural distinction that accrue to zine publishing by producing her own zine-like publication in ignorance of zine-cultural history. She encounters not an already-existent subculture but a dominant, technologized culture that suggests to her ways of self-valorization not open to her previously. By diminishing social and cultural distance such media practices are able to access the specificities of the everyday lives – their meanings, practices and values – of individuals sociated in 'occasional communities'.

Notes

1. Jary, Horne and Bucke are careful not to hitch all football fanzines to the subcultural wagon. They stress another category of fanzine that 'merely reflect[s] the commitment to team and locale of ardent supporters' (1991: 584). It is difficult to construe such publications as subcultural equivalents of Hebdige's fanzines.

2. This is a different form of gift relationship than that found by Kollock amongst cyberspace communities, where the gift lies not in the exchange of a publication, but in information, advice or help received.

3. Duncombe (1997: 55) finds that zine editors rarely talk in instrumental terms; it is important to make a distinction between the zines discussed here and, for example, the alternative media of new social movements. The latter certainly share production characteristics of the zine and can also be understood in terms of their ability to transform social relations. We might term them 'activist zines': they were especially prominent amongst the anarchist community in the 1990s. Zines and activist zines share an interest in the establishment of community, the search for self- and group identity, and in the validation of personal experience and culture, but activist zines tend to have explicit instrumental ends (raising consciousness, mobilizing resources, campaigning and organizing, 'revolutionizing the traditional order').

4. On-line journalling has itself become formalized as a practice on the Web. The MetaJournals web site (http://www.metajournals.com/main.html) offers tuition in setting up and maintaining an on-line journal, as well as providing essays and discussion lists for on-line journallers to share their experiences.

5. Some zines, though, find an economic benefit in moving to the Internet. The experimental music zine *Rubberneck* became an e-zine in 2000 after 15 years as

a printed publication. Its editor always insisted on it being free of charge. To achieve this he needed advertising revenue from the tiny independent record labels whose releases he reviewed. When that dried up, he was unable to subsidize the printed version himself. Moving to the Internet ensured the zine's continuance as a free publication and, whilst it required subsidy from its editor, at least this meant less personal financial commitment than maintaining the print version would have incurred. In correspondence to me he bemoaned the lack of readers signing his guest book and was concerned that his readership would drop. Yet he was prepared for this and to lose his own money in order to keep to his principle of producing a free publication. John Marr (1999), editor of the zine *Murder Can Be Fun*, believes that if he were starting a zine for the first time 'no way would [he] mess with hard copy – [he]'d go straight to the net. It's cheaper, easier, and faster.'

6. Defining and identifying e-zines are subject to the same problems we encountered with printed zines. The same arguments about the differences between fanzines, zines and niche publications apply, as do those surrounding the co-optation of the term by various interests. We will see, however, that further and more severe problems arise around the notion of e-zine.

7. Labowitz has since indicated his 'retiral' from maintaining the list and has offered the list to any non-profit organization committed to its upkeep.

8. This is not to say that there do not exist others that do resemble printed zines in these ways. Whilst many netsurfers would use Labowitz's list, many others might well use more idiosyncratic means such as personal recommendation, review in a printed publication or linking to e-zines from other sites. I have not attempted to replicate these types of searching here.

©📖📄💾🖥📁📹®

4

alternative media and new social movements

I now want to move from examinations of the personal and the individual in communities to broader sociopolitical applications of alternative media. In this chapter and the next I explore some of the ways in which the transformation of roles and responsibilities I have proposed as a theoretical construct is developed in practice by contemporary alternative media producers. I shall focus on the use of alternative media by new social movements, in particular by the various groups, alliances and pressure groups that comprise the contemporary, radical environmentalist movement in the Britain of the 1990s. In the present chapter I shall examine the aims of a range of alternative publications and explore how these are variously realized through their approaches to organization and production. The following chapter will look at the writers of these publications. It will discover the extent to which readers are enabled to contribute and the impact that radically democratic notions of participation can have on the coherence and coverage of these publications and on the production of knowledge within new social movements.

The British New Social Movement Media in the 1990s

The 1990s saw an upsurge in the alternative media that built on the 'zine explosion' of the 1980s. A large proportion of these titles were linked with environmental protest movements. The impetus for much of the campaigning on these issues has come from a broad sweep (coalition is too formal a term for it) of groups that are anarchist in nature, if not in political intent. In his study of the involvement of anarchists in movements for social change, Andy Chan observes that '[r]ecent years have seen a considerable degree of intellectual traffic flowing both ways between anarchism and environmentalism' (Chan, 1995: 48). Welsh and McLeish's (1996) study of anarchism and road protest finds a high correlation between the two. Anarchist commentators have pointed out the anarchist contribution to new social movement activity.

Numerous publications have grown up around the various groups and movements, documenting their actions as well as providing strategic and tactical discussion, and theoretical and ideological debate. Many protests and actions have spawned their own publications, such as the *McLibel Update* (giving news of the libel action taken by McDonald's against two activists), its on-line successor, *McSpotlight* (examined in Chapter 6) and *The Roadbreaker* (the 'No M11 link road' campaign newsletter). Others are published by specific groups engaged in a range of activities (for instance, the radical environmental group Earth First!'s *Do or Die*). Larger, less focused movements have established their own titles, such as *Pod* and *Scottish Anarchist*. There are also many general, non-aligned publications such as the free news-sheets *Counter Information* and *SchNEWS*, as well as more substantial newspapers such as *The Law* and *Squall*. A video magazine, *Undercurrents*, was also established: this aimed to provide an activist-directed alternative to television news. It appears that, just as a CIA report on the American underground press astutely observed, 'the vitality of the "alternative press" [is] directly proportional to the health of the radical movement in general' (from the CIA's 'Situation Information Report: the Underground Press', quoted in Rips, 1981: 73). If the alternative press flourishes in tandem with the movements it supports and documents, then in order to better understand the role and nature of the alternative media, we need to look at the context of these movements, which arises from what has been called the 'New Protest'.

The New Protest describes a plethora of diverse groups and movements that developed in the 1990s to espouse direct action to further their causes. These coalesced and combined or split as choice or necessity dictated; most are organizations without formal memberships, such as Earth First!; or temporary formations that come together for specific actions, such as the Earth Liberation Front and the radical cyclists' campaign, Critical Mass. Others lead a shadowy existence in an attempt to evade police surveillance, such as the militant animal rights group the Justice Department. Most have no leaders, no hierarchy. Some employ only non-violent direct-action tactics (NVDA) and are known as 'fluffies'; others do not balk at violence against property and sometimes people ('spikies'). Protests can take the form of marches, occupations (in tunnels, in trees, on tripods), street parties, 'guerrilla squats', the setting up of illegal sound systems. Locations are both urban and rural: protests may take place in offices, factories, building sites, fields and on nature reserves. Yet we should not consider these protests as entirely new phenomena: they are, as George McKay suggests, 'the latest in the line of living, indeed thriving, cultures of resistance, ones that offer their resistance through direct action' (McKay, 1996: 158). Where, arguably, they are new is in the nexus of alliances that have come together – animal rights, environmentalism, anti-capitalist critiques, squatters' rights, rave culture – and in the highly visible networks of communication and action that they have developed.

McKay notes the employment of diverse tactics in protests: tunnelling, tree-house building, demonstrations, occupations and 'celebration as a struggle'. He helps us understand the multiple voices and ideas that offer so many perspectives on the New Protest at the same time as they cohere as a 'patchwork' into a larger sociopolitical phenomenon. Independent self-creation is paramount, as is manifested by the practice of 'D.I.Y. politics' (*D.I.Y. Politics*, 1996). The individuals and groups participating in these movements do so from a position of non-alignment with political parties and groupings. They usually operate singly or in temporary alliances: what Richard Gott has termed the 'hit and run left' (Gott, 1995). The two major themes here – self-organization and 'DIY politics' as 'channels of resistance', rather than the more traditional avenues of political parties and organized pressure groups, and bricolage (as diversity) as a strength 'deriv[ing] from the refusal to grant primacy to any particular site or mode of struggle' (Welsh and McLeish, 1996: 32) – are useful starting points for an analysis of the contemporary alternative media. The application of the first feature should be clear enough: it points to media that are set up explicitly to fill gaps left by the mass media, where the alternative media hold that the mass media have failed to represent certain issues or social groups. The application of the second is less clear; superficially it might be considered as an explanation of the non-competitive nature of alternative media, but it also has to do with methods of organization within and across media that typically operate via a network. The aim of this chapter is to examine how alternative media organize themselves within this network:

> a network of *active relationships* between actors who interact, communicate, influence each other, negotiate, and make decisions. Forms of organization

and models of leadership, communicative channels and technologies of communication are constitutive parts of this network of relationships. (Melucci, 1996: 75)

In Melucci's reading of social movements the role of the network and that of communication – of media as activators of that network – assume a key position. Organizational forms are the building-blocks of the network. These forms, as Melucci asserts, tend away from the traditional, hierarchical and bureaucratic forms of social organization; in this respect, they demonstrate Welsh's claim that collective action 'eschews existing channels of resistance' (Welsh and McLeish, 1996: 30) and maintain 'an informal and irreverent posture towards the established norms and rituals of mainstream politics' (Scott, 1990: 34). It is these radically organized groups that make manifest the 'hidden networks' that ultimately define social movement activity (Melucci, 1996). These forms of organization are characterized by loose internal structures and by autonomy of the groups thus organized. Loose structures are most commonly realized in social movements by the absence (or at least, the reduction) of hierarchy and by an anti-authoritarian ethos. Job rotation is common, as is the sharing of jobs and skills. Membership is fluid: often there are few if any criteria for membership, save active involvement in the group. Consensus and collective decision-making are preferred over voting. The extent to which the alternative media of new social movements have adopted such forms of organization, to what ends and with what success is the subject of this chapter.

My focus is on the activist-run, grassroots alternative press of the UK. I will examine four nationally distributed titles that best exemplify the relationship between the non-aligned sociopolitical movements and the alternative media that support them. These titles comprise a broad category of 'environmental anarchist' publications, which were a distinguishing feature of the British alternative press in the 1990s. With the exception of *Green Anarchist*, all were founded in the 1990s. All continue to publish in printed form, except for *Squall*, which ceased quarterly publication in 1997, becoming *Squall Magazine Online*. The information on *Squall* in this and the following chapter relates only to the printed version.

Do or Die, subtitled *Voices from Earth First!*, was founded in 1992 and, though it hoped to appear more frequently at its outset, has now become an annual digest of reports and features based on the activities of one part of the environmental activist movement, the radical direct action group Earth First!. It has experimented with format and size, having been published in A5 and A4 formats, settling on A5 in 1996. It is currently the only alternative press title to be perfect-bound. It is also the longest of these four titles in extent; each new issue has been longer than its predecessors.

Its extent enables it to offer a wide content: detailed news reports from home and abroad, lengthy theoretical and philosophical articles, book reviews and features on tactics for protests.

If *Do or Die* can be said to have a single, overarching aim it is that described in the lead sentence of an editorial that appeared in its second issue, namely that it 'is dedicated to direct action to protect the biological diversity of this planet from the bigness of human development' ('Short Blah', *Do or Die*, 2, April–May 1993, unpaginated). It is explicit about encouraging activists to contribute to the magazine, not only to discuss ideas but to enable them to provide 'in depth reporting'. *Do or Die* hopes 'to create a space where the people behind the news stories get to put their message across unmediated' (from *Do or Die – Voices from Earth First!*, http://www.hrc.wmin.ac.uk/campaigns/efhtmls/dod.html). The strapline on the front cover of the first issue calls *Do or Die* 'The voice of the British Earth First! movement'; by issue 2 it is simply 'A voice', by issue 5 plurality within the movement is explicit: 'Voices from Earth First!'. In 1999 it broadened its scope further to encompass 'Voices from the ecological resistance'. In the words of 'Dom', a member of the editorial collective, the aim is 'to have pieces that broaden the focus and step outside of the ideological ghetto, to have something for everyone, a grab-bag ... to give people a sense of possibilities, to not succumb to dogma'. Dom also makes a nice distinction between two types of 'activist': the 'professional activists' who work for such organizations as Friends of the Earth and Greenpeace and who take part in large-scale actions to raise awareness of issues through media exposure, and activists who are 'ordinary people', undertaking actions to effect an immediate change:

> and the strongest campaigns have always been those with a tightly knit, resolute community of 'ordinary' people at their heart – and they often show up the 'professionals' or 'activists' as ineffectual or playacting. I would like to help engender such community struggles, and to represent them and their aspirations. (Dom, from an interview conducted by the author)

Green Anarchist is a quarterly tabloid of 20 pages (on average). It was founded in 1984 (for the first half of its life it was produced as an A4 magazine), and represents another strand in the anarcho-environmentalist movement with its vision of an anti-technological, primitivist society. It does, however, draw on the events, campaigns and protests of the wider environmental and anarchist movements. Its range of articles is similar to that of *Do or Die*, though its lengthier articles almost all deal with theory and philosophy within the 'green anarchist' movement.

Throughout its life it has been the subject of much controversy and criticism both within and outside the anarchist and the environmentalist movements. Such criticism has come mostly from its increasing support for violent activity, against people as well as property. The 'Gandalf' conspiracy trial of three people responsible for the production of *Green Anarchist* centred on the magazine's alleged incitement of its readers to violent action (Atton, 1998). The 1990s saw the magazine move increasingly towards an agenda that supports and promotes violent direct-action tactics. It has published instructions for making 'your own shotgun' (*GA* 27, Summer 1991), bombs and caltrops (GA 30, Summer 1992). More recently it has offered support to the radical animal rights group the Justice Department, Timothy McVeigh and the Unabomber. Its current strapline is perhaps the most accurate summary of *Green Anarchist*'s present purpose: 'For the destruction of Civilization'. Its strategy, a blend of cultural, political, social and economic interventions, had already been given a name in an earlier editorial: '*Green Anarchist* strategy is revolution on the periphery' (*GA*, 11, April–May, 1986: 2). It aims to function as a means of communication, to 'provide a forum for [committed activists] to find out what's going on in their own and other resistance milieus and to discuss this via our pages' (from an interview with Oxford Green Anarchists, the group primarily responsible for *Green Anarchist*).

In spite of its chosen medium, the weekly free-sheet *SchNEWS* (founded in 1994) appears distrustful of the printed word. A slogan often repeated in its pages is: 'A single act of defiance is worth a thousand angry words.' Its primary aim does not appear to be the straightforward act of reporting, but to promote political activism amongst its readers: 'Ultimately the idea of *SchNEWS* is to encourage people to get off their bums, go see things for themselves and make up their own minds' (untitled article, *SchNEWSround*, 1997, unpaginated). The reason for this is found in *SchNEWS*'s origins. It grew out of an activist collective based in Brighton whose members came together in 1994 to oppose the Criminal Justice Act. Their first high-profile action was the squatting of Brighton courthouse. Consequently, Justice? (as the collective is known; the ironic question mark is part of the name) has remained active, organizing parties, maintaining a collective allotment, running street stalls and other events (McKay, 1996: 175–177). From this perspective, its collation of 'unique weekly snapshots of the phenomenal rise of positive direct action' (statement from the back cover of *SchNEWS Reader*, 1996; also reproduced on an advertising flyer for the book) is less to be considered as news, more as 'information for action', as goads to personal involvement and empowerment. In relation to the radical community press of the 1970s, Brian Whitaker calls this 'useful information' (Whitaker, 1981: 105). Media researchers in the US call it 'mobilizing information' (MI). By this they mean information, appended to or embedded in a news report, that provides the reader with the wherewithal to pursue the story further; typically, to become actively involved in the issue being reported. This usually takes the form of details of a meeting or demonstration, giving time, place and date and contact details for further information (Bybee, 1982; Lemert and Ashman, 1983). It has been found that alternative newspapers are more likely to supply MI than their mainstream counterparts, and that of these, the 'activist' alternative newspaper supplies it most frequently (Stanfield and Lemert, 1987). In the present cases, information for action often goes much further than this, encouraging readers to develop their own tactics, which can range from 'blockades' of 'guilty' companies and government departments (telephone and fax numbers are published), to more militant techniques (*Green Anarchist* has, over the years, published articles on how to build police radio jammers and primitive firearms; *Do or Die*'s 'Dear Nora' column is dedicated to techniques for disabling earth-moving equipment and other ways of disrupting road-building activities (known as 'ecotage')).

SchNEWS does not set out any further aims or objectives; an interview with its editors elicited no more than a reiteration of these sentiments and in particular that of 'information for action'. However, the sentiments it expresses in an editorial statement resemble those of *Do or Die* in its more explicit objectives. Just as *Do or Die* recognizes diversity of opinion, so too does *SchNEWS*: 'diversity is our strength' ('*SchNEWS* – As It Is', *SchNEWS Reader*, 1996, unpaginated). It seeks to involve as many people as possible through its pages: 'The DIY media has exploded and there are many views, many sources ... from the heart of a fluid, organic, evolving movement of empowerment – "DIY culture"' (ibid.). The opening of an article entitled 'Underground Overground' approvingly quotes 'Jamie', a member of the Small World Media alternative news video group:

> The underground media is produced by activists – bored of not being given a platform, we create our own; bored of being misquoted, we quote each other; bored of going on actions, then rushing home to find the news either disregarding us, or distorting our deeds and words. ('Underground Overground', *SchNEWS*, 101, 13 December 1996)

Whilst focusing on environmental activism, *Squall* also provided coverage of and for the 'new travellers', the free festival scene and the squatting movement in the UK. Its size (from 1995, an average of 64 pages per issue) enabled it to report in much more detail than *SchNEWS*, though its frequency meant that it was inevitably less current. As with *Do or Die* and *Green Anarchist*, it found a place for the cultural activities of these movements, whilst being less focused on theory and philosophy. Its longer features showed a tendency to blend the political with the 'human interest' story, spotlighting initiatives by named groups and individuals within their local communities.

Squall operated in the same broad area as *SchNEWS*: both had a remit wider than the environmental issues that are at the heart of *Do or Die* and *Green Anarchist*'s coverage. *Squall* was keen, however, to express its closeness to the environmental movement, stating its main aim as '[t]o battle for a better environment – countryside, urban and psychological' ('Information Is Your Weapon', *Squall*, 9, Winter 1995: 3). In common with *SchNEWS* it has grown out of an activist collective 'lowLIFE?! [*sic*], based in London. After two years organizing 'large cultural events in London squats' the first issue of *Squall* was produced in 1992 on the collective's computer (Carey, 1998: 60). It began as a magazine 'for the squatter-homeless' (masthead on *Squall*, 2, August (1992)), widening its audience to 'squatters, travellers and other itinerants' (masthead on *Squall*, 5, October/November 1993) and publishing articles of wider interest to those involved in environmental and non-aligned political activism. Also in common with *SchNEWS* it presented its news and features not merely as information (and certainly not as entertainment) for a passive reader, but as information 'to tool you up', that is, to furnish materials with which readers could achieve certain practical objectives. This 'tooling up' is itself a metaphor taken from warfare (meaning 'to arm oneself') and the theme of struggle continues in the title of many of its editorial statements (as in the reference above): 'Information Is Your Weapon'. Like the other titles, *Squall* was concerned with increasing access to this mobilizing information.

This is not provided in a unilinear fashion by a controlling medium; instead it is the product of discussion, debate and other communications between participants in the 'action' itself. As a medium for communication within the alternative public sphere, such papers and magazines hope to build agendas and develop opinion. This will come from as wide a range of participants as possible; communication is encouraged across movements and communities, including those potentially in conflict; the media space available is to be open to a wide array of voices and opinions. These, at least, are what the aims of the alternative media as explicated in these four titles indicate. In such ways agendas and opinions are, ideally, to be shaped by a wider participation in the pages of the alternative media than is usually the case in the pages of the mainstream media. Here we see exemplified John Downing's four theoretical principles that we met in Chapter 1 (an emphasis on the 'multiple realities' of social life, freedom from party and intelligentsia, the privileging of movements over institutions, prefigurative politics). Even though the grand aim of 'changing the world' might not easily be achieved (if it ever is achieved), the provision of 'information for action' within an organizational model that is based on empowerment might at least 'provide staging posts along the way, moments of transformation, however small' (ibid.). The value of such activism can only come from the involvement of as many people as possible; by multiplying those 'moments of transformation' and by encouraging their profusion through self-education and a culture of activism, the alternative media hope to meet their aim of empowerment through 'information for action'. All four titles carry the implicit opportunity for any activist (and possibly, if not practically, all activists) to be part of the processes of creation, production and distribution. Activists are never to be mere readers or consumers; they are encouraged to be organizers, producers and writers. How these media are organized to permit such opportunities is the subject of the next section.

Approaches to Organization and Production

Do or Die

Do or Die is explicit in that it is a collective, in this case one that centres around one group of the British Earth First! movement, Mid Somerset Earth First!. However, this collective is only responsible for the collection, editing and production of the magazine; it relies on the remaining Earth First! groups (and other sympathetic organizations and individuals) to submit news and features. (Number 5 acknowledges the contributions of 36 groups and 'countless individuals'. A flyer for this issue begins: '*Do or Die* No. 5 has been written by over 60 activists from the British and worldwide environmental frontlines', a similar flyer for no. 7 claims 'over 80 activists'.) Problems with co-ordinating such a diverse – and deliberately unorganized – network led to difficulties in ensuring punctual submission of copy: 'due to the difficulty of getting campaigns to write reports to deadline, we have set up a network of regional reporters', who also act as 'collection points' for campaign reports from the regional Earth First! groups (from an interview with Dom). Whilst the editors of *Do or Die* seek to involve as many people as possible in all aspects of the magazine's production, at the time of my interview with Dom (March 1997), there were only three regular members of the collective. They were assisted by occasional contributions from a handful of other people, who often worked with them for one issue only. There was little division of labour: everyone involved in an issue 'wears many different hats':

> We're all responsible for soliciting pieces, editing them, writing stuff, laying out, gathering graphics and photos, publicity, mailing out free copies, answering orders, physically selling, you name it.

Dom admitted that their working methods were 'haphazard': 'I'm not quite sure how we do it, which may partly explain why we're so bloody irregular.' He continued: 'our different hats have a worrying tendency to slip off, cos we've got so much more important things to do instead' (such as the activism that is at the heart of the Earth First! movement and simply 'having a life, mmm, that would be nice', as he put it). He is in no doubt that improvements could be made. Indeed, they favour 'a more conscious, structured approach' which, whilst espousing the collective as the main method, would nevertheless eschew the random 'free-for-all' that Landry et al. (1985) find in many collective endeavours. At the same time *Do or Die* hopes to increase the number of people involved. Although the current editorial collective admits to feeling 'possessive' about their roles, Dom wants to encourage more people to contribute skills (as well as articles) in order to promote diversity of opinion within the movement and to prevent it from falling into inertia ('I'd actually like to have a lot more views in it that completely contradict my own, and set the cat amongst the radical pigeons.') It is the tension between that possessiveness and its openness to new people and ideas that may well save the magazine from the worst collective inefficiencies.

Do or Die is the only title to provide specific 'instructions for authors' and is prepared to accept all that it receives, of whatever length, as long as it conforms to these instructions. Its ability to encourage so much material is a direct result of its flexible approach – expanding to whatever size it needs to accommodate what it chooses to publish. It is no surprise that the magazine is particularly interested in first-person accounts of environmental destruction: '[w]hen you discover an incidence of eco-rape, immediately write down a description of it, what you feel, and what you believe you can do about it' ('Short Blah', *Do or Die*, 2, April–May 1993, unpaginated) Although 'discovery' need not entail physical proximity to the event, the authenticity of immediate reaction to it is crucial; certainly there is no expectation of objectivity. More than simple reporting and reaction, the magazine also wants its writers to supply suggestions for action to improve the situation. Empowerment is explicitly mentioned: 'articles should empower people to do something' (ibid.). Yet the magazine is not recommending the privileging of subjective accounts above accuracy; it expects the rigour of references: 'any facts or statistics quoted *must* carry references to their sources – without these an article is useless' (ibid.).

Only this single editorial provides detail on how to present an article; subsequent calls for submissions are much more general ('Send your material to us now!' shouts the editorial in issue 4). Little is said about content. Underneath such liberality, however, runs a current of concern about the 'dilution' of the magazine (and the movement): 'other groups have been swamped by well-meaning but naive recruits and lost their original radicalism' (ibid.). Despite its openness to diversity of opinion, information and proposals for action within its pages, *Do or Die* is concerned with the 'recuperation' of radical groups into mainstream environmental protest groups (such as Friends of the Earth and Greenpeace), where direct action by anyone save nominated 'professional activists' is discouraged. Within *Do or Die*, readers are expressly warned against contributing anything that might be accused of recuperation or reformism ('If you don't like it, do your own mag', they are told ('Idiotorial', *Do or Die*, 3, late 1993: 2).

A major part of the production of the magazine, Dom admitted, is in 'commissioning' articles and chasing up writers when they fail to deliver promised copy, which seems to be a regular occurrence. He is sympathetic, though, since he knows that the writers – like the editors of the magazine themselves – are primarily activists: 'to be fair, most people give their all to campaigns and are physical and mental wrecks as a result of it, so to expect them to write an article about it as well may be a bit much'.

Most of the articles that appear in *Do or Die* are commissioned; very few are unsolicited. Whilst the flexible length of the magazine can always accommodate whatever the editors choose to publish, it is wrong to assume that its length has continually increased due to the number of articles it happens to receive. Instead, it is the result of a conscious effort by the collective to encourage (and provoke) activists to write for the magazine and to be more 'ambitious' (Dom's word) with each issue. The magazine's guidelines may not be as formal or as precise as those of, say, academic journals, nevertheless they indicate that the editors have expectations of their writers that must be met. Despite its collective approach to production, distribution and editing, *Do or Die* places responsibility for the writing firmly on the writers themselves, offering 'positive suggestions of criticism' (Dom's words) where necessary for writers to improve their own contributions. That individual writers are expected to take responsibility for their own work is also evident in the editorial collective's statement that the magazine 'does not pretend to be the official voice of EF!' nor are its contents 'automatically the views of the editorial collective, the Earth First! movement, Earth First! groups or individual

Earth First!ers [*sic*]'. (Though in its zeal to emphasize editorial neutrality such a denial itself denies that the views must belong to someone.) The emphasis on the personal, the individual, rather than the corporate view is borne out by further examination of the magazine's guidelines, where the general rubric of any submission is sketched out. The emphasis is on the involved, activist writer reporting from within the event, describing it in personal terms, 'what you feel, and what you believe you can do about it'. This, along with the avoidance of editorial responsibility for content, might also be judged by the absence of the editorial statement as a vehicle for opinion on particular issues. The editorials mostly concentrate on guidelines, apologies for lateness and encouraging submissions. The very titling of *Do or Die*'s editorial as an 'Idiotorial' speaks of a self-deprecating, self-ironic view of the editors as knowing no more (perhaps even less?) than their writers and readers, while taking an ironic view of the practice of editorial writing in general.

Squall

The editors of *Squall* were less forthcoming, in print, about their work practices, which might be put down to their more 'professional' image and commitment to journalistic standards that resemble those of mainstream newspapers more than any of the other alternative titles in this study. For all that, they favoured a resolutely non-mainstream approach to organization: all editing and sub-editing was done collectively by a group whose membership varied 'according to availability'. Once more, the publication took its place behind more pressing commitments, such as activism or daily life. In *Squall*'s case, this could easily mean editors finding a place to live, since many of those involved were squatters. As with *Do or Die*, however, *Squall* was conscious of the weakness of full collective organization, and was developing towards a situation that recognized the different talents of different people 'where people perform the tasks to which they are most suited' and where more defined roles based on ability and skill can interlock: 'Together we are spokes in a wheel that rolls' (from an interview with the editors). Whilst the roles of editors, reporters and production workers were shared, they were shared by a relatively small group of people (five or six, though once – with *Squall* 11 – nine individuals could be considered as comprising the collective) in a single location, London ('The State We're In: a Notice to Readers', *Squall*, 14, Autumn 1996: 12). No staff lists were available, but it was possible to identify a small number of people, of which two

(Sam Beale and Jim Carey) were the most prominent and might be considered as the paper's main editors and writers. Even within this small group, *Squall* found room for improvement. Its size meant that many tasks were shared, that a small number of people had many responsibilities. *Squall* hoped to be accepted as an equal of the mainstream media in terms of the professionalism of its reporting and its design:

> [w]ere the magazine to lie on the shelves next to any other, the casual browser should not immediately be able to tell that one was produced by a fully paid commercial staff and one by a bunch of committed volunteers. (Carey, 1998: 66)

Consequently, sharing too many tasks was felt as an obstacle to that professionalism. An editorial hoped for:

> a *full* volunteer staff ... to be assembled to run the magazine. Each with only a small number of defined roles, rather than the multi-storey car park of duties currently taken on by each of the *Squall* posse ... with a wider team of writers, photographers and designers. ('The State We're In' p. 12; emphasis added)

Squall's organization centred around a small editorial group of five people, though others were encouraged to write for it: 'anyone can write for *Squall* but obviously the magazine has a criterion of expression quality' (from interview). Its features are the closest any of the four titles comes to 'professional' writing (some of *Squall*'s writers also write for mainstream publications), in that they demonstrate the conventions of news schemata and, despite the advocacy of activism and direct action protest, they seek to provide information that can go wider than their interest groups. *Squall*'s letters page frequently included (approving) letters from MPs and sympathetic mainstream journalists and campaigners (it is the only title where such correspondence appears): evidence that the paper was not only reaching the political mainstream but that its messages were being read and supported by some within that mainstream. Sam Beale, one of *Squall*'s editors, has spoken of 'writing to the bridge': 'to me that means MPs not being able to say they don't know [i.e., that they have not been informed of the issues *Squall* writes about]. I want my mum to read it, so she can be informed' (Wakefield and Grrrt [*sic*], 1995: 7). Anyone therefore 'may' write for *Squall*, but the editors placed a stress on 'nurturing' prospective writers to enable them to write in a style harmonious with the rest of the paper. This 'effectively operates as a training scheme', but since the editors did not have much time to spend on such training – being activists as well as writers, – the group of regular writers tended to stay small. The emphasis was on developing 'an evolving body of feature writers whom we know write well'. This pool of writers presented ideas at editorial meetings and then particular writers were 'commissioned' (so to speak; little or no payment was involved) to write on certain topics. This was not a closed group, but still one whose new writers were carefully selected by the editorial group. The editors admitted that they received 'masses of stuff, from scribbles on the backs of chip wrappers to mighty tomes of ideological treatise'. They would publish none of this, preferring to identify topics of importance to their readers and choosing (or training) a specific writer to produce a feature.

SchNEWS

For *SchNEWS* even the term 'collective' is perhaps too formal. Its organization is extremely fluid, the number of people involved in its production contracting and expanding almost on a daily basis. At one time it comprised as many as 25 people (Jay Griffiths, cited in *SchNEWS Reader*, 1996, unpaginated). In addition to the members of this group – any or all of whom might take part in every aspect of the paper's production – the collective is open to the possibility of transient members 'who'll bash in a few hundred words' ('*SchNEWS – As It Is*', *SchNEWS Reader*, 1996): 'It's *not* a clique. Nobody is a "member", you won't be given a membership form to fill in, and nobody tells you what to do' ('About Justice?', from the *SchNEWS* web site; http://www.cbuzz.co.uk/SchNEWS/justice/index.htm).

Rather than spending its time criticizing mainstream business practices or even promoting the values of the collective, *SchNEWS* disparagingly – yet celebratorily – calls itself a 'disorganization', publishing weekly out of apparent chaos, out of that 'hectic mayhem called, ominously, "the office"' ('*SchNEWS – As It Is*'). We should be wary of reading too much into what is surely meant (at least partly) ironically. After all, the publication, for all its brevity, does appear regularly every week. Though its distribution is occasionally haphazard (subscribers have complained that at times no issue appears, then the last three appear in one envelope), the concerted effort required to produce such a publication should not be ignored. However fluid, however casual the editors may seem to be, however random their methods may appear from their own descriptions, the work gets done. I believe that their deliberate self-effacement springs from a desire not to be seen as autocratic decision-makers, nor to be considered a clique. By presenting an image of amateurism and disorganization, they seek to attract people to participate who might otherwise be put off by a more 'professional' approach. For *SchNEWS is* organized: whilst no single person or group wishes to be considered 'in charge', a handful of people in *SchNEWS*'s Brighton office co-ordinate the paper's editorial and production, and others oversee distribution and the paper's World Wide Web site. Yet these people do not wish to set themselves above others as 'experts': they want to share their knowledge and skills with as many as want to work with them. They also want to share the knowledge and skills of others.

I experienced this at first hand when, following my interview with Warren of *SchNEWS* and correspondence with its 'webmaster' Toby, I was asked by them to provide an index for the paper's third collection of *SchNEWS* in book form (*SchNEWS Annual*, 1998). It gradually emerged that what they really wanted me to produce was a 'guide to indexing *SchNEWS*' so that they (and other workers on the paper) could produce their own indexes in the future. For *SchNEWS*, such empowerment is central; specialists are useful to the degree that they can offer education and training to others. The specialist is perceived not as a remote expert, but as a co-worker. *SchNEWS* offers training days for prospective reporters. These take place in Brighton, where *SchNEWS* is based, and provide training in writing stories, desktop publishing and database management. The paper hopes to break down the barriers that an 'expert culture' often puts in the way of grassroots empowerment. *SchNEWS*'s preferred self-image of disorganization and chaos is part of this demystification and promotes access to the paper for all those who want it. It is clear, however, that, in common with *Do or Die*, *SchNEWS* generally suffers from a lack of people who are regularly involved, with predictable results: 'There will be no *SchNEWS* next week cos not only are we really busy, but we knackered [*sic*] and we need more people to get involved!' ('*SchNEWS* Training Day', *SchNEWS,* 153/154, 6 February 1998).

SchNEWS collapses writing and editing into a single, collective process: 'Someone will start writing, someone else will add a little nuance, a factoid or two.' An overall style is identifiable, nevertheless: final writing irons out individual quirks and voices, leaving a 'communal voice' that is irreverent, colloquial, plain-speaking and often self-ironic. But this too is deceptive, since the process generates far more copy than will fit in the two sides of A4 that comprise a typical issue: 'Before long it's grown to ten times ... and half of it disappears again' ('*SchNEWS* – As It Is', *SchNEWS Reader*, 1996). However, it is impossible to know which half 'disappears'. For all its lack of reference to the editing process, it is obvious that *SchNEWS* is edited, just as for all the talk of 'disorganization', there is a work schedule of sorts, though this takes its place as part of a wider schedule of domestic work, activism and play, described in a leaflet produced by the Justice? collective and summarized by George McKay (1996: 177):

> Monday is for gardening at the Justice? allotment; Tuesday is a day off; Wednesday is for weekly meetings ending up in the pub; Thursday is for putting SchNEWS together; Friday is printing and distribution day, followed by the pub; Saturday there's a street stall; Sunday is for chilling out. Actions and parties are fitted around these regular events.

In practice, SchNEWS is put together over two days, Wednesday and Thursday. The regular members of the collective:

> rely on people coming in [to the SchNEWS 'office'], ringing up, writing stories, passing us bits of paper in the pub, taking bits from the paper [i.e. the mainstream press], [and from the] underground press. Someone starts a story, someone else adds a bit, someone else has their say – means you can't have an ego or say 'that's my story'. Sit around on Thursday evening – people shouting out headlines. (Warren, from an interview conducted by the author)

Here we see alternative media production taking its place in everyday routines amongst subsistence and leisure. For its producers SchNEWS appears as important as their more mundane activities. By preserving the production of the paper as an unprofessionalized and deinstitutionalized activity its producers weave it into the quotidian fabric of their lives. If the content of SchNEWS is about changing lives and defending the environment in order to better enjoy life, and its form a model for enabling others to participate in it or indeed produce similar media, then it is appropriate that the publication itself should be an inextricable part of living, not something to be bracketed off in 'the office'.

Green Anarchist

In 1984 Green Anarchist's organizational beginnings centred around three people, two editors and a designer and paste-up artist, Richard Hunt. This lasted for two years, during which time Hunt began to make significant editorial contributions: the magazine's economic analysis, for example, is largely his. Hunt was also responsible at this time for developing the magazine's support of violent direct action. It was this last that effectively split the editorial group. Albon and Christo departed in 1986, leaving Hunt in sole charge until 1988. A short-lived attempt to establish an editorial group in Oxford, the magazine's home at the time (and the city itself, not the university), 'detonated after 2 issues' in 1987 ('*Green Anarchist*: the First Ten Years', *GA* 36, Winter 1994: 7).

Another attempt at collective decision-making was made in 1988, with a group of local contributors and supporters persuading Hunt to develop the magazine on more anarchist lines, in accord with its manifesto. A collective approach would be an appropriate way of putting its prefigurative politics of 'revolution on the periphery' into practice. A partial form of collective decision-making and editorial responsibility was developed, prompted by the arrival of Paul Rogers (like Albon, an anarcho-pacifist) and Kevin Lano (of the Anarchist Sexual Liberation Movement). This was only partial, as from 1986 until his departure in the autumn of 1991, Hunt was effectively the magazine's owner, controlling its bank account and overseeing its administration and production. Indeed, it was the exercise of this control that forced the other members of the editorial collective to agree to the publication of Hunt's 'support our boys' editorial on the Gulf War in *GA* 28. They were able, however, to have a right of reply beside Hunt's piece, rebutting his opinions. In the face of the dissent of the majority of the collective, Hunt left the magazine: 'he couldn't take criticism and so resigned' ('*Green Anarchist*: the First Ten Years').

Less than a year after Hunt's departure, in 1992, the magazine was relaunched as 'a magazine and a movement'. First, there was the division of the organization of *Green Anarchist* into three functions: 'the magazine and the movement', street-selling and subscriptions, and the mail order catalogue. Each group worked autonomously with no overall control. Co-ordination of activities and all decision-making were made collectively. Furthermore, the groups were geographically separate, based in three English locations: Oxford, Lancaster and Camberley (Surrey). (Camberley is around 40 miles south-east of Oxford; Lancaster around 200 miles north-west of Oxford.) In the following year there was further decentralization of the magazine's editorial functions. As from *GA* 33 (Autumn 1993) the receipt and editing of copy was also divided into three: general editorial (remaining in Oxford), news editorial and 'counter-culture' (the magazine's review pages). The last two were further divided into categories, news into eight and counter-culture into four. Given some overlap between divisions (for instance, the Oxford editorial collective was also responsible for two of the counter-culture 'departments'), the magazine was now edited from seven geographical locations in England and Scotland. Contributions to the 'core' (the dominant theme in any issue) were edited by the groups in rotation. By the time of my interview with the group responsible for co-ordinating the production of the paper (Oxford Green Anarchists) in February 1997, there had been some consolidation of roles and duties, since this extreme form of decentralization had proved inefficient for the timely production of copy. The number of news departments had shrunk to four ('community resistance', 'ecodefence', 'animal liberation' and 'sexual politics'); instead of an entire group being responsible for 'the core' a single member of a group was now nominated and this post rotated for each issue.

Despite the clawback in the decentralized editing of the magazine, the expansion of the magazine into a movement prompted a further phase of decentralization early in 1994. It was Paul Rogers who, since his arrival on the magazine, 'had been working to turn the magazine into a movement, promoting local groups' ('Green Anarchist: the First Ten Years'). These local groups were first listed in GA 34 (Spring 1994) with the establishment of nine local co-ordinators (and 'additional contacts' for each area) in the British Isles, an international co-ordinator, and a handful of international contacts. Again, there was some overlap between the roles of co-ordinators and editors. At this stage, Green Anarchist (the movement *and* the magazine) was organized from 34 locations in the British Isles (plus five international locations). Since this drastic decentralization, some slippage has taken place: the list of local co-ordinators has lost three of its original nine regions. GA 40–41 (Spring 1996) reverted – without comment – to the single editorial address in Oxford for all contributions: articles, news, reviews and letters (this is preferred operationally: material received centrally is then distributed to the relevant editor). It still maintains its initial tripartite functional split, however, and the magazine (now referred to, in the spirit of the times, as a 'zine') and the movement are still considered as separate functions of a single organization (this is emphasized by the regular editorial and informational pages at the back of the magazine, one headed 'GA: the Zine', the other 'GA: the Network').

The present editors do not consider their activities to be collectively organized (in response to my question: 'Are editing and production done collectively?' the answer was brief: 'No'), though many people are involved. The organization is certainly highly devolved, and might well entail collective activity at a local level – many of the local groups in the UK that contribute to the running of Green Anarchist (both the movement and the magazine) are run on a collective basis and are effectively 'affinity groups', that is, not formally connected or formally part of Green Anarchist. Collective activity thus takes place at a level removed from the core group that co-ordinates the production of the magazine (Oxford Green Anarchists). Isolated individual activity also plays a part: Noel Molland has described how, as an animal rights activist, he compiled the 'Diary of Animal Liberation' for the magazine without having met 'anyone else connected to Green Anarchist' (Molland, 1998: unpaginated).

The decentralization of *Green Anarchist*'s organization may be viewed as a realization of its own desideratum for society as a whole. This break with hierarchy is stressed by one of the present editorial collective: 'I don't see a society which is hierarchic ... is a viable or sustainable one' (cited in Chan, 1995: 49). It is perhaps not reading too much into this particular history to view it as a microcosm of the way in which many anarchists predict the development of anarchism in society at large, as the limits on individual and collective freedom that are placed by hierarchical methods of organization become intolerable. It is to transcend such limits that those individuals organize for their mutual benefit. Such is the case with *Green Anarchist*. Are there other benefits to decentralization? Beyond its prefigurative and empowering values, *Green Anarchist* itself is explicit about the economics of decentralization: it 'make[s] it cheaper to get UABs [Urgent Action Bulletins] circulated nationally and to speed up production time of the mag' ('Editorial', *GA* 33, Winter 1993: 17). A magazine such as *Green Anarchist* gets little of its revenue from advertising; it has no capital reserves, surviving precariously from issue to issue. It needs to economize everywhere it can. Even though none of its 'staff' are paid, finances are never healthy. By decentralizing the circulation of its Urgent Action Bulletins (supplements to the magazine and a mainstay of communication and participation in 'the movement'), a single large postal bill is avoided. Local distributors can be ingenious, using other groups' existing mailings (many local co-ordinators also co-ordinate local anarchist groups) or handing out bulletins at meetings and events in their areas. Organizationally, devolving the receipt and the editing of copy places less burden on a single group; promised reports can be chased up, closer contacts established within smaller groupings of writers and editors. Edited copy for an entire section of the magazine can then be sent ready for typesetting to the main editorial group. These approaches harmonize well with the philosophy of *Green Anarchist*: 'Bigger isn't better – never organise on the principles of mass. If a group's getting too big ... split it. If one group in a network is developing monopoly, get them to teach what they know to everyone else or share their sources' ('Revolution on the Periphery', *GA* 33, Winter 1993: 6).

Participation and Control

Many alternative publications in previous decades – regardless of their provenance or their particular version of collective organization – have suffered tensions and difficulties in their organizational methods: the problems of autocratic decision-making; the unwieldiness of consensual decision-making processes; the split between the core of regular writers or members of an editorial collective and a larger group of less permanent contributors; and the differences in commitment that such a split can bring. Comedia (1984) and Landry et al. (1985) hold that such non-hierarchical, collective methods can only disadvantage alternative media, because they are always adopted for ideological, never economic, ends. This argument is not a new one in radical milieux. Jo Freeman's (1972–73) classic critique of structurelessness in the women's movement, though not concerned with economics, makes much the same points in the wider context of political organizing. Freeman argued that structurelessness inevitably led to political impotence, since the 'more unstructured a movement is, the less control it has over the directions in which it develops and the political actions in which it engages' (p. 161). Neither is freedom from structure any guarantee of freedom from the creation of elites or stars within the movement. That they do arise without the movement taking deliberate, rational action to create them makes them more difficult for the movement to disperse or direct, since they are already outside its control.

John Downing (1984) has argued for self-management of the media by activists themselves, where editorial and production decisions are made collectively, and communication is horizontal (both within and between publications). For him the importance of collective organization and horizontal communication does not reside solely in some notion of ideological purity or anti-managerial theorizing; he is making a case against inappropriate bureaucracy and stiflingly hierarchical methods of doing business. Here he is in agreement with Traber's (1985) notion of the alternative media concerned with social and political activism amongst 'ordinary people'. It is these concerns that differentiate Downing's approach from that of Comedia and Landry et al. The latter seem to consider the alternative press simply as an impoverished form of commercial publishing; for Downing self-managed media are about participation and communication through self-awareness, through reflexivity amongst the members of a collective, who must remain sensitive to the cultural and political conditions that affect their organizational choices. It is this style of self-management that we see, in various ways, in the four titles.

Moreover, it seems that these titles have not encountered severe organizational problems because they have not employed any of the more extreme methods of democratic decision-making. Whilst *SchNEWS* is apparently open to anyone who wishes to contribute, it does not advertise or hold the kind of open meetings that led to democratic paralysis for the likes of the *Liverpool Free Press* (Whitaker, 1981) and *Aberdeen People's Press* (Minority Press Group, 1980a). In its place, we find a core group that co-ordinates rather than controls. This is also the case with *Do or Die. Squall* preferred a stabler organization; for both, membership of the core group is essential if people want to be involved in decision-making. This is not to say that the desideratum of increased participation is necessarily abandoned, rather that each title has found different ways of squaring the circle of participation and control, at the same time avoiding some of the deeper pitfalls encountered by their predecessors. All are keen to involve new contributors: *SchNEWS* perhaps most conspicuously by its easy-going 'come-all-ye' approach to its production.

An especially useful way to view the balance between participation and control is through Robert Dickinson's (1997) notion of 'formalising' and 'informalising' impulses. Drawing on Bernice Martin's assessment of the underground movement of the late 1960s as inherently 'anti-structure', Dickinson finds in subsequent generations of alternative press activity a continuance of this approach yet a growing recognition of the value of more formal structures that might 'turn a publication into something increasingly efficient and conducive to a calculated readership' (1997: 228). Formal structures do not necessarily supersede informal ones; Dickinson is careful to identify the value of informalizing impulses in engendering the creative energy of a publication. He emphasizes the 'close proximity' of these two impulses, particularly in the early stages of a publication, where creative energy provides inspiration but more formalizing energies are soon required for 'stabilising and perpetuating the publication in terms of design, research, producing copy, sharpening a style, selling advertising, and so on' (p. 230). I would argue that both tendencies are also to be found in the later stages too; once formalizing impulses have provided a structure and encouraged the development of skills, informalizing impulses can be released once more to ensure the vitality of a publication. These impulses do not necessitate two separate types of worker; they may be present in the same person, to varying degrees.

With regard to zine publishing, Dickinson goes further, observing that where there is a single editor/writer, his two types of editor ('structure-grazer' and 'structure-builder') might well be found in the same person. I would argue that even in larger organizations such as *Squall* and *SchNEWS* this is very likely to be the case: individuals working for both these titles are able to take advantage of (and relish) the creativity that comes from their 'structure-grazing' (even their 'anti-structure' attitude) whilst appreciating the necessity for tighter organizational controls on, say, copy dates and distribution networks. In this light, what I called the 'professionalism' of *Squall* need not be seen as detrimental to its aim of empowerment. Instead, it is a recognition of the importance of structure in order to give that empowerment meaning and to ensure that it breeds results (in the form of 'useful' information written by those actively involved). *SchNEWS* offers an example of the close proximity of formalizing and informalizing structures: the news reporting and writing of the paper might well benefit creatively from an informal working method, whereas to enable the paper to go to press a formal structure is required to ensure that copy is typeset to deadline, copies mailed out and the paper's web site updated. The healthy tension that enables both to contribute equally and appropriately to the work of the paper is sustained by the participatory ethos of the organization that permits such variety to flourish.

The balance between participation and control is further demonstrated by the use of the network; indeed, Dickinson identifies this as an engine of the alternative press. He observes how the network is often 'uncontrolled, non-hierarchical, and open' (1997: 101), reflecting many papers' internal structures. But amongst the titles in my study there exist networks *within* each title, which act as 'empowering engines' (to coin a phrase) for the paper itself, and which further embody the dialectic of structure/ anti-structure. *Do or Die* and *Green Anarchist* have developed networks of independent groups which are able to function as news-gatherers and writers and which, in the case of *Green Anarchist*, also have an editorial function. Decision-making can be made locally, thereby empowering those away from the centre without the unwieldiness of fully open meetings.

In her critique of radical organization Jo Freeman (1972–73) presents seven 'principles of democratic structuring': (1) the delegation of authority; (2) taking responsibility for that authority; (3) the distribution of authority; (4) the rotation of tasks; (5) the allocation of tasks along rational criteria; (6) the diffusion of information; and (7) equal access to resources (pp.163–164). These principles are broadly found in the titles studied in this chapter, to varying degrees. Where they are not fully developed, their deficiency is at least recognized (as in the case of *Do or Die*). *Green Anarchist*'s present structure exhibits them most precisely, indicating that by taking a critical approach to its own organization and eschewing the 'structurelessness' of much free collectivization, it has succeeded in producing a democratic, participatory model for radical organizing.

Participation and control are also significant in the preference for small editorial groups. *Do or Die* and *Squall* each has a small, stable membership (anything from three to ten), but they are willing to admit new members as long as they are prepared to get involved and develop the necessary skills. *Do or Die*, *SchNEWS* and *Squall* offer training and help to such people, as well as to new writers. *Squall* was comfortable with its size of around ten (*Squall*'s editorial collective was smaller than this but the figure rises when the regular 'staff' writers are included). The three editors of *Do or Die* are less happy with their situation and hope to involve more people: to provide more 'voices' as well as to ease the continual problem of contributors missing deadlines. By encouraging more people to take responsibility for the publication they hope to improve their receipt of copy. Though *Green Anarchist* does not call itself a collective, its decentralized, highly inclusive methods of working ensure that many people have the opportunity to become involved. *Green Anarchist* is also looking for ways to involve more people in more decisions, hence the commitment to rotating the editor's role. *SchNEWS* encourages all-comers to get involved, and is the freest and easiest of all, editorially speaking. But there are still core members from the Justice? collective who are going to be there to ensure the paper comes out on time, even though their editorial hand is light. The membership of its editorial/writing group changes continually.

Here we see the alternative media of new social movements reflecting the organizational and social structures of the direct-action movements they document. They exhibit the primary characteristics of the New Protest: direct participation and local, grassroots decision-making where resources are diffused and shared within and between groups. They have as their main function the empowerment of activists in their communities of resistance. Such media also appear creative, involving individuals and groups in reflexive practice, enabling them to become communicators. In his account of the Polish dissident press of the previous decade, Jakubowicz observes that when groups and individuals are radicalized they tend to become 'communicators in their own right', establishing autonomous media, or 'information seekers, eager to seek out media giving expression to their views and experience' (1991: 158). Such media then more closely reflect the everyday practices of the decentralized, directly democratic, self-managed and reflexive networks of 'everyday-life solidarity' that Melucci finds at the heart of social movement activity. How the new social movement media encourage their readers to become 'communicators in their own right', what knowledge is produced by them and what readers do with this knowledge are all addressed in the next chapter.

© 📖 📄 💾 📑 📹 ®

5

writers, readers
and knowledge in new
social movement media

Readers as Writers

A publication that is predicated on the practice of resistance by its readers can encourage those readers in one of two ways. First, it can follow the example of the Communist media of the former Soviet bloc and seek to enthuse its readership into action, whilst those writing remain above the readership: a writing elite editorially and organizationally controlled by a hierarchy (*Morning Star* and *Socialist Worker* are of this type). In this model the readership remains passive, only able to contribute to the publication financially or through its letters page. Communication is hierarchical and vertical; influence and propaganda flow downwards. Any upward flow is against the tide: letters to the paper will be selected and edited, their impact on the publication's contents or editorial policy unknown, but probably minimal. The weakness of this approach is that the very agents of resistance (the working class, in this instance) can be isolated and alienated from those directing them.

In 1928 a proposal was circulated for 'worker correspondents' in a pamphlet published by the periodical *Workers' Life* (*Workers' Life*, 1928/ 1983). Such contributors have continued to be sought by the working-class press, though with limited success. This problem was recognized by the editorial staff of *Socialist Worker* from its earliest days. In his history of the paper, Peter Allen notes that as early as the second year of its life, the number of articles written by workers was increasing, but he gives no indication as to the size of the increase or whether it continued

(Allen, 1985: 211). By the mid-1970s Tony Cliff, the leader of the Socialist Workers' Party, was insisting that '[w]orkers' names will have to appear in the paper ... more and more often and less and less often the by-lines of the Paul Foots, Laurie Flynns and Tony Cliffs' (cited by Sparks, 1985: 145). Allen notes that a general appeal to its worker-readers 'did increase the number of articles written by workers, [but] the increase was neither dramatic nor sustained' (Allen, 1985: 220). This clearly caused some anxiety amongst the party's Central Committee, not least to its leader, Tony Cliff. Writing in 1982, he noted that 'to a large extent work-ers' writing is limited to a small area of the paper'. His solution was to propose that the paper became 'a workers' diary' (Allen, 1985: 216), but Allen provides no evidence to show that the paper evolved even partially along the lines that Cliff was demanding. It is likely that by the time the paper recognized the value of readers' contributions, the professional ethos of the staff writers had all but closed off the readership from feel-ing that they could contribute any more than a letter to its pages. Letter-writing aside, readers at most had been paper-sellers at factory gates and in high streets; to move from this to becoming writers was perhaps too ambitious a leap to expect 'mere workers' to make.

There is a second way. If the true aim of such publications is 'revolution' or 'liberation', then 'we cannot imagine them as liberating forces unless they are open to lateral communication between social beings, with their *multiple* experiences and concerns' (Downing, 1984: 19; emphasis in orig-inal). Turn to the 'non-aligned' alternative press and there is a very differ-ent approach, prompted less by a centralist, party-led ideology and having more to do with 'the search for community, and the construction of alter-native value systems' (Rau, 1994: 13). As the *Rochdale Alternative Paper* (*RAP*) exhorted its readers: 'use RAP to tell your own story... tell us what you know: what happens in your factory, office, school or area of Town. tell us what you want or what you hope for' (cited in Dickinson, 1997: 80).

In this chapter I shall argue that knowledge production has become the province of the activist and the 'common reader' in media that hope to be participatory and non-hierarchical. I shall also show how a variety of approaches has developed to offer critical spaces to 'narratives of resis-tance' written by activists themselves and to theoretical work written by readers, and examine the implications of such 'equal' platforms and ques-tion the utility of this subversion of the 'hierarchy of access' to the media. Are such platforms automatic guarantors of a comprehensive set of dis-courses? Are all types of knowledge represented? In particular I will ask how – if at all – discourses of resistance are enriched by such an approach. To the four titles from the previous chapter will now be added a wider range of activist-run alternative media.

Knowledge Production and Knowledge Producers

In their account of cognitive praxis within social movements, Eyerman and Jamison (1991) offer an extremely inclusive definition of 'knowledge production', the process whereby social movements create identity and meaning for themselves and their members. For Eyerman and Jamison, the movements themselves are 'producers of knowledge' and 'knowledge is ... the product of a series of social encounters' (p. 55). Knowledge production can thus encompass 'the heated debates over meeting agendas and demonstration slogans and specific organisational activities' (p. 58) as easily as it can philosophical, theoretical and strategic writings and speeches.

I shall first examine knowledge production in alternative media as a function of the type of 'knowledge producer', before looking at the nature of the various types of knowledge produced, how they are articulated and their value to the movements. In using the term 'knowledge producer' I focus more narrowly than do Eyerman and Jamison, and refer not to movements as a whole, but to types of individual knowledge producer. The most explicit category established by Eyerman and Jamison is that of 'movement intellectual'. Eyerman and Jamison (1995: 450) define movement intellectuals as those individuals 'who through their activities articulate the knowledge interests and cognitive identity of social movements'. This category itself is open to broad interpretation: I turn first to the contributions made to radical social movement media by 'traditional' or established movement intellectuals, that is, by those intellectuals whose primary activity is intellectual, who either make a living from their writing and speaking or who at least have gained prominence through such activities as opposed to through activism. Direct-action newsletters such as *SchNEWS* do not admit of such contributions at all (though on occasion they do use brief quotations by movement intellectuals such as George Monbiot). In part, this is due to their being collectively and anonymously written and edited, though *SchNEWS* at least has declared itself to be anti-intellectual: 'it's written by activists – not academics' (*SchNEWSround*, 1997, back cover). Earth First!'s journal *Do or Die* similarly has little room for such figures: only in its first issue does one such appear: Derek Wall, academic and prominent member of the Green Party. Of the wide range of writers appearing in *Squall*, the best fit for movement intellectual is the professional writer (for example Steve Platt – former editor of *New Statesman and Society* – and once-*Guardian* columnist, C.J. Stone), though the number of contributions by this type is small at less than 5 per cent from issues 1 (1992) to 14 (Autumn 1996). *Green Anarchist*, shows the highest percentage of movement intellectuals writing for it (16 per cent since the magazine's founding in 1984). These include prominent figures from the British anarchist movement such as Colin Ward, Donald Rooum and Peter Cadogan, though these names appear only in early issues, to be replaced in the 1990s by members of the current wave of anarchist intellectual such as John Moore and, from the US, Bob Black and Hakim Bey.

The lack of established intellectuals in social movement media should come as no surprise. Eyerman and Jamison affirm that there is a significant place for the 'nonestablished intellectual' and go on to identify three types: the counter-expert, the grassroots engineer and the public educator (1991: 104–106). It is arguable that Colin Ward falls into at least the first and the second category, being known as much for his radical, 'counterexpert' views on social housing as he is for his commitment to writing with the 'common reader' in mind. The members of professional groups writing in *Squall* (lawyers, information managers) and those representing advocacy or pressure groups can also be considered as members of one or other category of unestablished intellectual. However, such contributions are infrequent. *Squall* can hardly be said to rely on such people as main contributors, except where the organization is less a bureaucracy and more an activist-run organization (such as the Advisory Service for Squatters).

The writers and editors of sustainable technology magazines such as *Clean Slate* are 'grassroots engineers'. Those interested in disseminating information on ecotage and monkeywrenching (the disabling of, for example earth-moving equipment on road construction sites) might be similarly defined. All are, to use Edward Said's term, 'amateur' or 'critical intellectuals' (Said, 1994): we might call them 'activist intellectuals'. In *Do or Die* these are mostly from the US, where Earth First! was founded, and include Judi Bari, whose article on 'the feminization of Earth First!' is reprinted from the American *Earth First! Journal* in the second issue of *Do or Die*. The US journal is used elsewhere in *Do or Die* as a source of reprints and its status as an intellectual repository for the movement is unchallenged: no other magazine or newspaper has its articles reprinted in *Do or Die* (though an article is sometimes developed from one in another publication). The 'activist intellectual' appears briefly elsewhere: a communiqué from the Zapatistas is printed in issue 4. The Zapatistas were the peasant guerrilla movement (most of them Indians, but with the support of urban intellectuals such as their spokesperson, Subcomandante Marcos) active in the Mexico of the 1990s, who had endured expulsion from their native lands in the Mexican state of Chiapas, as well as forced resettlement and the gradual erosion of their legal rights since the early 1970s. They take their name from Emiliano Zapata, the Mexican revolutionary champion of landless peasants at the turn of the last century. Their work has been reprinted in numerous anarchist and class struggle publications. An article by John Zerzan, radical primitivist philosopher, is reprinted in issue 5. Perhaps the only unarguable intellectual 'pure and simple' whose work appears in the magazine is Proudhon: a brief extract from his writing on government appears in issue 3. A small number certainly, yet they attest to an acceptance – however slight, in *Do or Die's* estimation – of the role of the intellectual in activist politics.

Eyerman and Jamison note how in the 1960s unestablished intellectuals emerged from within the student body itself and that these individuals took the place of intellectuals coming from outside the struggle. Here the movement intellectual becomes more of a 'facilitator, interpreter, and synthesiser, rather than ideological leader' (Eyerman and Jamison, 1991: 116); 'individuals without formal training and credentials' were thus enabled to 'have the opportunity to learn new skills and to practice them' (p. 119). In the media of contemporary radical environmentalism and anarchism this category of intellectual is pre-eminent. The bulk of the writing in *Squall* was done by its editorial collective who, though some have gone on take night classes in journalism, began as activists – and emphatically remain so. At its height, in *Squall* 11, there were nine collective members writing under their own names, three of whom contributed more than one article: Andy Johnson, Sam Beale and Jim Carey contributed four, three and three articles respectively to this issue.

A far smaller number of articles were written by activists who are not part of the collective. These include Kit Nash, 'a squatting activist' (writing in *Squall*, 9); Patrick Field, a cycling activist involved in the Critical Mass demonstrations (also *Squall*, 9); Catherine Grivas, who provides 'a personal account' of the eviction of protesters from Stanworth Valley in Lancashire, the proposed site of the M65 (*Squall*, 10); Jason Royce, who 'lived at the Fairmile road protest camp' in Devon (*Squall*, 14); and 'Johnny Minor', one of 60 activists who entered the garden of Michael Heseltine (then President of the Board of Trade) to protest against open cast mining (*Squall*, 11). Others have written articles while in prison for their actions: animal rights activist Keith Mann (*Squall*, 12) and Andrea Needham, one of four women who disabled a Hawk aircraft in a protest against arms sales to Indonesia (*Squall*, 13).

Whilst the anonymity and pseudonymity of almost all the articles in *Do or Die* mean it is difficult to make any detailed claims about individual authors, from an interview with one of its editors and from internal evidence in editorials and the articles themselves it is clear that the majority of the articles are written by activists. Articles written by the editorial collective show no discernible move towards attribution: the number of such articles fluctuates from issue to issue (seven, three, seven, four and 13 articles respectively in its first five issues); none are attributed to any single member of the collective. The 'Action updates' (sometimes called 'Regional reports') take up an increasing amount of space. These are at the heart of *Do or Die's* function as a magazine providing news and information to members of Earth First!, since they document the latest actions undertaken by Earth First! groups around the country (a further section, 'Other islands', does the same for other countries). They are always credited to a regional or local group (for example, South Downs Earth First!) rather than to individuals, and should therefore be considered as anonymous collective products of those groups.

These reports are produced by activists. For instance, *Do or Die* claims that its fifth issue was written by over 60 activists. In this light, the relatively small number of reports from identifiable individuals need not be seen as limiting the opportunities for activists to have their voices heard. Roughly half of these in any issue are named individuals from Earth First! groups, but typically they provide only their first names (Phil of Merseyside EF!, 'Slippery' Steve of North Downs EF!) or pseudonyms ('Rabbix' of the 'Vegan Retribution Squad', 'Boudicca' and 'Snufkin' of Camelot EF!). Only eight writers offer their full names. Of these, four write from overseas, one from prison in the UK (HMP Holloway) and one as a member of the Caledonian Green Circle. Only two activists from Earth First! give their full names (George Marshall of Oxford EF! and Lesley de Railiver of Upper Nene EF!). The preference for keeping one's identity either hidden (whether under a collective identity or under a pseudonym) or only partially revealed is understandable in a movement where many have been arrested for criminal offences. Earth First!'s explicit espousal of sabotage of machinery and destruction of property makes the movement careful about revealing too much about its operations and its members.

In the case of *SchNEWS* the collective and anonymous approach to editing and writing obscures these different categories further, resulting in a collective activist-intellectual enterprise. Developing Eyerman and Jamison's flexible concept of knowledge production, we might also consider the participatory and collective forms of organization adopted by many social movement media as extensions of activist-intellectual activity. (Perhaps anonymity and pseudonymity, despite their obvious value to activists involved in illegal acts, also continue the Enlightenment notion of rational truth and demonstrate a concern with promoting anti-individualism and a democracy of the intellect.) This is supported by Eyerman and Jamison's argument that the work of activists is to be considered knowledge production 'because through their activism they contribute to the formation of the movement's collective identity' (1991: 94); in social movements 'knowledge creation [is] a collective process' (p. 57), a process that articulates with the collective action typical of new social movement activity.

SchNEWS claims that 'attributing articles would be an impossibility' ('SchNEWS – As It Is', SchNEWS Reader, 1996) and prints no bylines to any of its stories. The given names of three regular (at least, for the present) writers and editors are known from interviews: Cheryl (Zobel), Warren and Peter. Of these three, only Zobel has any professional training in journalism, but she still considers herself primarily as an activist. This self-definition is shared by the other two and by everyone else who is involved in SchNEWS, however temporarily (indeed, the transient nature of their involvement often demonstrates their commitment as activists who have decided to devote most of their time to protest, not to reporting it). Yet this is not to exhaust the number of contributors. It is clear from SchNEWS's promotion of training days that it wishes to expand the numbers and range of its reporters; even without such training, potential contributors and 'informants' regularly supply news stories. Within its first year of publication, SchNEWS was receiving 'up to forty phone calls per day' (Jay Griffiths, cited in 'SchLIVE!' SchNEWS Reader, 1996) as well as letters and faxes, giving news and mobilizing information. SchNEWS was connected to the Internet in March 1996: since then, an increasing number of reports have been sent to the paper via email (no doubt due in part to SchNEWS's World Wide Web site and an email version of the paper itself). In April 1998 this amounted to 'over 200 e-mails a week' and a plea to potential contributors 'to send a very short story' (from the header to the email version of SchNEWS, 164, 24 April 1998). Ultimately, though, the number and nature of contributors is impossible to identify, since all such contributions are inevitably transformed by the writing and editing of the editorial collective.

In Green Anarchist, editorial contributions comprise 25 per cent of the total articles in the magazine. Such a large percentage should come as no surprise; after all, it is the editorial group who have developed the manifesto of green anarchism through its editorials and features. The three-part manifesto 'Where We Stand' in GA 2 was the work of Albon and Hunt. As the person behind the magazine's economic philosophy, Hunt was the most prolific of the three, contributing many articles on economics, class and the Third World right up to his departure. Paul Rogers began contributing significantly upon becoming a member of the editorial collective in 1988 (he had been writing letters and short articles for a couple of years before this). In contrast to Hunt, he does not seek to develop 'the party line'. His work includes criticisms of *Green Anarchist*'s aims, as well as interviews with other groups, such as the Legalise Cannabis Campaign and Earth First!. In the 1990s, the anonymity of many of the editorial group and the use of pseudonyms made identification more difficult. Recurring names include Rabid Eigol (an anagram of Logie Baird) writing on the media and 'Rob a.k.a. Arthur Mix'.

As if in spite of the editorial hierarchy, from its earliest issues *Green Anarchist* solicited three types of contributions from its readers: the traditional letters to the editor, the 'designed page' and articles for 'themed issues', otherwise known as 'the core'. There is no indication of how many readers' letters the magazine received, nor how many of these were published, until 1991. In *GA* 26 (Spring 1991: 18), presenting three pages of letters, the magazine simply states that 'we print all letters received'. Given that the magazine's open policy on other contributions from readers had been in existence since its earliest days, I assume that a similar policy on letters was also in operation long before this announcement. One reader at least saw the benefits in 1989, being 'impressed by [the] unbiased views and [the] ability to publish letters slagging [the magazine] off' (*GA* 22, Late Summer/Autumn 1989).

The 'designed page' is the most radical form of readers' contribution (yet the most short-lived). A little over a year after its founding, *Green Anarchist* exhorted its readers to 'design a page!'. 'Say what you think needs to be said. Type it. Write it. Illustrate it and send us the complete camera-ready page.' The request asks for 'plenty of reading matter in it' as well as 'a striking design' (*GA* 8, September/October 1985: 2). The editors would have no control over the content or layout of that page (save to reject it completely, though there is no evidence that they did). The first such page appears in the same issue, extolling the value of art in anarchy. The next issue includes two such pages (an illustrated account of police harassment at an anti-apartheid rally in London and a more reflective piece titled 'Don't Let Green Die'). Other examples are information about the Legalise Cannabis Campaign in *GA* 16, and the 'psychedelic thoughts of a green anarchist' in *GA* 17. The designed page appears less frequently in the late 1980s, its significance apparently dwindling in the face of the decentralization that saw many more readers taking an active part in all aspects of the magazine.

The themed issue gives the reader much more scope for contribution. Given only the title of a forthcoming theme ('The follies of science', 'Anarchy and culture', 'Women and men'), readers were encouraged to contribute articles of under 500 words. These would be reproduced verbatim as part of a larger feature (at times, in pre-tabloid issues, the reproduction was literal, the author's typescript being pasted directly onto the page). Readers have frequently been encouraged to contribute, even during Hunt's control of the magazine. *GA* 22 (Late Summer/ Autumn 1989) calls for articles on 'Anarchy and Culture'; *GA* 26 (Spring 1991) for articles for a critique of the Green Party. Such requests continue to the present and had great success in the 1990s. *GA* 42 (Summer 1996) celebrates the volume of readers' contributions to that issue's 'technocracy is tyranny' theme: 'The brill response to our appeal for copy last issue means that we've got enough to continue this theme into the next [issue].' Letters apart, the contribution of readers to the magazine is high, at 46 per cent. Most of this comprises themed contributions which continue to be a significant proportion of each issue.

There is a difference in content between these contributions and those submitted by readers to a magazine such as *Do or Die*. Rather than the first-person, activist accounts found in the latter, readers' contributions to themed issues of *Green Anarchist* tend to deal with the philosophy and theory of (green) anarchism; often they are simply readers' opinions on the chosen topic. Though such perspectives are not explicitly recommended by the editorial group, its choice of topics does encourage less practical and tactical writing: 'The collusion of state and industry', 'The green and black economy', 'Primitivism' and 'Anti-ideology'. (Though there has been a 'double core' issue dealing with strategy and tactics and 'survival scams', as if to redress the balance.)

All four titles have found different ways of admitting a diversity of voices into their pages. The admittance of the reader-writer into the same part of a publication as that of the movement intellectual (that is, the reader-writer who is not relegated to the letters page), offers a challenge to intellectual discourse as well as the opportunity to discuss the ideas in that discourse to an extent unknown in the mainstream media. Such a strategy not only introduces new forms of knowledge from a much wider writing base (so to speak), it also introduces many more social actors, and offers them the same empowerment as it offers the intellectual: an equal platform for their ideas (whether the ideas are equal is another matter). In this way, the 'hierarchy of access' (Glasgow University Media Group, 1976: 245) normally found in the media – where an elite of experts and pundits tends to have easier and more substantial access to a platform for their ideas than dissidents or protesters – is subverted, even inverted. The notion of writing for the media is transformed into an egalitarian, devolved communicational tool for theory and for action.

The 'activist-writer' is the other significant additional social actor empowered through the alternative media and is especially conspicuous in *SchNEWS*, where activism seems more important for membership of the editorial collective than a proven ability to write. Involvement as a writer can only come with being an active participant in the entire process of reporting, writing, editing and production. Similarly, whilst *Do or Die*, *SchNEWS* and *Squall* recognize the importance of encouraging or training potential writers, they are primarily interested in what these writers have to say from their perspective as activists. Dealing with events and actions, their contributions superficially resemble eyewitness reports in the mainstream press. Rather than marginalize them as the contributions of 'mere readers', it is profitable to consider these as radical forms of reporting, what I shall call 'native-reporting'.

Conceptualizing Alternative News as 'Native Reporting'

'Native reporting' can usefully define the activities of alternative journalists working within communities of interest to present news that is relevant to those communities' interests, in a manner that is meaningful to them and with their collaboration and support. *SchNEWS* has similarly termed its contributors 'activist-reporters' and 'native-journalists', though it has provided no further comment on how it understands these terms. The origins of the latter term lie, however, in mainstream journalism. It was coined by Robert Chesshyre to describe his return to Britain following his posting as the *Observer*'s Washington correspondent (Chesshyre, 1987: 13): 'coming home, one had to learn again the native idiom'. For Chesshyre, this meant relearning a method of reporting about local, everyday 'situations with which readers can personally identify' (p. 31). He observes how such reports inevitably draw many letters from readers:

> who have something to say and want to join in .... They know more than their masters do of what it is like to have a child in a comprehensive school, or to be unemployed, to try to start a business. They are the reliable witnesses. (1987: 31–32)

However reliable those witnesses, in the forum of mainstream journalism they still need their Robert Chesshyres (and their John Pilgers) to argue on their behalf. And however powerful their arguments might be, such professional journalists are firmly within the advocacy tradition, mediating on behalf of those whose lives they understand – perhaps very well. But 'native-reporter' also evokes those local grassroots journalists of the South by whom Michael Traber sets so much store, whose value lies not in their role as message-creators for a passive audience, but as members of a community whose work enables the entire community to come together, to 'analyse one's historical situation, which transforms consciousness, and leads to the will to change a situation' (Traber, 1985: 3). The experience of colonialism is not far from here, in particular its legacy of 'dualism': 'a dual culture, a dual economy and a dual polity' (ibid.). In all these instances, and in particular in relation to the media, this duality is expressed by 'participation and alienation'. Local communities under colonialism found themselves unable to participate in the media that ostensibly reported on matters of concern to them; they were alienated from the methods of production as well as from the nature of the report-ing. They were not involved in the media, either as creators of stories or as actors within them. Instead there was the colonizing journalist, described by David Spurr as 'placed either above or at the centre of things, yet apart from them' (Spurr, 1993: 16). Spurr argues that the power relations inherent in this relationship between observer and observed are grounded by standard narrative practices in journalism that, by adopting these perspectives, 'obviate the demand for concrete, practical action on the part of its audience' (p. 45). By contrast, native reporters are at the centre of things as participants, and their work is precisely to feed discussion and debate from the perspective of the colonized and, crucially, to provide 'information for action'.

How native reporting situates activists in both the texts they produce and in the sociopolitical contexts in which they place them (and are themselves placed) can be shown by the following example taken from a feature in the video magazine *Undercurrents*. *Undercurrents* was espe-cially interested in promoting what one of its founders calls 'witness video' (Harding, 1997: 1) and in encouraging 'activist editing' (p. 148) – an interest in politicizing programmes through subjective testimony, often by the subjects representing themselves. In the opening moments of the news feature 'New Labour, New Arms' (*Undercurrents*, 8, December 1997), the activist reporter 'Jen' presents herself conventionally enough along mainstream lines. She is apart from the action, whether in front of an Air Training Corps building, outside the Labour Party conference, or at times as a voice-over ('above' the action). Her introduction has nothing of the testimonial at this point. As the report develops, however, Jen's identity as an activist becomes clearer – critical comment becomes more frequent (Foreign Secretary Robin Cook's address to his party's confer-ence is 'just a pacifying speech'; 'I just don't think that it's good enough'). During her brief, backstage interview with Cook she infracts more reporting rules: the interview is unplanned, opportunist. Cook is caught on camera hurrying a sandwich before turning to speak. Jen's nervousness is apparent. After Cook's departure, her to-camera remarks are candidly personal, perhaps naïve ('he seemed human – he was eating a sandwich'; 'I would have liked longer to talk with him').

Her comments situate her as a non-professional reporter, reacting ordinarily and spontaneously much as her audience might do in a similar situation: a little overawed, nervous, yet committed to criticism and action. There is a strong sense of the quotidian here. An epilogue to the feature constructs two scenes that emphasize the everyday nature of activism. The first depicts Jen at her breakfast table, reading a newspaper. Though clearly rehearsed, her testimony to camera is sincere enough; she is responding to a statement by Cook that appears to contradict his ethical foreign policy ('I can't quite believe my eyes'; 'blatant hypocrisy'). We cut to the final scene where Jen is perched on a high wall overlooking an arms factory. She is filmed through barbed wire. The shift from domestic to military is shocking, yet logical: her message is 'Go down to your local arms factory and take direct action.' In a little over seven minutes Jen moves from conventional reporter to activist, throughout representing herself not as a simple professional, not even as a simple activist, but as a vulnerable, brave individual, situated in the everyday yet capable of remarkable actions, whether interviewing a senior politician or taking direct action against the military-industrial complex. She is oppressed and activist; witness and critic. Her words and actions are, in the end, those of her audience, her movement through identities and relationships in this brief feature as complex as any in everyday life.

Such a performance accrues further power through 'underproduction':

> Keep those long shots. Don't worry if it's a bit wobbly; it will feel more authentic. In general, turn your weaknesses (few resources, little experience) to an advantage by keeping your feature simple but powerful. (Harding, 1997: 149)

In her study of AIDS video activism, Alexandra Juhasz (1995) argues for the employment of mainstream media forms such as the documentary to claim authority over the radical content of a programme, content that would never be thus presented through mainstream channels. Like Harding, she emphasizes production processes that involve members of the communities for which (and in which) the video is being produced: 'Alternative AIDS media ... actively situates itself *within* the object of study ... to look is to see and know *yourself*, not the other – an entirely different route to pleasure and power' (Juhasz, 1995: 138; emphasis in original).

Reading 'native reporter' in a colonial sense declares that the news gathered and presented by such reporters as part of their own lives is not catered for by the colonial power wielded by mainstream reporters, nor have their issues been taken over by these 'invaders'. Native reporters seek to take back what is 'their' news, just as the grassroots journalism that Michael Traber discusses seeks to empower local people in Latin America, India and Africa. This second interpretation is perhaps more powerful than Chesshyre's, since it suggests the actualization of his 'reliable witnesses' as recorders of their own reality, empowered as participators in the very construction of their own media as resistance to colonialism. Here I do not want to force an exact correspondence between the power relations of the colonizer and the colonized and those between the mainstream and alternative media; I simply want to show that a comparison is instructive. The native reporter as construed in the alternative press is Other, what Spurr has his colonizing journalist call 'the antithesis of civilized value' (1993: 7). This highlights a struggle within the politics of representation, a 'politics of struggle and power in the everyday world', to use Edward Said's phrase (Said, 1982/1985: 147), where the native reporter gains self-respect and moral and political strength through self-representation, thereby drawing power away from the mainstream back to the disenfranchised and marginalized groups that are the native reporter's proper community.

Native reporting can also be seen at the heart of local community media. The radical local press of the 1970s in the UK was concerned with 'the production of revelatory news' (Franklin and Murphy, 1991: 106) that directly affected the lives of working people in their communities. The non-aligned nature of these presses encouraged reporters to investigate all political parties equally, with no restriction of political allegiance. Where such allegiance was observable it was not at party level, but at grassroots level; many radical papers sought support from local Labour Party and trade union activists, though this did not prevent investigation of the senior members of these organizations. Broadly speaking, this radical press was interested in promulgating left-wing views, as Franklin and Murphy assert, but it was far from the propagandist approach of the Party newspapers that Colin Sparks (1985) terms the working-class press. Where the alternative local press did acknowledge its propaganda value was in presenting its practices of media production as propaganda of the deed, a sociopolitical argument deriving from reflections similar to those presented by Duncombe in his exploration of Benjamin's duality of position and attitude, as presented in Chapter 1.

'Breaking two sorts of silences' is how Franklin and Murphy (1991: 113) sum up the project of the radical local press. The first silence – of elite groups on corruption within their ranks – is broken by investigative and revelatory news reporting. From the breaking of the second silence springs a recognition that such news is not merely there to titillate or to sell papers: it is there as an instance of news that is relevant to the lives of ordinary, unprivileged people. Breaking this second silence is about giving voice to those people, about reporting news from their perspective, presenting stories where they are the main actors, where they are permitted to speak with authority, as counters to the mainstream's regularized interest in public figures as the only authoritative voices, the predominant sources of 'validating information'. Through the radical local press of the 1970s it was revealed to readers and writers alike that all news was socially constructed. Whereas the mainstream local media privileged news constructed from the perspective of those in positions of authority, the radical local press constructed its news from the perspective of those of low status, producing what have been termed 'parish magazines of the dispossessed' (Harcup, 1994: 3). And in answer to Tony Harcup's question: 'Whose news is it anyway?' (Harcup, 1998: 105) we might answer: 'Their news.' Local people would not only become primary sources and major interviewees in stories, they could also become news-gatherers. Reporters would build up networks of local people – not only political activists, but local residents' groups, parents, workers, the unemployed, the homeless – and encourage them to supply leads for stories.

We might also consider the alternative news sources in Northern Ireland produced within the Republican community. As David Miller (1994: 215) demonstrates, such sources as the weekly republican paper *An Phoblacht/Republican News* and the nationalist weekly *Andersonstown News* were and continue to be key sources. The majority (eight out of ten) in the group of nationalist residents in West Belfast taking part in Miller's examination of mainstream news values in the coverage of the Gibraltar shootings of 1988 cited such alternative media as part of their sources of news. Here we find a redefining of community media as agents of national identity, where political communities seek valorization of their identity, community and political strength through the production of their own media. Miller has shown how, following then Secretary of State for Northern Ireland Roy Mason's attempt to close down *Republican News* in 1978, the Republican Press Centre and *Republican News* became more 'overground', their editors and workers taking more visible roles in political media production (1994: 85). Liz Curtis (1984) examines *An Phoblacht/Republican News* in terms of its significance as the major engine of Republican publicity. Far from the massive propaganda machine alluded to by much British journalism, she finds an operation that has much in common with the economic and cultural characteristics of the alternative media under discussion in this book: ramshackle, squatted premises, extremely limited resources (the acquisition of a hired telex machine in 1974 was a major leap forward for the Republican Press Centre in West Belfast), 'underground' printing, hole-and-corner publishing, on occasion producing single-page emergency editions 'on the run'. There was little or no subsidy, yet there remained space for innovation: the hunger strikes of 1980–81 saw the production of the first Republican video, which was shown in community centres throughout the province. This period also saw an increase in the range of materials produced: posters, badges and pamphlets – largely for local use – which supplemented the weekly newspaper. (A similar situation might be outlined for the Unionist media.)[1]

Other types of community media might also be seen as comprising 'native reporting', though these often appear to have little interest in political activism of any kind. A first broad group would include the web-based network of community reporters established under the aegis of Steve Thompson at the University of Teesside. These initiatives involve a high proportion of local, non-professional people in their news-gathering, reporting and production – the *Newcastle Community News* website (www.ncn.org.uk/) boasts a youngest writer of only eight years. There is little interest here in courting controversy. Instead we find the promotion of more neutral, 'universal' values of local communities. History, in the form of recollection and reminiscence, is encouraged: much of the reporting in these web sites is to do with the preservation of tradition, with community journalism as the practice of a demotic local history. Other initiatives resemble more closely the alternative community newspapers of the 1970s. Grimethorpe's Electronic Village Hall and London's Tower Hamlets Community Network E-base seek to make Internet technology accessible to local communities in order to assist in the regeneration of economically deprived areas. These can directly benefit local economies by enabling small businesses to access e-commerce. They also offer access to Internet resources to enable campaigning on social issues such as housing through networking with similar organizations, holding discussions on-line, communicating with local officials, and publicizing causes and issues. As Christopher Mele (1999: 292) has found in the case of a North Carolina residents' group, the technology enables members of a community to 'operate as agents outside the local and exclusive pathways of information, social discourse and social action that were either controlled or influenced by the institution of the housing authority or other local elite groups'.

Radical Populism and Language

Peter Golding (1999: 51) has argued that the 'demotic and casually convivial tone of the popular press [is itself] rooted in the evolution of a journalism of the market from a more socially anchored journalism of community or movement'. Here he is drawing on Raymond Williams's (1970: 21) argument from history that the English Radical press employed colloquial language 'with colour, vitality and force; very often without the restraints and qualifications of highly educated writing'. This style was exploited by the commercial popular press to mask a very different social voice, so that a paper with a very different model of 'ownership and political opinion [has] been made to sound popular' (ibid.). Far from subscribing to this latter, reactionary and disempowering model of spectacular consumption (in its recent manifestation as tabloid journalism) that claims to represent the majority of people, the grassroots alternative media are returning to the source of the model and rediscovering a popular discourse that is grounded in popular writing for social action. It is tempting to go further, arguing that the tabloid newspapers' values are the aberration from a press that was historically and socially grounded in the struggles of ordinary people. The Radical press should be considered the central form of democratic media, with subsequent dilutions such as the tabloid press as 'marginal' in democratic terms.

This offers an instructive complement to the argument made by Theodore Glasser (1974) in his evaluation of the language used by the American underground press. He found that, rather than employing an inclusive language that encouraged a wide audience, the underground press 'resorted to the use of a modified and self-limiting language, one that was unintelligible to a great many in their potential audience' (1974: 201). Whether we attribute this to its (arguable) origins as a language of 'drug addicts and criminals' or consider it as a strategy to exclude the older generation (specifically parents), it is far removed culturally and historically from the populist Radical press and its successors. Elsewhere we can find examples of alternative media that consciously draw on populist forms of address and presentation at the same time as they subvert those forms for the purposes of political consciousness-raising and mobilization. The British anarchist newspaper *Class War* (published by the Class War Federation in the 1980s and 1990s as 'Britain's most unruly tabloid') drew on the common style of the tabloid press by producing news articles and features that were irreverent and often humorous, all couched in a language of self-righteous anger and moral certainty familiar to us from papers such as *The Sun*. The Class War Federation has explicitly acknowledged its debt:

> There is a reason why people like to read *The Sun*. It's not because they're ignorant, it's because a lot of the time all you want is a light entertaining read... there is a lot to be said for a paper that is simple, entertaining and easy to read, and that's what *Class War* should be like if we want people to read it. (Class War Federation, 1991: 18)

To this end, in common with many tabloid newspapers, *Class War* employed what Norman Fairclough (1995: 72) has termed a 'public-colloquial' style of discourse, a hybrid style that is able to function both interpersonally (solidarity is formed between paper and audience through a shared, non-intellectual, non-specialist style) and ideationally. In a paper like *The Sun* this entails the transformation of official discourse into a colloquial setting; in the case of *Class War* it means representing anarchist positions on class colloquially. In both, as Hall et al. (1978: 61 and cited in Fairclough, 1995: 71) have shown, this not only makes the viewpoints more widely available to a larger, 'uninitiated' public, it also 'invests them with popular force and resonance, naturalizing them within the horizon of understanding of the various publics'. But *Class War* is hardly interested in using the mainstream press as a political model; its borrowings of language, stylistic devices and modes of address typically subvert tabloid conventions through irony or sarcasm (at the same time subverting their political modalities). Its long-running 'hospitalized copper' photo-feature subverted the common appeal made to tabloid readers to join together in condemning violence against police officers, in empathizing with their families and in assessing such violence as symptomatic of political hooliganism. By contrast the 'hospitalized copper' series revels in such violence, encouraging its audience to support it as emblematic of violence against the state and as symptomatic of successful class struggle. Similarly, where the tabloid press often promotes ordinary people as vigilantes, taking the law into their own hands against criminals (or alleged criminals), *Class War* 'feature[s] people fighting back in the paper to show that it happens all the time ... giving people the confidence they need to take on capitalism and the State' (Class War Federation, 1991: 19). Whilst this fighting is real enough (often resulting in the 'hospitalized copper') its tactics are to refer ironically to the tabloid language from which the Class War Federation hopes to draw much of its popular strength: the label 'Rentamob', used by the tabloid press to refer to a stage-managed, typically left-wing group of 'troublemakers' (van Dijk, 1991) is used by the Federation to refer to its own members – a group of *Class War* supporters is photographed carrying a banner emblazoned with

'Class War – Rentamob – On Tour' (*Class War*, 73 Summer 1997: 8). Here an expression of moral outrage is ironically reversed and transformed into a celebration of demotic power.

Perhaps my choice of example is an extreme one – I certainly do not intend *Class War* to be taken as the ideal or only model for such transformation. Seen though, alongside other forms such as those found in *Undercurrents* and in the colloquial and irreverent forms of address used by *SchNEWS*, we see how a radical, popular journalism may be recovered from an aberrant, populist form in the mainstream tabloid press.

Activists as Intellectuals

Let us now return to the notion of 'activist intellectual' we met earlier. Are we to ascribe the term 'activist intellectual' to anyone who has ever written anything – however slight – for the radical media, or who has ever pasted up a page of that same publication? Whilst Eyerman and Jamison assert that 'most activists are movement intellectuals in one form or another and at one time or another' (1991: 106), they argue that this dissolution of categories is succeeded by the full professionalization of movement intellectuals. As evidence they cite the evolution of the British environmental social movement in the 1970s into hierarchical social movement organizations (SMOs) such as Friends of the Earth and Greenpeace, each with its own professional intellectuals established within the organization.

The frequent use of anonymity and pseudonymity in new social movement media suggests an aversion to the professionalization of intellectual activity based on personality and reputation. There are few signs that this democratization of intellectual activity is about to be succeeded by intellectual professionalization. In the direct-action networks of the 1990s there was no move towards the status of SMO; indeed, it is contrary to the principles of DIY culture that such a shift should occur. (Retaining such activity within the movements themselves is emphasized by Jim Carey's (1998: 63) proposal that better than 'DIY culture' we should call it 'DiO culture' – Do it Ourselves.) Far from intellectual activity being promoted within the new social movements, there is much scepticism of it. Thinking and writing about activism usually trail a poor second to the practice of activism. *SchNEWS* declares that 'it's all about participation and activism', that writing and publishing are only part of the picture; to complete it 'you have to go out and see it for yourself' (from my interview with Warren). An editorial in *Squall* declares that it is 'written and produced by people who live the issues, not observers looking for a commission' ('It's Still Serious', *Squall*, 7, Summer 1994: 2).

Does a culture where intellectual activity is of so little value not render 'movement intellectual' and 'activist intellectual' mere analytical categories to be employed by researchers alone? Are they as empty as that? I believe they are not. Such low status is not borne out by an examination of the content of the radical media. The negative comments on writing made by the editors of *Do or Die* must be balanced against their careful request for articles to be submitted according to certain criteria outlined in an editorial in their second issue. Whilst these highlight the notion of 'information for action' ('articles should empower people to do something') they also stress the value of references. Moreover, an examination of the content of articles in *Do or Die* finds that a significant amount are emphatically products of movement-intellectual activity and correspond well with Eyerman and Jamison's assertion that the role of the movement intellectual 'is that of providing a larger framework of meaning in which individual and collective actions can be understood' (1991: 115) and that of 'drawing out and helping to make conscious the core identity of a social movement' (Eyerman, 1994: 199).

Examples of Knowledge Production

In *Do or Die* issue 5 (1996) a 4,000-word article presents major theories of biodiversity loss in island populations and suggests differing types of action to combat such loss required by SMOs such as Friends of the Earth and Greenpeace and grassroots groups such as Earth First!. The article, whilst anonymous (as are all the articles in this issue bar one) has the style of many an undergraduate essay in its blend of personal opinion and secondary research, of colloquial first person and scholarly quotation. A further anonymous article, on the radical cyclists' movement Critical Mass, examines the philosophy of that movement, its history, strategy and tactics, and addresses the notion of how the movement is able to 'build community' amongst its members and supporters. The only attributed article, written by Martin Miriori of the Bougainville Interim Peace Office, discusses Bougainville in the Solomon Islands and examines the islanders' demands for political self-determination in the face of continuing economic exploitation. (The island was placed under colonial rule first by Germany from 1899, then by Australia as part of its territory of Papua from 1919. Even when Papua New Guinea gained its independence from Australia in 1975, Bougainville remained under Papuan administration.)

Perhaps the most politically astute article – in terms of an understanding of the tensions that can arise between political groupings involved in a campaign – is 'Shoreham – Live Exports and Community Defence', which examines the strategies and tactics employed during the protests against live exports at the port of Shoreham, on England's south coast. This is not simply a description of the protests, but an account of community organization that is critical of the involvement of media celebrities and highlights contradictions in community struggles. It alleges aloofness from the protest by 'Brighton politicos' and is especially critical of the Socialist Workers' Party's (SWP) 'workerist' philosophy that prevented the party from 'connect[ing] to Shoreham'. Scepticism about organized left-wing parties and Trotskyites in particular appears throughout the radical environmental and anarchist movement media: a group calling itself Trotwatch has produced an irregular magazine and pamphlets dedicated to such critical work. Whilst some publications – notably *Aufheben* and *Counter Information* – do take a class-struggle perspective on activism, there is a general lack of interest in class (as George McKay, 1998, has also noted). The article is sensitive to differences in such groups, however – its author writes favourably of members of Militant, because they became involved in the protest as individuals rather than as Militant ideologues. The author is also critical of other DIY groups, in particular of the Brighton direct-action group Justice?'s alleged inability to connect with working people and middle-aged citizens, since the group is primarily interested in (and drawn from) the young middle-class unemployed. (Such a critique could also form the basis of a more fundamental analysis of how inclusive and participatory such groups – and their media – really are.)

In the next issue (1997) amongst the 86 pages of feature articles (compared to 33 pages in issue 5), there are lengthy pieces on Reclaim the Streets, the Luddites, the future of Earth First! and activists' accounts of three prominent British protests (Fairmile, Newbury and Manchester Airport). The feature on the Reclaim the Streets (RTS) movement is in fact three articles in one, all anonymous, totalling around 5,500 words. It examines the political and social issues of the movement, its history from 1991 to the present and its rationale, identifying an historical basis for its 'street party' tactics drawn from the events of Paris in 1968. It argues that RTS's critique of the commodification and privatization of public spaces is based on the theoretical writings of Adorno, Debord and Vaneigem: 'to "reclaim the streets" is to enact the transformation of the [road] to the [street]. In this context the anti-roads movement is also a struggle for the human-scale, the face-to-face, for a society in harmony with its natural surrounding.' The article on the Luddites is a synthetic reading of Kirkpatrick Sale and John Zerzan's writings on the Luddites and Guy Debord's theory of spectacular society which draws implicit parallels with British activism in the 1990s.

'Earth First! – But What Next?' notes the limits that the movement has placed on potential activists (for instance, it requires them to be physically fit and able-bodied); it is critical of the common 'fuck you' attitude on protests, exemplified most vividly by the hard-drinking and disruptive element known as the 'Brew Crew'. It argues for links with a wider range of groups, including community groups. It suggests talking to the local Women's Institute, an interesting tactic for a group often portrayed in the mainstream media as uncompromising and 'extreme', and encourages involvement in local economic initiatives such as the Local Exchange Trading Schemes (LETS). It even finds inspiration in the strategies of SMOs, noting the success of Friends of the Earth 'who score by being well connected, wealthy and strategic'. Finally, it recommends using and working with other movement media (it cites *Corporate Watch*) to improve education within the movements. I shall return to links between media below.

The three activists' accounts might best be thought of as critical narratives of resistance since they not only recount the experiences of protesting but critically engage in its successes, failures and contradictions. Though admitting that it is 'not intended as any kind of history or analysis', the anonymous account of the protest against the Newbury bypass reinforces many of the points made in the earlier critique of Earth First!. Similarly, the account of the road protest at Fairmile addresses problems of elitism, questions of function, media coverage and future strategies for similar protests. The final account – of the protest against the building of Manchester Airport's second runway – also offers a critical account of 'Brew Crew culture' and notes the lack of strategic planning in many protests: 'there's a lot to be said for thinking, planning – rather than just throwing yourself into the first idea that comes into your head ... tactical thinking'.

These two issues of *Do or Die* present an eclectic set of articles that variously combine twentieth-century cultural and radical philosophy, critiques of activism, historical parallels for contemporary activism, economic and political critiques, self- and movement analyses and accounts of ecology. The length and detail of the articles suggest a commitment from their authors to intellectual activity. The range of approaches, sources, inspiration and theories does, however, raise some questions. Does the writing comprise a coherent philosophy for Earth First!? Is it expected to? Is a co-ordinated approach to movement-intellectual activity necessary in a non-hierarchical, participatory network of protest? Co-editor Dom's notion of the magazine as 'a grab-bag ... to give people a sense of possibilities' does not address how these possibilities might come together as a coherent knowledge base for the movement, nor is there any acknowledgement that such a 'grab-bag' might well lead to incoherence.

Whereas *Do or Die* has attained high professional standards in proofreading and reproduction, the reader coming to *Green Anarchist* for the first time (as to many alternative publications) will immediately note that its standards of layout and production are far from professional. *Green Anarchist* began as a cheaply printed magazine with a mix of typewritten and hand-written copy originated and pasted up by the editors. Since *GA 32* (Summer 1993) it has been produced in an offset tabloid format, yet this is no guarantee of error-free professional standards. Columns are often misaligned and at times laid out in the wrong order; sometimes paragraphs are absent. Typographical errors abound; illustrations are frequently poorly reproduced. To the professional eye, *Green Anarchist* bears all the hallmarks of a publication produced by amateurs, and less than competent amateurs at that. Nor are such failings only of aesthetic importance: a letter in *GA 51* (Summer 1998) from Michael William, the author of a piece on Quebec in *GA 47–48*, points out that several literals in the typesetting of his article significantly altered the sense of the piece; most notable was the confusion between 'francophone' and 'francophobe'. William also draws our attention to the fact that the magazine received his article as a '22-page handwritten version' and was obliged to type it from scratch. Whilst there are those who would argue that mistakes of the number and significance as appear in *Green Anarchist* detract from its value, we should remember that it is the product of people who are primarily activists, neither professionals nor technicians. In terms of content *Green Anarchist* is an odd blend of the colloquially pragmatic (often expressed confrontationally), the densely theoretical and at times the simply baffling. *GA 51* exhibits all of these characteristics.

The front page leads with an editorial about the Gandalf trial under a typically confrontational headline: 'Fuck you, pigs!'. The following three pages are taken up with the magazine's regular 'diaries': of animal liberation, ecodefence and 'community resistance'. Each attempts to list all examples of actions (both violent and peaceful) that have taken place in support of these causes since the previous issue. 'Community resistance', though the shortest, is the most varied. It includes food riots in Indonesia, peace protesters in London, the 'Mardi Gras' bombings against London supermarkets and a pro-ETA rally in Bilbao. In microcosm this list exhibits much of the magazine's confused blend of support for terrorism, for the oppressed and for peaceful protest. By implication, *GA* appears to consider them all as manifestations of anarchism, which they clearly are not. The feature articles that follow are divided into a number of sections; an issue usually has one or two 'cores' (key themes). *GA* 51, unusually, is a 'triple core' issue. The first deals with the Gandalf trial and comprises pieces written by members of the editorial group. On the second theme, 'the Unabomber trial', there are only two articles: a letter from Ted Kaczynski (whom *Green Anarchist* believes was framed as the Unabomber); and a critique of the Unabomber manifesto by John Moore. The final theme is 'direct action', on which there are three articles: Steve Booth's article on the 'irrationalists'; an article on 'poetic terrorism' as direct action (actions that delight rather than destroy) and 'a crypto-anarchist manifesto'. Whilst previous issues of *Green Anarchist* have dealt with more fundamental debates in direct action (such as the future and purpose of Earth First!), this collection seems oddly focused – whether the last article of the three has any relevance to the others is difficult to say. *Green Anarchist* seems to be moving towards a blend of theoretical critique (Moore, Zerzan) and the (apparently indiscriminate) support of terrorist violence.

Inevitably, *Do or Die* and *Green Anarchist* also present more pragmatic and tactical information ('mobilizing information' or 'information for action') as well as 'diaries' and news reports of actions and protest world-wide (in the case of *Do or Die*, such information can also be found in the Earth First! *Action Update* and on its web site). In these cases, knowledge and mobilizing information appear as equal partners, exemplifying 'an activist concept of intellectual activity, a sense that knowledge must be put to good and better use' (Eyerman and Jamison, 1991: 116). In other media, such as the journal *Aufheben*, the two are fused. *Aufheben* characterizes itself as a 'class struggle anarchist' journal that offers 'revolutionary perspectives' (according to the footer on its front cover) and straddles the radical environmentalist and anarchist movements. It was founded by activists who 'wanted to develop theory in order to participate more effectively' (from 'Aufheben' on the *Aufheben* web site lists.village.virginia.edu/~spoons/aut_html/auf1edit.htm) and it critiques and theorizes protests as well as the objects of protests and the tactics of groups such as the SWP (again). *Aufheben* has developed its theoretical perspective from a blend of situationism, the work of the Italian *autonomia* and Marx. (The title of the journal is taken from a concept employed by Hegel and used by the early Marx to describe the dialectical process of supersession, through which a higher form of thought or being may replace a lower one while retaining its 'moments of truth'.) It has its roots in a reading group dedicated to Marx's *Capital* and *Grundrisse* and is published 'as a contribution to the reuniting of theory and practice'. The same aim had been attempted by the Class War Federation through its simultaneous publication of two titles: 'Britain's most unruly tabloid' *Class War* and its theoretical journal *The Heavy Stuff*. Before this, the anarchist Freedom Press had for many years published alongside its long-running newspaper, *Freedom*, a theoretical journal, *The Raven* (though perhaps more weakly theoretical, since much of it is taken up with commentary on mainstream topics from an anarchist perspective).

Though not set up together with the explicit aim of offering a balance of theory and practice, the critical journal *Here and Now* and the class-struggle anarchist news-sheet *Counter Information* are seen as complementary by Jim McFarlane, who is a member of both publications' editorial collectives. McFarlane has written about the contradiction of being involved in two projects, 'one [*Counter Information*] requiring a certain suspension of disbelief, the other [*Here and Now*] rooted in skepticism' ('Heresay', *Here and Now*, 13 [no date]: 2). He reveals a 'political tension' in producing material that is meant to 'enthuse and inspire' its readers into action, at the same time as producing 'semi-scholastic articles' whose politics are 'elevated' and 'less accessible'. A search for such a tension in other media and their sociocultural contexts may well prove useful to an understanding of the nature of their 'intellectual coherence'.

Coherence and Coverage

Publications such as *Aufheben, Counter Information* and those of the Class War Federation and Freedom Press offer information and knowledge from more or less ideologically determined positions. The 'grab-bag' of *Do or Die* and *Green Anarchist*'s placing of dense, theoretical texts alongside readers' briefer, personal writings generate critical spaces where freedom of expression is privileged over intellectual coherence (for instance, the editors of *Green Anarchist* claim that they publish on a 'no platform, no censorship' basis). When these two positions are taken together (and remembering that these represent only a fraction of the movement media, albeit a conspicuous fraction), intellectual coherence is unlikely. Do such media present any coherent vision or identity of a movement? Should we expect them to cohere?

The anonymous author writing about the future of Earth First! in *Do or Die* noted the value of a journal such as *Corporate Watch* to the movement. In the spirit of DIY culture this journal – an investigative and critical journal about corporate activity world-wide – arose spontaneously. As we have seen, outside the tighter organizational structures of the SMO, such media develop independently and unco-ordinated (except where links are forged latterly). An editorial in the alternative review journal *Bypass* argued that decentralization 'may prove a key strategy for the survival of dissent, or even just plain old independent thinking' (cited in Atton, 1996a: 101). Given the primacy of the network in DIY culture, can we expect these diversely differentiated media to co-ordinate for the further-ance of the movements? What links are maintained between media? We have seen that some groups and movements produce two complementary titles. In addition, many list each other's titles in a spirit of mutual support and networking, but there is little evidence of the media actually working together. More noticeable are the antagonisms and the rivalries. *Green Anarchist* is the most vociferous in this regard and appears to have aliena-ted itself from many other anarchist and environmental groups in the UK. Even during the conspiracy trial in 1997 of three of its 'editors', opinion was ambivalent towards the charges. Whilst *SchNEWS* was supportive, *Squall* ignored the case. Tyro readers find their way through such myriad media only with the greatest difficulty; the lack of an overarching publi-cation and the necessity to understand the various rivalries and alliances mean that making sense of the new social movement media is hard and that getting access to – and assessing – their contents problematic.

Furthermore, there is a danger that some areas of knowledge will be dealt with hardly at all. There is little discussion of gender, sexuality, race and class, though the occasional article may be found: *Green Anarchist* has published articles highly critical of feminism and articles supporting extreme libertarian views of sexuality, some going so far as to support paedophilia. Race tends to be discussed as a function of fascism (*SchNEWS*'s reports about the status of immigrants in Dover typically focus on (white) activists' attempts to disrupt marches by the local branch of the National Front.) The multi-racial character of the Exodus Collective – championed at length in *Squall* and examined in Tim Malyon's (1998) essay from George McKay's *DIY Culture* collection – is hardly touched on by the various reporters who have written about them. The general absence of interest in class has already been noted. There is a danger that so many disparate theories, philosophies and strategies will be posited that it becomes impossible for a movement to progress evenly, especially in a culture that is (at least partially) sceptical of intellectual activity. If there is little enough time to edit a journal between bouts of activism, where is the time to reflect on the issues raised by the articles in even a single issue of *Do or Die* or *Aufheben*?

Finally, we should ask: Whom do these media aim to represent? The large numbers of activists who contribute to *Do or Die* and *Green Anarchist* certainly have an outlet for their contributions, yet the letters pages of both titles crackle with voices critical of these contributions. Offering a space for discussion is no guarantor of consensus. A journal such as *Aufheben* offers no such space and presents itself as the product of a closed group. How valuable it is to the wider movements is impossible to judge from its own pages. And what of the silent voices, those of non-contributors? Are they alienated by such diversity and dissent? How many activists reading the movement media have no interest in large parts of it?

Readers as Readers

A small-scale survey of *SchNEWS* readers (around 50 self-selected respondents) that I undertook in 1999 suggests that most are looking for the two commonplaces of alternative media: mobilizing information and news of events ignored or marginalized by the mainstream media. A little under half of the respondents claimed that they read *SchNEWS* for the second reason. The assertion that issues are not covered elsewhere might be as much an assertion of the respondent's own 'alternativeness' as an assertion that they know that certain stories are not covered by the mainstream media. One respondent referred to the importance of 'defiance' in alternative media and said that, for them, that position was crucial. Choosing to read the alternative media as an act of defiance, as a proclamation of alternativeness, may well underlie assertions regarding coverage.

No respondent, however, presented this as the sole reason for reading the paper. For many respondents *SchNEWS* provides contacts, acts as a directory, enabling networking amongst like-minded activists: it 'does not merely inform, it activates its readers' (rather, this reader values the activating potential of the paper). A Finnish reader used *SchNEWS* to promote DIY culture in her own country; another found in it inspiration 'for other groups to start their own *SchNEWS*-type news-sheet'. Of all British alternative publications in this milieu it is the most frequent and reliable, appearing every week in paper form, by email and on its web site; it can be more up to date with country-wide actions and campaigns than any other single medium (though some email discussion lists and bulletin boards are more current in narrower fields, such as the McSpotlight web site). Consequently it is considered of great value for activists and potential activists alike. *SchNEWS* is also thought to be useful for increasing readers' understanding of the political, social and economic issues underlying many of the reasons for protest. It is respected for its ability to deal with 'heavy issues' in simple language, its accessibility to readers without any sophisticated prior knowledge of the topic. Though the range of issues covered and the space available force its writers and editors to deal with topics in brief, this brevity is generally praised as contributing to the paper's accessibility. Even within these limits readers find a variety of writing styles that appeals to them, often in the same article: the writing is 'snappy, to the point and fun to read'; 'passionate, serious, hilarious'. The sense of humour that abounds in *SchNEWS*, its irreverence, its use of slang, are all commented upon favourably – they contribute to the communication process, even when present in articles where one might expect humour to be absent (as in the paper's coverage of marches by fascists in Dover). It is tempting to find similarity here between the variety of style and language employed and the variety of methods some respondents identified that *SchNEWS* promotes, 'a lot of different ways of working to positively create a better world'. A wide range of issues (educational, environmental, ideological, economic, cultural), a wide range of writing styles (telegrammatic, listings of mobilizing information, satire, humour, passion, gravity) and a wide range of tactics (demonstrations, ecotage, letter-writing, fax blockades, setting up local groups, self-education) – the autonomous, networked multiplicity of DIY culture is figured in the form, content and (hoped for) outcomes of *SchNEWS*'s weekly two pages.

Credibility and bias figured high on respondents' evaluations of *SchNEWS*. The predictable cry was that the mainstream media was biased and could not be trusted; *SchNEWS* on the other hand, was 'trustworthy'. Trust was frequently invoked, not only by activists who felt part of the culture from which *SchNEWS* has developed (crudely speaking, young, middle-class unemployed activists, often living in squatted premises). Readers far from this milieu praised the paper for its 'honesty': it has 'nothing to gain by bullshitting', said one. This of course is arguable: *SchNEWS* has explicit aims centred on radical social change that could just as easily be pursued at the expense of veracity or credibility. 'Bullshitting' can, after all, be simply another word for propaganda. This appears to be appreciated by some readers who, whilst making the expected claim of bias in the mainstream media, also find bias in *SchNEWS* (this is the nearest any respondent came to negative criticism). Here, though, the bias does not obstruct reading, it encourages it.

What is perhaps more revealing is the statement, made by several respondents, that *SchNEWS* 'can be trusted because it's free (in both senses of the word)'. Here again we find it argued that profit-making within media institutions is essentially corrupting, or at least that it distorts the ethical values writers and editors might wish to uphold. This harmonizes with the prevalent suspicion of taking advertising within the alternative media, even where its absence leads to the extreme of 'barefoot economics'. To this we might add the value that appears to accrue from an unpriced publication ('free' in a second sense), as if a publication that does not ask for our money is somehow less corruptible than one that does. This argument is rather weak: the extensive networks of free 'community' newspapers that are little more than vehicles for advertising argues against it. But taken together the two senses of 'free' as applied to alternative media reveal more: for those who find it valuable, to be able to read a paper such as *SchNEWS* without having to pay for it and to be at the same time signally aware of its independence from other sources of funding is to participate in an enterprise that is courageous in a capitalist world, an enterprise that exhibits – and exhorts its readers to join in – an alternative economy. To participate in such a radical (anti-)economic world is to construct oneself radically, defiantly. Reading *SchNEWS* engenders solidarity: 'readers know that they are not alone', as one respondent put it. All the readers questioned intimated that they engaged with the content of the paper (its extrinsic, instrumental value) as well as appreciating it as an act of defiance, for its intrinsic alternativeness (its news values, its production values, its economic values). Often this is regardless of its bias, or even of agreeing with its message: 'I don't always agree with *SchNEWS* but at least they are "free".'

Who makes up this community of readers? I have already alluded to the 'typical' activist reader and these (predictably) appear to constitute a significant group within the readership. Further, as one respondent put it, *SchNEWS* acts as a 'lifeline' to former activists to the extent that it offers continuously updated information on protests and actions, enabling readers not only to remain informed but to rejoin (or join anew) a protest when circumstances permit. But this is to homogenize activists and their activity; there is much differentiation within such a category and consequently many different uses to which *SchNEWS* is put by its readers. In addition to its use as an information resource for such as environmental activists and hunt saboteurs, it is of value to an activist-run music and arts collective as a source of information for events run by other groups, information on those groups (and therefore it has a networking value) and as a site for publicizing the collective and its events. A former member of the group responsible for *Corporate Watch* found *SchNEWS* valuable as a source of leads for that journal's more detailed pieces as well as providing formal and organizational inspiration ('I don't just read the things, I produce them!'). But there are others far from this milieu, far from DIY culture and transient protest who also feel a sense of solidarity with the paper. Some readers apologized for not adhering to the stereotypical activist-reader ('I'm not an activist or campaigner'; 'I'm a "fluffy" liberal'). Others went further, citing attitudes or social milieux that might appear to exclude them as part of the paper's readership: '[I'm] much more an apathetic cynic type'; '[I] even have friends who hunt'. Once more, there is defiance here: not against corporate media or global capitalism, but against their own, local sociocultural settings. Not necessarily to deny them nor even to rebel against them, but to show that it is possible for individuals to construct themselves, accommodate themselves – apparently contradictorily – within a number of settings. We may see here a further instance of the disruption of purity that we first met in Chapter 3 in the discussion of Jody's personal web page. Here we see readers of alternative media who do not all fit easily into a single category (activist or member of a subculture). Just as we might look for alternative media in settings beyond the new social movements or zine culture, we should also consider that their audiences might be drawn from other settings. (What this study lacks is any evidence to gauge how – if at all – the knowledge and information gained in the *SchNEWS* 'community' is employed within any such individual's local milieu.)

This chapter has shown how the range of contributors and their various styles have led to a diversity in knowledge production. An emphasis on independence, autonomy and freedom of expression across these media, whilst it clearly encourages a range of critical intellectual activity, leaves some topics unaddressed. There are contradictions between media – even within a single publication – about the status of intellectual activity. The profusion of titles and their often divergent (if not conflicting) agendas can hinder the dissemination of knowledge. In their effort to avoid dogma and 'the ideological ghetto' they run the risk of embracing a plurality that can be just as stifling in its welter of competing discourses. McKay (1998: 44) has urged the movements 'to greater consideration and reflection' of such crucial issues as the 'coherence of ideology'. How is this to be achieved when faced with so many perspectives?

Elsewhere I have argued that the success of radical media need not be based simply on the circulation and readership of specific titles. Instead we must consider the networked totality of such media; individual calculations are less important than the decentralized, participatory mechanisms that enable a diversity of voices to be heard through a wide range of media (Atton, 1999b). This argument must be tempered by a consideration of the reach and impact of these media. If readers are ignoring the theory and philosophy they present, what is being achieved?

If such material is only being read by fractions and coteries of the movements – or by self-selected 'movements within movements' (which *Green Anarchist* appears to promote), then a possible outcome is a further alienation of the bulk of movement actors from those types of knowledge. I do not assert that the movement media are failing; the evidence is not sufficient. I have not examined the other critical spaces where knowledge presented in the media might be disseminated and reproduced: meetings, demonstrations, protest sites and the 'free universities' that have arisen spontaneously and temporarily at such sites. Such further examinations – along with deeper analyses of readers and reading – will enable a more accurate assessment of the success or failure of movement media. The evidence presented here demonstrates at least that there is much intellectual work going on in the radical media. How effective such work is to the movements themselves remains to be seen.

Note

---

1. The Northern Ireland Political Collection of the Linen Hall Library in Belfast is the single most valuable resource for any study of such material. Given the extent of this collection – over 2,000 political newspaper titles, over 10,000 locally published pamphlets and books, around half of which are unique to the collection, as well as thousands of posters and other ephemera – and its significance not only to alternative media studies but to sociological, cultural and political studies – it is surprising that Northern Ireland has not been examined in terms of media production in these communities – particularly when the quantity and range of materials held in the Linen Hall suggest it as the locus for the most intense production of alternative and radical media in the UK throughout the last quarter of the twentieth century. Joanne Wright's (1991) study of terrorist propaganda draws on *Republican News* and a handful of other documents and is one of the few studies to engage in any detail with the media. Her central interest, however, is in the use of such propaganda, not the social and cultural circumstances and significance of its production.

© 📖 📄 📠 💾 📑 📹 ®

6

information and communication technologies (ICTs) in alternative media

he use of the Internet by the Zapatista movement in Mexico to send communiqués out to the rest of the world has been an especially potent demonstration of autonomous electronic communication (Wehling, 1995). Manuel Castells (1997: 79) has called the Zapatistas the 'first informational guerrilla movement'. Worldwide mobilization came in the form of protests, letter-writing and the sharing of information about the situation in Chiapas and to this extent – the use of the Internet as the primary channel for autonomous communication – the movement was informational and (if only metaphorically) 'guerrilla'. It is as this electronic complex of informational and communicational possibilities which is itself linked with other complexes of previously existing technologies (face-to-face communication, print, music, political demonstrations and marches) that the Internet holds out such potential for oppositional groups. Since Chiapas we have seen a range of groups, movements and causes based in actual struggle, but having at their communicational, informational and organizational heart the deployment of information and communication technologies (ICTs), using them to present mobilizing information, alternative news reports, video and webcam feeds, Internet radio, archives, discussion lists, chat rooms, bulletin boards and sound files.

In this chapter I shall extend the discussion of ICTs from zines to new social movement media. I shall show that the deployment of ICTs appears developmental and progressive: an additive set of processes that supplement and exponentially increase opportunities for sociality, community, mobilization, knowledge construction and direct political action. To begin I have chosen to examine the use of the Internet by anarchist groups. I do so not only because this offers a range of interventions, but also because within a social movement such as anarchism attitudes, beliefs and ideologies have a pragmatic bearing on the adoption of the technology under consideration. We are therefore able to see how arguments for and against technology and the range of applications of that technology link with the wider sociocultural and political features of the movement. I shall go on to show how the use of ICTs by alternative media groups encourages us to reassess the notions of 'alternativeness' and 'radicality' under the conditions of new technology.

Anarchist Perspectives on the Internet

Anarchist critiques of the Internet may be divided into two broad categories (following Burgelman, 1994): 'boom' and 'doom'. These mirror the categories Burgelman finds in the greater part of the literature on the information society and its attendant technologies. The first ('boom') examines the Internet 'from a perspective of discontinuity: a radical and better society will emerge.' This is most apparent in the variety of magazines devoted to the Internet (such as .net and Wired) that have brought to a wider public the concepts and the lexicon of technological utopianism. Mike Peters (1996) argues that it is precisely the tone of such writing that is central to any understanding of its message. Its proponents espouse a 'cybertheory' that is 'an entirely *linguistic* phenomenon' in that what they are describing – a replacement for the lived world of social relations – has no existence beyond its dependent technology. This tone will also be found in studies of the new technology, where a euphoric idealism is typical (Rimmer, 1995 and Rushkoff, 1994 are two very different examples of this). Even where such optimism is alloyed, the tone remains generally positive (Hafner and Markoff, 1991; Rheingold, 1994). Some anarchist groups and commentators see in the structure and 'openness' of the Internet the prefiguring of an anarchist society. The British anarchist newspaper *Freedom* has noted the frequent appearance of the word 'anarchy' in a positive sense, as used by many commentators and Internet users to describe the *modus operandi* of the system. Remarkably for an anarchist organization, an editorial in *Freedom* even quoted Ian Taylor (then the UK's technology minister) approvingly: 'because the Internet is anarchic it's virtually impossible for us as a government to say what can and cannot be done on it' (Anon., 1995a). Given the legal action taken against some anarchist groups using the Internet in Britain shortly before this editorial was published (see Atton, 1996b for a discussion), *Freedom*'s view must be considered somewhat naïve. The paper itself was slow to see the potential of the Internet for its own activities. Anarchist use of the Internet can be traced back as far as 1988 (with the establishment of the Anarchy List), yet it did not touch *Freedom* until seven years later.

Burgelman's 'doom' commentators consider such developments 'from a perspective of continuity ... in line with the existing (unequal) power relations'. They view the democratic potential of the Internet pessimistically, citing the problems of access to the required technology for the disenfranchised, the poor and, in some cases, the entire populations of countries that lack the necessary communications infrastructure. The dangers of the rise of an information elite exercising absolutist control over a communications system is one outcome of this scenario (Haywood, 1995; Panos, 1995). Certain anarchist groups (such as some 'primitivist anarchist' groups and neo-Luddites) have strong ideological objections to using the technology, which are developed from this argument. The anti-technology stance of the American anarchist newspaper *Fifth Estate* is instructive here. Arguing for 'the elimination of the information age', a member of its editorial collective warns against espousing a technology that he considers as: 'the last frontier for the imperial project of late capitalism. If relative autonomy and abundant piracy flourish today, the legal apparatus of the corporate information state remains poised to control this exchange in the name of profit' ('Sunfrog', 1995).

Even putting aside such control, he believes that the optimism of such as *Freedom* is misplaced, to the extent that the Internet 'further imposes mechanized intervention in the antiquated realm of activity known as live[d] experience' and engenders a 'depreciation of sensual reality and deterioration of communities'. This is not a solitary view. An anonymous article in the anarchist zine *Black Cat* (Anon., 1995b) also emphasizes the alienation that such technology can bring, finding in the Internet not a force for liberation but another manifestation of 'the spectacle', a debilitating convergence of consumption, control and pseudo-communication.

Noam Chomsky (1994: 261) who, although he admits his reaction is emotional rather than analytical ('These are intuitive responses,' he warns), is especially sceptical: '[e]xtending that form of abstract and remote relationship, instead of direct personal contact ... [is] going to have unpleasant effects on what people are like. It will diminish people, I think.' Chomsky warns against what Hakim Bey (1991: 110–111) has approvingly called 'cyberpunk utopianists, futuro-libertarians, Reality

Hackers and their allies', those who, by living out their lives materially via electronic communication, adopt codes and practices that do not equip them for unmediated direct human contact. Peters dismisses the desiderata of the cybertheorists (a 'post-biological humanity', a 'post-human' world) as possessing merely the 'aura of radicality'. Rather than actually subverting the 'order of things ... [they are] exactly identical to where capital is driving at the moment'. Just as 'Sunfrog' finds, this is no new threat, simply the old one in a new guise.

Anarchists' Use of the Internet

Even amongst those who advocate using the Internet, there is a divergence of applications. Freedom Press (http://www.ecn.org/freedom/) uses the Internet as little more than a means of publicity for an established publishing programme (in the case of Freedom, this includes a fortnightly newspaper, a quarterly journal and an extensive backlist under the Freedom Press imprint). It claims to provide indexes to its two serial publications, the fortnightly *Freedom* newspaper and the quarterly journal *The Raven*. 'Index' is perhaps the wrong word, for what we have under both are links to the full text of a small number of articles (for *The Raven* the aim is to include only one article from each issue). The criteria for inclusion in the 'index' are obscure. Are these texts any more than tasters for the printed version, and this part of the site little more than advertising?

Others have made available existing print periodicals in their entirety, though even these differ substantially in their *modus operandi*. The American journal *Practical Anarchy Online* was the first anarchist periodical to become available solely in electronic format, replacing its original paper version in 1992. It also offered a form of subscription; its editor would send subscribers an email alerting them to the appearance of a new issue on its web site (now a common practice in web serial publishing). Some journals are located on web sites that must be browsed in order to discover whether a new issue had already appeared, posted to discussion lists such as the Anarchy List or emailed directly to subscribers (of course, a periodical may be 'published' simultaneously by all these methods). Another US journal, *Wind Chill Factor*, based in Chicago, declared in 1993 that 'the cost of printing 5000+ copies per issue [per month] on newsprint is prohibitive' (10 December 1993, copy in author's possession). It decided to publish in print quarterly, and to issue 'Info-Bulletins' in between as necessary, available as a page in a radical Chicagoan magazine

Lumpen Times, as a freesheet distributed around the city and electronically for Internet and BBS distribution.

Most anarchist titles continue in paper form. Since their relevance is largely limited to local or regional audiences, these titles use the international distribution afforded by the Internet only contingently; it is not of prime importance. Journals here include *The Anarchist* (Australia), *The Anarchives* (Canada), *Counter Information* (UK), *Love and Rage Newspaper* (US) and *Sekhmet* (an anarcha-feminist magazine from New Zealand). It is difficult to judge the effect of such distribution (anecdotal evidence apart), since no access figures are available for these titles. (That *The Anarchives* and *Counter Information* are posted to the Anarchy List does however ensure their distribution to at least 500 subscribers worldwide.)

There is no reliable or comprehensive directory of anarchist journals in either the US or the UK (*The Anarchist Year Book* only ever offers a fraction of those in circulation), nor are they systematically collected by any library (the Labadie Collection at the University of Michigan is one of the rare attempts by the academy to preserve an anarchist heritage). Many titles do benefit from being preserved electronically on the numerous sites dedicated to archiving anarchist writings and illustrations. Pre-eminent amongst these is Spunk Library (formerly Spunk Press), which archives many of the above journals and acts as a distributor for numerous anarchist news services. Its significance and value to the anarchist community does not stop there. Established in 1992 in Holland, but with an international editorial group, its avowed aim is 'to act as an independent publisher of works converted to, or produced in, electronic format and to spread them as far as possible on the Internet and in the BBS society free of charge' (Spunk Library Manifesto, available from Spunk Library at http://www.au.spunk.org/info/manifest.html). As such it claims uniqueness. Jack Jansen, the founder of Spunk Press, believes so:

> As far as I know, we're the only group working this way, i.e. distributing globally by using the net as our communications medium. There are other groups with similar subject matter, but they tend to be one-person projects. There are also groups who make documents available, like Project Gutenberg, but they are funded. (Quoted in Campbell, no date)

Spunk Library's catalogue contains essays, speeches and lectures from prominent anarchists, both historical (Bakunin, Goldman) and contemporary (Bookchin, Chomsky). Works by 'dissident' anarchists such as Hakim Bey, Bob Black and the situationists will also be found here. An 'alternative section' includes works that, whilst not strictly anarchist in outlook, might be held to inform the debate, such as items on alternative education, environmentalism and nuclear issues. At present the collection is largely of articles, essays, speeches and letters; in general there are no full-length books or collected works (except where these are brief). There are archives of electronic anarchist journals (and partial archives of some print journals). It contains a comprehensive list of anarchist groups, along with selected reviews of anarchist books and selections of anarchist poetry. There are also collections of anarchist images and symbols and portraits of famous anarchists.

The rationale behind the inclusion of an item in Spunk Library is at once very loose and very restricted. The editorial collective recognized the need for a collection development policy (there is such a heading in Spunk Library's World Wide Web pages) but no policy has apparently ever been finalized. Anyone is at liberty to suggest items for inclusion. If they are deemed relevant to Spunk Library (i.e. they are broadly anarchist in outlook) then they will be accepted. How easily the material becomes part of Spunk Library is dependent on whether any copyright adheres to the original document and the original format of the information – whether electronic or print. If the latter, then resources and time will be needed to scan the document, to proofread it and to mark up the text in HTML. All tasks, from the selection of a document to its final appearance in the archive, are undertaken by an international collective of volunteers, largely using borrowed equipment or equipment used primarily for other purposes (i.e. full-time work). In common with much of the media examined in this book, it seeks to involve as many people as care to become involved, particularly those with technical skills to donate. And in common with most alternative publishing ventures, Spunk Library is run in spare time, at no profit (the service is free and accepts no advertising). Resources and time are at a premium. There are currently almost 2,000 items available for reading and downloading (according to Spunk Library Numerical Catalog (http://www.spunk.org/cat-us/numeric.html), last updated 13 April 1999). Although it seeks to make available documents originally published in electronic form, the majority of its publications are converted from print.

Assessing the Constraints

Many commentators believe that the advent of the Internet marked a dissolution of constraints on freedom of expression and on the monopoly of publishing and distribution. We have already seen how economic and other constraints can prevent alternative media from reaching even their intended audiences. Some would argue that the Internet provides these media with the means to escape such constraints and to gain unprecedented opportunities for disseminating ideas and information. James Hamilton (2000a) notes that the use of the Internet appears to lower the costs of production and distribution, if only because there is no physical product to move around. He does remind us, though, that the Internet remains an elite medium that is far from universally available. Professionalized skills are still required to create and distribute material, and the purported global reach of the medium falls far short in reality. From my earlier discussion of economics we can identify two major constraints: (1) Low capital, leading to low print runs; (2) poor access to mainstream distribution and limited opportunities for independent distribution. It is in the light of these constraints that the potential of any new form of publishing needs to be assessed. The opportunities apparently afforded by electronic publishing on the Internet might enable publishers to overcome them. The limits of small print runs and distribution do not apply to the dissemination of electronic information; nor does economy of scale. The problem of low print runs is very real for anarchist publishers and prevents widespread dissemination of their titles. Though no precise figures are available for the circulation of anarchist journals, Chan (1995) provides the following estimates of readership: *Class War* 12,000, *Direct Action* 500–1,000, *Freedom* 500–1,000, *Green Anarchist* 2,000. One would expect the actual copies printed to be at least half of these figures. Even where a title has a substantial print run, it often proves difficult to sustain (for example, *Wind Chill Factor*'s print run of 5,000). Publishing on the Internet requires that only a single 'copy' of any document exists to provide mass circulation. It not only dispenses with the notion of circulating copies, it also blurs the distinction between production and distribution, since the origination of a document in a format suitable for uploading on the Internet entails the second. Whilst the Internet does away with the capital requirement for print runs, it nevertheless requires capital and time to enable the origination of documents in machine-readable format. Such a requirement is hardly trivial. For a venture such as Spunk Library, which receives no income from its work, these resources must come from personal funds or be offset by the use of equipment intended for other purposes, e.g. scanners and computers used in the course of paid employment.

Just as 'print run' is a meaningless term in electronic publishing, so is 'distribution'. Freedom from the vagaries of a distribution network and from unsympathetic wholesalers and bookshops is guaranteed, but is only worth having if the public have access to a publisher's stock in some other way. In terms of the World Wide Web, we talk of access rather than distribution, the distribution of multiple copies of a document being replaced by the placing of a single copy of a document at a single site. Detailed figures of access to all Spunk Library publications are not available, but general figures suggest that the archive is well used. It has been keeping a hit count since May 1996 and at the time of writing (September 2000) has had over 17,000 hits. The most current figure indicates that in one month well over 500 documents were accessed from Spunk Library's Netherlands site (no figures are available for the US site). More than half the items in the catalogue are downloaded at least once a month. Whilst these figures tempt favourable comparison with the small-circulation anarchist papers and journals, it is not possible to compare them directly with the distribution and sales figures of the anarchist presses represented in Spunk Library, for a number of reasons. In the main, documents archived on the site are extracts from publications, not the publications themselves (with the exception of journal archives, which are a mixture of complete issues and extracts from the larger journals, such as *Anarchy: a Journal of Desire Armed*). For many publishers Spunk Library is a shop window, and is not intended to replace print publishing. Finally, many documents exist only in Spunk Library: they were created specifically for it, they only exist electronically or they are out of print in other formats. In many ways, then, Spunk Library, like many similar archiving projects, is quite unlike the passive repository that is the physical archive. Its visibility on the Web (in spite of its less than popular philosophy, it has been recognized by the *Rough Guide to the Internet* as being 'organized neatly and with reassuring authority') enables it to function as a promoter for anarchist book publishers, newspapers and journals. It is a supplier of many of these publications (in part if not in whole) to individuals and groups seeking out information, education and entertainment. It exists as an advertisement for a socially responsible anarchism with a significant intellectual pedigree. In a world where anarchism is still largely derided or maligned by the mass media, that is an important function.

When I first examined the use of the Internet by anarchists (Atton, 1996b), I referred to it 'as simply one more method of communication, one more weapon in the armoury of the activist, the dissident publisher, the disenfranchised individual or constituency' (p. 120). There are those in the anarchist community who still appear to see it like that. For a few it is a replacement. What is the status of Spunk Library, though? It is many things: an archive, a distributor, a communication node, a virtual meeting-place, a publishing house, even a talking-shop. It is certainly closer to a site like the Mid-Atlantic Infoshop in its multivalent character and functions than it is to an archive or a publisher (whilst being both). Those working for it might be seen as authors, editors, publishers, disseminators, 'facilitators', organizers – moreover, it offers those roles to a multiplicity of individuals and groups, presenting a shifting population of – what do we call them? – contributors? communicators? activists? archivists? reporters? readers? Although it remains convenient to talk of centres, of nodes, the notion of centrality (especially when construed as a function of authority), of an organizational hub, is eroded in a cyber-space characterized by interdependent linkage and a lack of hierarchy. Coupled to a political philosophy such as anarchism, such notions are made even more fragile. Ownership is similarly problematic. Whilst we may talk of 'webmasters' and 'site administrators', ownership in terms of who is responsible for content, for links, for organizing resources is dif-fuse and uncertain – appropriately enough for systems that operate on anarchist principles and perhaps liberatingly so. And this apart from any operation of anti-copyright principles. No faceless cyberspace this. The complex of relations initiated in cyberspace – intellectual, social, cultural, political, economic – is overlaid and interpenetrated by a further complex in the lived world. In practice the distinction between the two is far less clear than some cybertheorists would have us believe.

Kriha (1994) gives the name 'cyberanarchism' to what he considers the ideal application of the Internet: to establish 'confederal' structures of community and communication, free from the 'external coercion' of the state and commercial providers of Internet access and the limits of com-puter ownership and literacy. Kriha finds benefit where others find only detriment: 'by insulating individuals from the need for physical contact, members of a cybercommunity are insulated from the worst effects of any potential coercion'. This is to ignore the possibility of other types of coer-cion, 'patterns of inequality and forms of division' arising within cyber-space. There is no guarantee that all such forms will disappear under computer-mediated communication (CMC). We have already seen how networks are sustained through donations of equipment, itself often aged, and of intangibles such as free webspace. There is no guarantee that such gifts will be endless, nor that the potential participants in the net-works have easy and regular access to the technology. On economic grounds alone, there is reason to note the 'fragility of the set of circum-stances that [leads] to... access' (Mele, 1999: 306).

Kriha's position does offer some purchase in understanding the role and value of a site such as Spunk Library. In common with numerous sites estab-lished by new social movements (GreenNet, PeaceNet, McSpotlight, sq@t!net, contrast.org), Spunk Library exhibits multiple and simultaneous functions at the same time as it exhibits few of the characteristics of a pub-lication, or even those of an institution. Its 'membership' ('contributors'?) is diffuse, in many cases anonymous – whether for reasons of (perceived) personal security or because personal identity and circumstances are deemed irrelevant. It occupies no single physical space; neither an office nor a library, nor a meeting-place. Such features are of course common to many net-based 'organizations' – what is striking in the case of Spunk Library is the extent to which a 'given' technology is fully integrated into anarchist praxis. The anarchist affinity group model of sociopolitical organization appears remarkably congruent with the technological model.

The history of the deployment of information and communication technologies has not always been so congruent. Early efforts to establish radical television were severely hampered by restrictions on access to broadcasting frequencies, not to mention the capital-intensive require-ments of equipment and the necessity for trained operators. The inclu-siveness and reach of such projects as the American Videofreex were severely limited (Boyle, 1997). Whilst theatrical screenings in community centres and educational establishments (a recurring feature of alternative video production) took the material out of its narrow field of production, the size of audiences increased only when producers were able to place their material with public access stations. Given an economy of scale and a regulatory system that promotes both a Public Broadcasting System (PBS) and public access cable TV, it is not surprising that attempts to deliver programmes nationally are most common in the US. Paper Tiger TV began producing video programmes for public access cable in New York City in 1981 (Halleck, 1984). Enabled by a grant in 1985, the group founded Deep Dish TV to provide its own video programmes and those of other grassroots media producers by satellite. Two of its members, Martin Lucas and Martha Wallner (1993) give an account of its Gulf Crisis TV Project series of the early 1990s that was offered to local access and the PBS by satellite. This account has much to say about co-operation and networking with local TV stations; it also has much to say about depen-dence: on public funds for equipment, staffing and running costs and on the technological and managerial infrastructures necessary for such elec-tronic media to survive. Political dependence may also be added to the list of constraints that limit many current radio and television initiatives on both sides of the Atlantic. In the US, low-power FM broadcasting up to approximately 3.5 miles is regulated by the Federal Communications Commission (FCC). Ownership is restricted to 'noncommercial govern-ment or private educational organizations, associations or entities, and government or non-profit entities providing local public safety or trans-portation services' (Hamilton, 2001b). Hamilton calls this 'institutional-ized dissent' and sees in it an obstacle to the creation of media operating on participatory, radically democratic lines whilst it pays lip-service to freedom of expression. A similar position obtains in the UK where the temporary licences available to local broadcasters under the government's

Restricted Service Licences (RSL) scheme prevent them from promulgating party-political or other non-aligned political agendas through the legislative limits set on the contents of their broadcasts. RSLs have been used by local groups, communities and event organizers (of music festivals, religious gatherings) as well as by universities and colleges, hospitals and prisons – over 2,000 RSL projects were set up in the 1990s. Under such legal constraints, community media here are prompted less by local politics and social change and more by a desire to improve the relevance of general content to a highly localized audience uninterested in the wider, regional programmes offered by the BBC and commercial broadcasters. The managing director of the Isle of Wight's TV12 describes it as 'a general entertainment channel' (cited in Scott, 1999: 12). Amongst its talk shows and DJ slots it offers a schedule already familiar from regional and national channels: talent shows, gardening and cookery programmes. For TV12, producing programmes made to industry standards of professionalism is essential: 'people don't want to see shaky cameras or home videos' (p. 13). This is far from the assisted amateurism of the alternative community newspaper, where the trained reporter took a significant, but ultimately empowering role in production.

Such initiatives are thus shackled to the prevailing models of local commercial broadcasting, in part due to the need to attract sponsorship and advertisers, in part due to government restrictions on political content. Though supportive of these initiatives, Steve Buckley, the director of the Community Media Association, finds here a 'dual strategy of co-option and marginalisation' that has led to the de-radicalization of the community media sector. He looks for co-operation and networking across the entire range of alternative media, erasing the polarities of advocacy/activism and local community/global struggles (in an email to the author). This is not to characterize all such projects as competing with the mainstream on the mainstream's terms; alternative artistic cultures have also taken advantage of RSLs. The London Musicians' Collective ran its Resonance FM station in the summer of 1998 for the first time, broadcasting experimental and avant-garde music from London's South Bank Centre. Kevin Howley (2000), though, still argues for the unregulated micro-radio movement in the US. In these cheap, low-power stations, a single person or small groups usually operate out of front rooms or on a local hillside on behalf of a local community, often a minority community. These unlicensed stations offer more than merely transmissions: their narrowcast capability and transience require close co-operation with the community in which they operate, for support as well as for the establishment of a word-of-mouth network to publicize transmission times (which often need to change to elude the authorities). They also provide legal challenges to the FCC, at times successfully arguing their right to broadcast. Unlike pirate radio these stations do not wish to remain clandestine; they celebrate their visibility (perhaps 'audibility' is better?) for the benefit of their community and to seek the removal of legal restriction on the freedom to broadcast.

We might also consider the value of emerging forms of broadcasting to community groups and political activists alike, such as Internet radio. Irational [*sic*] Radio (http://www.irational.org/radio/) supplies information on a range of radio initiatives, including information and contacts for setting up analogue pirate radio as well as DIY guides and software links for webcasting with RealAudio streaming software. Internet radio (usually 'net.radio') encourages a variety of strategies. This need resemble conventional radio only in the notion of broadcasting sound. Using streaming software, only encoding software is required to convert music or spoken word into streamed audio files. Jo Tacchi (2000) has called this technology 'radiogenic' and asks us to consider its products as 'radio'. Some webcasters couple it with live FM transmission; some capture other stations' streamed audio and broadcast that as FM radio. Irational Radio also recommends using archives of streamed audio to build up one's own programmes (just as we have seen new print media constructed from existing print media through strategies of anti-copyright and open distribution). The Open Radio Archive Network Group (ORANG at http://orang.orang.de/) offers hundreds of hours of such material for webcasters to upload and stream as part of their own programming. These initiatives, in their intertwining and redefining of media forms, in their blurring of creator, producer and distributor, of broadcaster and listener, suggest hybridized forms of media production particularly well suited to the multimedia possibilities of the Internet and the World Wide Web. Whilst more strategic in nature, even the networking and co-operation undertaken by Deep Dish TV to upload its programmes to satellite and have broadcasters use them required a hybridized approach to production and distribution. Hybridity in media form may also lead to a hybridity of intention, a hybridity of constituency and even – that Holy Grail of so many alternative media – a hybrid audience beyond the grassroots ghetto.

Progressive Librarians and McSpotlight

The N30 protests, held to protest against the World Trade Organization meeting on 30 November 1999 in Seattle (hence N30), prompted a multiplicity of sites that were for the most part unco-ordinated and decentralized. Here practices of computer-mediated communication highlight the extreme fluidity and hybridity there can be, whether as continual flux or temporary repositioning for a specific objective during a specific period. This might involve groups whose constituency might not be expected to move in certain directions. During the Seattle protests, a small group of radical librarians (numbering a little over 100 members) in the US became variously involved in the protests, engaging and informing each other and a wider audience through CMC as well as through direct action in Seattle: this was the Progressive Librarians' Guild (PLG). PLG embodies an apparent contradiction in its constituency. Its radical credentials include a strong interest in promoting free speech and combating censorship in libraries and, *inter alia,*

> encourag[ing] debate about prevailing management strategies adopted directly from the business world, propos[ing] democratic forms of library administration, [and] consider[ing] the impact of technological change in the library workplace and on the provision of library services... (from 'PLG's Commitment' at http://libr.org/PLG/index.html#statement)

Yet it is part of a profession that is usually represented as being staid, conservative and preservationist in its philosophy and actions. Above all, librarianship has hardly ever been a public site for political activism (unlike, say, the legal and medical professions). PLG's involvement in the radical politics of the collective actions taken in Seattle not only presents a largely unknown and surprising face of librarianship, it also indicates how members of such a profession can become radicalized in events that have little obvious connection to the principles and practices of their profession. During the days following the protest, many documents were posted to PLG's discussion list (PLGNET-L) containing details of where to obtain alternative news reports, video and radio feeds and op-ed features on the WTO and the protesters; many of these were available through the AlterNet (www.alternet.org), set up in 1987 by the US-based Independent Media Institute. AlterNet provides access to articles from over 200 alternative and independent newspapers and magazines. Here we see one aspect of radical librarianship in practice: providing alternative information and access to the sources of that information. The educational role that such a practice entails was also evident here in frequent discussion about media literacy and the media representation of the protesters. PLG members also became protesters: a three-person PLG contingent marched in Seattle, their 2,000-word report posted to the list functioning as eyewitness account, media critique and – importantly for the group – the valorization of librarians as agents of social change.

('These are the people who make sure Harry Potter stays in the library' and 'Aren't all librarians progressive?' are two of the approving comments they heard during their participation.) Though numerically insignificant in the protest, these three members of an organization on the margins of a profession that continues to struggle against a pejorative public image used CMC to publicize positive reactions to their protest. Other members built on this, praising a 'narrative [that] vividly place[d] in perspective the overwhelmingly positive and cooperative nature of the demonstration' and located their activities at the heart of both PLG's aims and, they argued, those of the profession at large, emphasizing a concern 'with our profession's rapid drift into dubious alliances with business and the information industry, and into complacent acceptance of service to the political, economic and cultural status quo' (from 'PLG's Purpose' at http://libr.org/PLG/index.html#statement).

The involvement of PLG in the N30 protests was necessarily temporary (though the consequences may well be long-lasting). Other organizations have developed more permanent approaches where the Internet is central as a hybridizing force in their communication, information and mobilizing strategies. The McSpotlight web site (http://www.mcspotlight. org/) shows how this works at an international level. In 1990 five members of the anarchist group London Greenpeace were served libel writs by the fast food company McDonald's for publishing and distributing a leaflet allegedly containing defamatory statements about McDonald's, claiming that the company was responsible, *inter alia*, for the destruction of rainforests to provide land for beef cattle, infringing workers' rights, cruelty to animals and promoting unhealthy eating. Three of the five apologized to McDonald's; Helen Steel and Dave Morris decided to fight the company in court. The defendants were unemployed and not eligible for legal aid and were therefore compelled to conduct their own defence. The 'McLibel' case, as it was known, became the longest British libel trial and, at its conclusion, the longest English trial. The action started in 1990; the judge did not deliver his final verdict until June 1997 (see McSpotlight's 'The McLibel Trial Story' at http://www.mcspotlight.org/case/trial/story.html). The McSpotlight web site was set up by supporters and sympathizers of the two in February 1996.

This represented a huge advance in the information and communication strategies so far used in the campaign, which had previously relied on small-circulation radical newspapers and magazines, and on the distribution of flyers and pamphlets produced by London Greenpeace. The communication networks that typify the culture of new social movements had already been complicated by the overlapping, various uses of telephones and fax machines. These were used as both intra- and inter-communication devices for movements, as well as weapons for direct action – the practice of 'blockading' a target organization with telephone calls and faxes. Freed from the constraints that the printed form places on the construction of networks beyond the local, CMC was able to significantly extend the opportunities for networking beyond the ephemerality of telephone call and fax paper.

McSpotlight was initially termed an 'on-line interactive library of information' by its founders – expanding the idea of the library to become a space where information is exchanged and created, not merely stored and consulted. The site contains two major archives: one is the full trial transcripts, the other an attempt to exhaustively archive print media references to McDonald's. It also hosts a 'debating room', a discussion list, DIY protest guides and campaign leaflets ready to print out 'in over a dozen languages' – even a compressed version of the entire site 'to help ensure that McDonald's will never be able to stop the dissemination of this information'. The site is 'constructed' by a network of volunteers working from 16 countries and continues to call for volunteers: 'HTMLers, programmers, typists, researchers, artistes [sic], people with skills we didn't even know we needed till you contacted us' (all references from http://www.mcspotlight.org/help.html). Compared to Spunk Library its hit rate is remarkable: at June 2000 it claimed to have 1.5 million hits per month. In its first year it estimates to have had well over a quarter of a million visitors (not merely hits, but individuals looking at the site; from information at http://www.mcspotlight.org/campaigns/current/mcspotlight/faq.html#1g).

The site's purpose was not exhausted by the end of the trial: it continued to campaign against McDonald's, as well as becoming a 'protest node' for a number of campaigns against anti-environmental corporations. McSpotlight not only connects activists to information, it enables communication amongst them. The grounding of the site's content in actual struggle is emphasized by the foregrounding of campaign information and leaflets and the assumption that these should be available in print for distribution at protest sites, on demonstrations, in high streets. A primary aim of the site was to publicize the McLibel trial in the face of a largely uninterested national media; yet it also delights in citing those media in its own publicity (the site claims to have the 'most press coverage of any web site' and refers visitors to its extensive press citations and awards). This ambivalence, coupled with the mass media's own fascination with the form and use of the site (over and above its content) complicate the site's characterization as 'alternative media', particularly in terms of its processes and its relation to the mass media. What first attracted the mass media to the site were its processes, not its content – it was through this publicity that the content of the site achieved a prominence that political and media lobbying might never have reached.

This raises some significant questions about the status and relation of alternative media and their audiences under the conditions of CMC. First, in the case of McSpotlight, we may note the apparent contradictions in the site's approach to publicity. The site seeks to publicize its causes to as wide an audience as possible (the site may be freely accessed at point of use; no membership or other fee is required), so it is also freely available to download. McSpotlight is attempting to bring in as many visitors as possible to view its contents. That it offers its site-download free of charge might also be seen as encouraging unlimited use, free of the constraints of on-line net access, line rentals and connection charges. Ostensibly, though, the download option is intended to frustrate any attempt by McDonald's to shut the site down. Here the appeal is to the committed audience, the environmental activist and the supporter of free speech. This plurality is only contradictory if we expect alternative media to adhere to some notion of 'purity' – to set limits on their audience and their reach either by economic or geographic circumstance (that is, by working with limited materials) or by design and purpose (desiring to build and retain an elite audience, whether for reasons of security or ideological purity). The very publicness available to a web site weakens the grip of such limits. The activities, information and involvement that McSpotlight promotes are available not simply to 'members' of an essentialized social movement or to an already committed audience – they are available to all: the sceptical, the uncommitted, the sympathetic, the antagonistic, as well as to the committed and the activists. And to all of these all at once.

Second, McSpotlight offers a centre. Its activities may be diverse, its audience and reach diffuse; in the end, though, it is a focus for a protest without a geographical or temporal centre. Around it (inspired by it, even) have arisen numerous sites, for the most part unco-ordinated. There is a tendency for protest nodes to arise, to gather information, offer spaces and resources for activists, and then either to disappear as the protests conclude or to evolve into other campaigns. Activists employing CMC can adapt their resources, to continually transform and reinvent themselves with a facility only partially available to print media. Whilst print media can make use of varied formats, make changes in frequency and produce 'emergency' issues, the processes of print production entail slower responses. There are also the conventions of periodicity (an audience expects regularity of publication in print) and of stability (few titles would vary a format indefinitely). The use of CMC by new social movements privileges fluidity, interpenetration and non-linearity. This strengthens the argument against essentializing new social movements as comprising fixed sets of aims, motives, strategies and tactics that are directed towards a clear, largely unchanging set of social-change objectives. It significantly weakens the vanguardist conception of a social movement, where an elite employs authoritative forms of discourse that are 'at the price of a deep separation between journalists and readers, producers and consumers. Acceptance and practice of distinction activates deeper kinds of social relation in capitalist societies, with perhaps the most disabling ones based in the notion of consumption' (Hamilton, 2000b: 361). In the previous chapter we saw how otherwise authoritative forms such as the eyewitness report and the documentary can be subverted: the vulnerable, self-conscious reporter at the Labour Party conference, her role further confused by being reporter, interviewee and pundit; the articles in *Do or Die* that blend colloquial, first-person address with scholarly writing. These show media that are combining (at times dissolving) genres and offering new approaches to representation through radical approaches to content, form and process, particularly where the stages of the production process are collapsed into one another and readers become writers. McSpotlight presents similar opportunities.

Third, where print media offer information directly and the possibility of communication only indirectly, CMC offers them both directly and thus confuses the two. Where sites still offer periodical publications as part of a wider structure of networked information and communication, periodicity is often eroded, only weakly present in the 'last updated' legend common to web sites. But there are also less liberating consequences of such erosion. Linking to other sites on the Net radically reinterprets the practice of editing a publication. Selection may well be made positively and thoroughly when choosing to link, but there is little evidence that the volatility of all web sites is taken into account by linkers. Linked-to sites might well change their content radically, yet still be considered 'editorially' part of the home site. Changing URLs (Uniform or Unique Resource Locators), lapsed telecommunications subscriptions and unpaid bills can all render these rhizomatic enterprises fragile and make them liable to collapse, disruption and incoherence. Further, the facility with which links may be made encourages 'saturated linking' – what is benignly termed 'surfing' can often be perpetual consignment to a maze of increasingly irrelevant data. Unmoderated discussion lists also present complications: the reliability of information in posts; the security of data; managing the information flow; dealing with inappropriate responses ('flaming' and 'spamming'); simply finding the time to make sense of it all. Boundaries dissolve, edges disappear – the very notion of 'publication' is challenged.

What are the distinctive features of alternative media under the conditions of CMC? Does it make any sense to talk of alternative media in cyberspace? Where the processes of production are available to anyone, where the horizontal, networked flows of information and communication are inbuilt, where anyone can become their own publisher, their own polemicist, does a specific set of media termed 'alternative' have any identity? Some distinctive processes of alternative print media production are no longer radical on the Web. Non-hierarchical methods of communication and ease of participation in creating and commenting on media texts are now normalized in Internet practice. The experimental nature of much alternative print publishing is called into question: either it is no longer a meaningful practice (the small print run) or it has become absorbed into a dominant practice of web publishing that ordinarily entails transformed roles and social relations that were once the province of alternative media production (anyone can be a writer or a publisher). Experiments with blending informational and communicational forms are a further instance of common web practice. The exclusiveness of alternative media as a communication process is also eroded. The narrowcast nature of much alternative media entailed small audiences (it guaranteed it) and restricted access to those who knew where to go for such media. Some media producers preferred this, either for reasons of elitism or for security. By contrast, publicity for many web sites is likely. For those with a message to the world this may be attractive; for such as Spunk Library it may be ambivalent. As one of the most visible advertisements for anarchism it has been the target of virulent (and perhaps even libellous) criticism (Atton, 1995). For others with more clandestine activities to protect, publicity can threaten the entire enterprise.

Whether desirable or not, the Internet entails publicness, though there persists the possibility that no one will find your information, so lost is it in the welter of electronic data. Perhaps the only significant constant in print and CMC versions of alternative media is content, particularly the origins of that content. For much alternative media, content comes from lived, local experience. Miller and Slater (2000) have argued that there is no such place as 'cyberspace'. The significance of Internet use proceeds not from a solipsistic and technocratic desideratum of value only to Hakim Bey's 'cyberpunk utopianists' but from 'locally contextualised [practices of] consumption and production' (Tacchi, 2000: 293). In order to sustain a notion of alternative or radical communication in cyberspace we must, as Kevin Robins (1995) has urged, let the real world break in on the virtual one. It is through the use of CMC by new social movements for collective political action that we best see such an irruption in action.

Hybridity and 'Purity'

Throughout this book, from the theoretical arguments over dimensionality to the examination of the varied approaches to alternative media organization and production and their aims and knowledge structures, we have seen difference at work. The dimensions explored in Chapter 1 do not merely serve to explain production and distribution strategies (such as innovations in form and reprographic techniques, and new sites for distribution), they also account for the realignment of social and professional relations that alternative publishing offers (such as methods of collective organization, writing and editing, the deprofessionalization of editing and writing). Whether within each media form or across forms; in the hybridized voices constructed from a range of contributions – from the movement-intellectual, the activist, the native reporter, the everyday narrative, the 'guerrilla semiotics' of the collage; collective writing and editing and anonymized multiple contributions – all work to dehomogenize alternative media as a single field of production, as a consolidated part of a single alternative public sphere. There is hybridity in audiences, too: the notion of the reader-writer transforms the Fiskean active audience from an individual engaged in a type of everyday social action to a creator and communicator of symbolic materials out of that everyday, at once a media producer, a witness and a media critic. Audiences are diffuse and divergent. The deployment of ICTs by a site such as McSpotlight presents a plurality of resources to an equally plural range of audiences. The publicness it can employ forces us to let go of any notions of purity in alternative media. Though Internet technology prompts us to do this forcefully at present, the problematics of purity, hybridity and difference have a longer history in alternative media.

In her study of two films made in the early 1970s by local community groups in the East End of London, Gillian Rose (1994: 49) recognizes that the marginalized cultures that are represented and which produced the films were 'neither the same as hegemonic cultures nor entirely different from them'. She identifies many dimensions of difference, amongst them the final purposes of the film: as a campaigning tool, as a consciousness-raising event, as a spur to public discussion, as a weapon against the bureaucrats, as a process of building self-confidence within a community – even as a method of renegotiating the identity of that community. The site of production of the films – just as much as the screening of the films – forms a space for discussion and negotiation. Rose discovers in these cultural interplays a version of Homi Bhabha's (1990) 'third space' where meaning and understanding emerge from a negotiation of cultural and political identity as the site of a hybridic excess of meaning. Whilst the deprofessionalization, decapitalization and deinstitutionalization proposed by James Hamilton are extremely useful concepts in developing a theoretical framework for alternative media, they should not force us into unwittingly perpetuating an untenable duality between alternative and mainstream. John Downing (2001) has drawn attention to the shortcomings of his earlier work (Downing, 1984) where he proposed a rigid binary model of alternative and mainstream media. As he has acknowledged, this offered little opportunity for considering the democratization of mainstream media, the application of skills and techniques from the mainstream, or the hybridic or subversive use (détournement) of mainstream media products and processes – to which many instances from this book attest.

Homi Bhabha (1994: 39) has talked of eluding 'the politics of polarity' and of 'the transformational value of change [that] lies in the rearticulation, or translation, of elements that are *neither the One ... nor the Other ... but something else besides,* which contests the terms and territories of both' (1994: 28; emphasis in original). To read such a possibility into alternative media has methodological implications for 'alternative media studies'. We need to consider not only form and content, but the processes and relations that inform them and are in turn informed by them. The study of alternative media needs to interrogate identities and practices that are negotiated across the terrain of a third space that hybridizes practices between hegemonized and marginalized cultures.

conclusion

The present study has repeatedly emphasized that the alternative media – as a major constituent in the dissemination of the views and opinion formation of 'subaltern counterpublics' (Fraser, 1992) – have the potential to offer even more than 'interpretation'; they provide readers with access to other readers' (activists') lived experiences and on occasion offers these as part of a network of sociocultural and sociopolitical projects (often aimed at social change through extra-parliamentary means). The alternative media can provide empowering narratives of resistance for those counter-publics that are written by those very counter-publics. If such counter-publics 'want nothing more than the writing of their own texts' (as Njabulo Ndebele expressed the desire of the repressed of South Africa; cited in Carusi, 1991: 103) then the contemporary alternative media appear able to realize that desire. A key feature of these media is the erosion of the expert who is dependent on formal education and professionalization, to be replaced by the autodidact, informally skilled often through collective experimentation. In Bourdieusian terms this autodidact has 'a relation to legitimate culture that is at once "liberated" and disabused, familiar and disenchanted' (Bourdieu, 1984: 84). The 'heretical mode of acquisition' (ibid.: 328) of cultural capital by the counter-cultural intellectual 'leads to a refusal to be classified, with the injunction to resist fixed codes' (Featherstone, 1991: 44).

We see here the erasure or weakening of the influence of educational accomplishments and social background that Bourdieu argues are necessary for entry into legitimate culture. These autodidacts are not entering legitimate culture at all; neither does their lack of cultural capital condemn them to the middle- or lowbrow– theirs is an oppositional culture. Frith (1996) has argued that low culture as much as high culture 'generates' cultural capital and its attendant cultural authority amongst its consumers (see also Fiske, 1992b; Thornton, 1995). Alternative media appear quite indifferent to formal education. They are as interested in education gained through action as in that gained through the written word. I have shown how within new social movements the production of the printed word is often an encumbrance that can get in the way of the 'real job': activism. But education can also come from involvement in the production and organization of the media. Education in the alternative media leads to self-reflexive practice. If the notion of mobilizing information, of information for action, is to be seen as 'action on action' (as Melucci has it), as the development of a reflexive practice that aims to change the 'lifeworld' of its participants, then self-reflexivity within a 'free space' such as an alternative media project may be seen as 'self-action on self-action' (Cox, undated), where all individuals are able to realize their own potential and develop the self-awareness that can arise from understanding one's position within the free space and one's own potential to create and contribute from that position. Experimentation and creativity with alternative possibilities of 'being' and 'doing' will form the heart of such activity; autonomy and the absence of unbalanced power relations can develop 'a reflexive habitus' (Cox, 1997) that can connect the self with the lifeworld: '[t]his grassroots intellectual activity of rethinking and reorganising everyday life links ... "transformation of self and transformation of social structures"' (ibid., incorporating a quote from Hilary Wainwright).

Such possibilities are strongly suggestive of the strategies promoted by Paulo Freire's (1972) critical pedagogy. Freire was concerned with achieving the educational empowerment of the oppressed, the disenfranchised and the marginalized through encouraging dialogue as a form of study, as horizontal communication that privileged empathy, hope, trust and criticism. This dialogue would be grounded in the everyday language and reality of the students and aimed to critique (and ultimately to change) the oppressive social forces that surrounded them without reproducing those oppressive structures in their own social practices. One of the many applications of Freire's approach is that of Ira Shor (1980) who worked with Open Admissions students at the City University of New York in the 1970s to engender an egalitarian form of education that was 'mobilizing, the pedagogical means to advance political consciousness' (1980: 95). The characteristics of many of the alternative media practices I have examined in this book – horizontal and dialogic forms of communication, an emphasis on self-reflexivity, the employment of everyday language, critical approaches to the media and its objects, mobilizing power and the significance of prefigurative politics – all suggest educational and transformational possibilities that might constitute an autonomous project of critical pedagogy.

The ability to express and publish opinions in the alternative media is radically different from the situation in the mass media. Whereas access to the mass media by readers is severely limited, in the main being through letters to the editor (the majority remaining unpublished, thus further limiting access), the alternative media claim a democratic, participatory ethos, where readers are very often able to contribute articles and take part in editorial decision-making, even becoming editors themselves. Such an ethos promotes what Ben Agger (1990: 36) has termed 'intellectual democracy' which, he argues, is essential to halt the decline in discourse that he identifies as a key element in the withering of the dominant public sphere. The alternative media, in offering their pages to activists and readers, enable the members of an alternative public sphere to function as Habermas argues they must if they are to be a public body: 'to confer in an unrestricted fashion – that is, with the guarantee of freedom of assembly and association and the freedom to express and publish their opinions' (Habermas, cited in Eley, 1992: 289).

Access to the alternative media encourages self-publishing, whereby readers may publish their own papers and magazines quite independently from one another (most often as zines), with minimal financial outlay. There is less restraint on form, too. The alternative media in their public sphere not only involve people directly in their production and distribution, but they do so with far less commodification than do the mass media, which have become, in John Durham Peters's words, 'a means for imagining community... just splendid for representation but horrid for participation' (Peters, 1993: 566). Alternative media actively elicit such participation by their very construction, offering it in the place of spectacle; identity instead of mere representation (p. 559). As social practices democratize involvement in media production, such roles are further eroded. The desires and demands of agents are articulated through alternative media by a set of transgressive practices that challenge dominant forms of organization and cultural and political practice, and that establish their own alternative frames of participation, power and creative action. Participants do not simply consume reflexively, but produce reflexively in an attempt to 'change the way in which we construct our selves, our actions and our lifeworlds' (Cox, 1997); 'as more people learn to communicate about communication, they revolutionize the traditional order' (Eder, 1993: 22). Raymond Williams has highlighted both the value of communication in social networks and its role in reflexive learning processes:

> What we call society is not only a network of political and economic arrangements, but also a process of learning and communication. Communication begins in the struggle to learn and describe. (Williams, 1976: 11)

I have argued that the alternative public sphere is an appropriate conceptual foundation from which to understand the production and reception of autonomously developed accounts of experience, critiques, information and knowledge. Here are Nancy Fraser's 'subaltern counter-publics' engaging in 'parallel discursive arenas' in order 'to invent and circulate counterdiscourses to formulate oppositional interpretations of their identities, interests, and needs' (Fraser, 1992: 123).

Within this sphere we might consider alternative media as instances of the 'free spaces' identified by Melucci (1995), who stresses the necessary independence of such spaces from government, the state and other dominant political institutions and practices – particularities they hold in common with a public sphere model – an independence that allows for their maintenance as experimental zones within which alternative means of 'sociation' may be developed. Cox (undated) similarly defines free spaces as 'situations of a relative weakening of determination by the logics of power and economics' and Bookchin considers the affinity group as the 'free space' *par excellence,* 'in which revolutionaries can make themselves, individually, and also as social beings' (Bookchin, 1986: 243). Such theorizations bear upon the characteristics and values we have found in the practices of alternative media; they centre on autonomy, solidarity and the development of reflexivity in the creative processes of democratic media production.

bibliography

Abel, Richard (1997) 'An Alternative Press. Why?', *Publishing Research Quarterly*, 12(4), Winter 1996–97: 78–84.

Achbar, Mark (1994) *Manufacturing Consent: Noam Chomsky and the Media*, Montreal: Black Rose Books.

Agger, Ben (1990) *The Decline of Discourse: Reading, Writing and Resistance in Postmodern Capitalism*, London: Falmer.

Allen, Peter (1985) '*Socialist Worker* – Paper with a Purpose', *Media, Culture and Society*, 7: 205–232.

Alternatives in Print: an International Catalog of Books, Pamphlets, Periodicals and Audiovisual Materials (1980) Compiled by the Task Force on Alternatives in Print, Social Responsibilities Round Table, American Library Association, 6th edn, New York, NY: Neal-Schuman and London: Mansell.

Anon. (1995a) 'Computer Anarchy', *Freedom*, 8 April: 5.

Anon. (1995b) 'Jerking Off in Cyberspace', *Black Cat* 1, September (unpaginated).

Atton, Chris (1995) 'Policing Electronic Information: Threats to Freedom of Expression', *New Library World*, 96(1122): 5–9.

Atton, Chris (1996a) *Alternative Literature: a Practical Guide for Librarians*, Aldershot: Gower.

Atton, Chris (1996b) 'Anarchy on the Internet: Obstacles and Opportunities for Alternative Electronic Publishing', *Anarchist Studies*, 4, October: 115–132.

Atton, Chris (1998) 'No More Dissent', *Index on Censorship*, 27(1), January/February: 15–16.

Atton, Chris (1999a) '*Green Anarchist*: A Case Study in Radical Media', *Anarchist Studies*, 7(1), March, 25–49.

Atton, Chris (1999b) 'A Re-assessment of the Alternative Press', *Media, Culture and Society*, 21: 51–76.

Atton, Chris (2000) 'Alternative Media in Scotland: Problems, Positions and "Product"', *Critical Quarterly*, 42(4): 40–46.

Aubrey, Crispin (1981) 'Beyond the Free Press: Recent Developments in the Radical Press'. In Brian Whitaker, *News Limited: Why You Can't Read All About It* (Minority Press Group Series no. 5), London: Minority Press Group. pp. 167–176.

Barker, Martin (1984) *A Haunt of Fears: the Strange History of the British Horror Comics Campaign*, London: Pluto.

Bellerue, Bob (1995) 'Zines: Independent Publishing in the Age of Widespread Mechanical Reproduction'. Unpublished essay distributed on the Internet. Copy in author's possession.

Benjamin, Walter (1934/1982) 'The Author as Producer'. Edited translation in Francis Frascina and Charles Harrison (eds), *Modern Art and Modernism: a Critical Anthology*, London: Paul Chapman in association with the Open University. pp. 213–216.

Bennett, Andy (1999) 'Subcultures or Neo-tribes? Rethinking the Relationship between Youth, Style and Musical Taste', *Sociology*, 33(3): 599–617.

Bennett, Tony (1982) 'Theories of the Media, Theories of Society'. In Michael Gurevitch, Tony Bennett, James Curran and Janet Woollacott (eds), *Culture, Society and the Media*, London: Methuen. pp. 30–55.

Berens, Camilla (1997) 'What it Means to be a Vendor', *The Big Issue*, 218(3–9 February): 18–19.

Bey, Hakim (1991) *T.A.Z.: the Temporary Autonomous Zone, Ontological Anarchy, Poetic Terrorism*, Brooklyn, NY: Autonomedia.

Bhabha, Homi K. (1990) 'The Third Space'. In J. Rutherford (ed.), *Identity: Community, Culture and Distance*, London: Lawrence & Wishart. pp. 207–221.

Bhabha, Homi K. (1994) *The Location of Culture*, London: Routledge.

Bonnett, Alastair (1991/1996) 'The Situationist Legacy', *Variant*, 9 (Autumn 1991). Reprinted in Stewart Home (ed.), *What Is Situationism? A Reader*, Edinburgh and San Francisco, CA: AK Press. pp. 192–201. Reference is to the latter.

Bookchin, Murray (1986) 'A Note on Affinity Groups'. In Murray Bookchin, *Post-scarcity Anarchism*, 2nd edn, Montreal: Black Rose, pp. 243–244.

Bourdieu, Pierre (1984) *Distinction: a Social Critique of the Judgement of Taste*, translated by Richard Nice, London: Routledge & Kegan Paul.

Bourdieu, Pierre (1993) *The Field of Cultural Production: Essays on Art and Literature*, New York: Columbia University Press.

Bourdieu, Pierre (1997) *Sur la télévision*, Paris: Liber-Raisons d'Agir.

Boyd-Barrett, Oliver (1995) 'Conceptualizing the "Public Sphere"'. In Oliver Boyd-Barrett and Chris Newbold, *Approaches to Media: A Reader*, London: Arnold. pp. 230–234.

Boyle, Deirdre (1997) *Subject to Change: Guerrilla Television Revisited*, New York and Oxford: Oxford University Press.

Burgelman, Jean-Claude (1994) 'Assessing Information Technologies in the Information Society'. In Slavko Splichal, Andrew Calabrese and Colin Sparks (eds), *Information Society and Civil Society: Contemporary Perspectives on the Changing World Order*, West Lafayette, IN: Purdue University Press. pp. 185–207.

Burt, Stephen (1999) 'Amateurs', *Transition*, 77: 148–171.

Bybee, Carl R. (1982) 'Mobilizing Information and Reader Involvement', *Journalism Quarterly*, 59(3), Autumn: 399–405, 413.

Campbell, K.K. (no date) 'Anarchy in More than the UK: Spunk Keeps Anarchist Torch Lit on Net'. Available from Spunk Library at http://www.spunk.org/library/comms/sp000725.txt.

Carey, Jim (1998) 'Fresh Flavour in the Media Soup: the Story of *SQUALL* Magazine'. In George McKay (ed.), *DiY Culture: Party and Protest in Nineties Britain*, London: Verso. pp. 58–78.

Carusi, Annamaria (1991) 'Post, Post and Post. Or, Where is South African Literature in All This?' In Ian Adam and Helen Tiffin (eds), *Past the Last Post: Theorizing Post-colonialism and Post-modernism*, New York and London: Harvester Wheatsheaf. pp. 95–108.

Castells, Manuel (1997) *The Information Age: Economy, Society and Culture. Volume II: The Power of Identity*, Oxford: Blackwell.

Chan, Andy (1995) 'Anarchists, Violence and Social Change: Perspectives from Today's Grassroots', *Anarchist Studies*, 3(1), Spring: 45–68.

Chesshyre, Robert (1987) *The Return of a Native Reporter*, London: Viking.

Chomsky, Noam (1994) *Keeping the Rabble in Line: Interviews with David Barsamian*, Edinburgh: AK Press.

Class War Federation (1991) *This is Class War: an Introduction to the Class War Federation*, revised and updated edn.

Comedia (1984) 'The Alternative Press: the Development of Underdevelopment', *Media, Culture and Society*, 6: 95–102.

Cox, Laurence (1997) 'Reflexivity, Social Transformation and Counter Culture'. In Colin Barker and Mike Tyldesley (eds), *Third International Conference on Alternative Futures and Popular Protest: a Selection of Papers from the Conference, 24–26 March 1997*, Vol. I, Manchester: Manchester Metropolitan University, Faculty of Humanities and Social Science, Department of Sociology and Interdisciplinary Studies, unpaginated.

Cox, Laurence (undated) 'Towards a Sociology of Counter Cultures?' Unpublished manuscript in author's possession.

Curran, James and Seaton, Jean (1997) *Power without Responsibility: the Press and Broadcasting in Britain*, 5th edn, London: Routledge.

Curtis, Liz (1984) *Ireland: the Propaganda War, the Media and the 'Battle for Hearts and Minds'*, London: Pluto Press.

Dahlgren, Peter (1997) 'Cultural Studies as a Research Perspective: Themes and Tensions'. In John Corner, Philip Schlesinger and Roger Silverstone (eds), *International Media Research: a Critical Survey*, London: Routledge. pp. 48–64.

Darnton, Robert (1990) 'What is the History of Books?' In *The Kiss of Lamourette: Reflections in Cultural History*, London: Faber & Faber. pp. 107–135.

de Certeau, Michel (1984) *The Practice of Everyday Life*, Berkeley, CA: University of California Press.

Dery, Mark (1993) *Culture Jamming: Hacking, Slashing and Sniping in the Empire of Signs*, Westfield, NJ: Open Magazine Pamphlet Series.

Dickinson, Robert (1997) *Imprinting the Sticks: the Alternative Press outside London*, Aldershot: Arena.

D.I.Y. Politics (1996) Supplement to *New Statesman and Society*, 1 March.

Dodge, Chris (1998) 'Taking Libraries to the Street: Infoshops and Alternative Reading Rooms', *American Libraries*, May: 62–64.

Dodge, Chris (1999) 'Words on the Street: Homeless People's Newspapers', *American Libraries*, August: 60–62.

Dowmunt, Tony (1993) *Channels of Resistance: Global Television and Local Empowerment*, London: British Film Institute, in association with Channel Four.

Downing, John (1984) *Radical Media: the Political Experience of Alternative Communication*, Boston, MA: South End Press.

Downing, John (1988) 'The Alternative Public Realm: the Organization of the 1980s Antinuclear Press in West Germany and Britain', *Media, Culture and Society*, 10: 163–181.

Downing, John (1995) 'Alternative Media and the Boston Tea Party'. In John Downing, Ali Mohammadi and Annabelle Sreberny-Mohammadi (eds), *Questioning the Media: a Critical Introduction*, Thousands Oaks, CA: Sage. pp. 238–252.

Downing, John (2001) *Radical Media: Rebellious Communication and Social Movements*, Thousand Oaks, CA: Sage.

Duncombe, Stephen (1996) 'Notes from Underground: Zines and the Politics of Underground Culture'. In Sanford Berman and James P. Danky (eds), *Alternative Library Literature: 1994–1995*, Jefferson, NC: McFarland. pp. 312–319.

Duncombe, Stephen (1997) *Notes from Underground: Zines and the Politics of Alternative Culture*, London: Verso.

Dyer, Sarah (no date) 'How to Order Zines: a Guide to Zine Etiquette'. Available at http://www.houseoffun.com/action/zines/ordering.html.

Eder, Klaus (1993) *The New Politics of Class: Social Movements and Cultural Dynamics in Advanced Societies*, London: Sage.

Eley, Geoff (1992) 'Nations, Publics and Political Cultures: Placing Habermas in the Nineteenth Century'. In Craig Calhoun (ed.), *Habermas and the Public Sphere*, Cambridge, MA and London: MIT Press. pp. 289–339.

Enzensberger, Hans Magnus (1976) 'Constituents of a Theory of the Media'. In *Raids and Reconstructions: Essays on Politics, Crime and Culture*, London: Pluto Press. pp. 20–53.

Eyerman, Ron (1994) *Between Culture and Politics: Intellectuals in Modern Society*, Cambridge: Polity Press.

Eyerman, Ron and Jamison, Andrew (1991) *Social Movements: a Cognitive Approach*, Cambridge: Polity Press.

Eyerman, Ron and Jamison, Andrew (1995) 'Social Movements and Cultural Transformation: Popular Music in the 1960s', *Media, Culture and Society*, 17: 449–468.

Fairclough, Norman (1995) *Media Discourse*, London: Edward Arnold.

Farseth, Erik (1998) 'Behind the Zines', *Paper Scissors Clocks*, 2: 33–55, 59–73.

Featherstone, Mike (1991) *Consumer Culture and Postmodernism*, London: Sage.

Fiske, John (1989/1991) *Understanding Popular Culture*, London: Routledge. Originally published by Unwin Hyman.

Fiske, John (1992a) 'British Cultural Studies and Television'. In Robert C. Allen (ed.), *Channels of Discourse, Reassembled*, 2nd edn, London: Routledge. pp. 284–326.

Fiske (1992b) 'The Cultural Economy of Fandom'. In Lisa A. Lewis (ed.), *The Adoring Audience: Fan Culture and Popular Media*, London: Routledge. pp. 30–49.

Fiske, John (1992c) 'Cultural Studies and the Culture of Everyday Life'. In Lawrence Grossberg, Cary Nelson and Paula A. Treichler (eds), *Cultural Studies*, New York and London: Routledge. pp. 154–173.

Fiske, John (1992d) 'Popularity and the Politics of Information'. In Peter Dahlgren and Colin Sparks (eds), *Journalism and Popular Culture*, London: Sage. pp. 45–63.

Foucault, Michel (1980) *Power/Knowledge: Selected Interviews and Other Writings, 1972–1977*, edited by Colin Gordon, Brighton: Harvester Press.

Fountain, Nigel (1988) *Underground: the London Alternative Press, 1966–74*, London: Comedia/Routledge.

Fox, Elizabeth (1997) 'Media and Culture in Latin America'. In John Corner, Philip Schlesinger and Roger Silverstone (eds), *International Media Research: a Critical Survey*, London: Routledge. pp. 184–205.

Franklin, Bob and Murphy, David (1991) *What News? The Market, Politics and the Local Press*, London: Routledge.

Fraser, Nancy (1992) 'Rethinking the Public Sphere – A Contribution to the Critique of Actually Existing Democracy'. In Craig Calhoun (ed.), *Habermas and the Public Sphere*, Cambridge, MA and London: MIT Press. pp. 109–142.

Freeman, Jo (1972–73) 'The Tyranny of Structurelessness', *Berkeley Journal of Sociology*, 17: 151–164.

Freire, Paulo (1972) *Pedagogy of the Oppressed*, London: Penguin.

Frith, Simon (1996) *Performing Rites: Evaluating Popular Music*, Oxford: Oxford University Press.

Gauntlett, David (1996) *Video Critical: Children, the Environment and Media Power*, Luton: John Libbey Media.

Gitlin, Todd (1980) *The Whole World is Watching: Mass Media in the Making and Unmaking of the New Left*, Berkeley, CA and London: University of California Press.

Glasgow University Media Group (1976) *Bad News*, London: Routledge & Kegan Paul.

Glasgow University Media Group (1980) *More Bad News*, London: Routledge & Kegan Paul.

Glasgow University Media Group (1982) *Really Bad News*, London: Writers and Readers.

Glasgow University Media Group (1985) *War and Peace News*, Milton Keynes: Open University Press.

Glasser, Theodore L. (1974) 'Semantics of an Alternative: the Language of the Underground Press', *ETC: A Review of General Semantics*, 31: 201–204.

Golding, Peter (1999) 'The Political and the Popular: Getting the Measure of Tabloidisation'. In *Proceedings of the AMCCS Conference, Sheffield, UK, 1998*, edited by Tessa Perkins, Sheffield: Association of Media, Communication and Cultural Studies. pp. 2–18.

Gott, Richard (1995) 'The Hit and Run Left', *Red Pepper*, August: 15–18.

Green, Malcolm (1999) *Brus Muehl Nitsch Schwarzkogler: Writings of the Vienna Actionists* (Atlas Arkhive: Documents of the Avant-garde No. 7), London: Atlas.

Hafner, Katie and Markoff, John (1991) *Cyberpunk: Outlaws and Hackers on the Computer Frontier*, London: Fourth Estate.

Hall, Stuart (1990) 'Cultural Identity and Diaspora'. In J. Rutherford (ed.), *Identity: Community, Culture and Distance*, London: Lawrence & Wishart. pp. 222–237.

Hall, Stuart, Critcher, Chas, Jefferson, Tony, Clarke, John and Roberts, Brian (1978) *Policing the Crisis: Mugging, the State, and Law and Order*, London: Methuen.

Halleck, Dee Dee (1984) 'Paper Tiger Television: Smashing the Myths of the Information Industry Every Week on Public Access Cable', *Media, Culture and Society*, 6: 313–318.

Hamilton, James (2000a) 'The Inter-not?', *M/C Reviews*, 12 April. <http://www. uq.edu. au/mc/reviews/features/politics/internot.html> (accessed 1 August 2000).

Hamilton, James (2000b) 'Alternative Media: Conceptual Difficulties, Critical Possibilities', *Journal of Communication Inquiry*, 24(4) (October): 357–378.

Hamilton, James (2001a) 'An Alternative Practice of Alternative Media'. Unpublished manuscript in author's possession.

Hamilton, James (2001b) 'Institutionalizing Dissent? The Dilemma of Legalizing US Low-power FM Radio as Alternative Media'. Unpublished manuscript in author's possession.

Harcup, Tony (1994) *A Northern Star: 'Leeds Other Paper' and the Alternative Press 1974–1994*, London and Pontefract: Campaign for Press and Broadcasting Freedom.

Harcup, Tony (1998) 'There Is No Alternative: the Demise of the Alternative Local Newspaper'. In Bob Franklin and David Murphy (eds), *Making the Local News: Local Journalism in Context*, London: Routledge. pp. 105–116.

Harding, Thomas (1997) *The Video Activist Handbook*, London: Pluto Press.

Haywood, Trevor (1995) *Info-rich – Info-poor: Access and Exchange in the Global Information Society*, London: Bowker-Saur.

Hebdige, Dick (1979) *Subculture: the Meaning of Style*, London: Routledge.

Held, John (1991) *Mail Art: an Annotated Bibliography*, Metuchen, NJ: Scarecrow Press.

Henderson, S.P.A. and Henderson, A.J.W. (1996) *Directory of British Associations & Associations in Ireland*, 13th edn, Beckenham: CBD Research.

Herman, Edward S. and Chomsky, Noam (1994) *Manufacturing Consent: the Political Economy of the Mass Media*, London: Vintage.

Hill, Christopher (1975) *The World Turned Upside Down: Radical Ideas in the English Revolution*, Harmondsworth: Penguin.

Home, Stewart (1995) *Neoism, Plagiarism and Praxis*, Edinburgh: AK Press.

Hopkin, Deian (1978) 'The Socialist Press in Britain, 1890–1910'. In George Boyce, James Curran and Pauline Wingate (eds), *Newspaper History from the Seventeenth Century to the Present Day*, London: Constable. pp. 294–306.

Hopkinson, Amanda and Tacchi, Jo (2000) 'Radiocracy: Radio, Democracy and Development'. Themed issue of *International Journal of Cultural Studies*, 3(2), August.

Howley, Kevin (2000) 'Radiocracy Rulz! Microradio as Electronic Activism', *International Journal of Cultural Studies*, 3(2), August: 256–267.

Jakubowicz, Karol (1991) 'Musical Chairs? The Three Public Spheres in Poland'. In Peter Dahlgren and Colin Sparks (eds), *Communication and Citizenship: Journalism and the Public Sphere in the New Media Age*, London: Routledge. pp. 155–175.

Jankowski, Nick, Prehn, Ole and Stappers, James (1992) *The People's Voice: Local Radio and Television in Europe*, London: John Libbey.

Jary, David, Horne, John and Bucke, Tom (1991) 'Football "Fanzines" and Football Culture: a Case of Successful "Cultural Contestation"', *Sociological Review*, 39(3): 581–597.

Jenkins, Henry (1992) '"Strangers No More, We Sing": Filking and the Social Construction of the Science Fiction Fan Community'. In Lisa A. Lewis (ed.), *The Adoring Audience: Fan Culture and Popular Media*, London: Routledge. pp. 208–236.

Juhasz, Alexandra (1995) *AIDS TV: Identity, Community and Alternative Video*, London: Duke University Press.

Kelly, Phil (1989) 'Counter Culture and the Small Journal'. In Norman Buchan and Tricia Sumner (eds), *Glasnost in Britain? Against Censorship and in Defence of the Word*, London: Macmillan. pp. 70–78.

Kettering, Terri A. (1982) 'The Alternative Press and the Mass Media: Two Case Studies'. In James P. Danky and Elliott Shore (eds), *Alternative Materials in Libraries*, Metuchen, New Jersey: Scarecrow Press. pp. 6–11.

Khiabany, Gholam (2000) '*Red Pepper*: a New Model for the Alternative Press?', *Media, Culture and Society*, 22: 447–463.

Kollock, Peter (1999) 'The Economies of Online Cooperation: Gifts and Public Goods in Cyberspace'. In Marc A. Smith and Peter Kollock (eds), *Communities in Cyberspace*, London: Routledge. pp. 220–239.

Kriha, Tomas F.J. (1994) *Cyberanarchism*. Text available from the Spunk Library at http://www.spunk.org/library/copyrite/comms/sp000877.txt.

Landry, Charles, Morley, Dave, Southwood, Russell, and Wright, Patrick (1985) *What a Way to Run a Railroad: an Analysis of Radical Failure*, London: Comedia.

Lefebvre, Henri (1947/1991) *Critique of Everyday Life. Volume I: Introduction*, translated by John Moore, London: Verso.

Lemert, James B. and Ashman, Marguerite Gemson (1983) 'Extent of Mobilizing Information in Opinion and News Magazines', *Journalism Quarterly*, 60(4), Winter: 657–662.

Lewis, Roger (1972) *Outlaws of America: the Underground Press and its Context*, Harmondsworth: Penguin.

Lievrouw, Leah A. (1994) 'Information Resources and Democracy: Understanding the Paradox', *Journal of the American Society for Information Science*, 45(6): 350–357.

Locke, Christopher (no date) *New Directions in Personal Publishing: from Point of View to Online Presence...* Available at http://www.rageboy.com/webwriting.html

Lucas, Martin and Wallner, Martha (1993) 'Resistance by Satellite: the Gulf Crisis Project and the Deep Dish Satellite TV Network'. In Tony Dowmunt (ed.), *Channels of*

Resistance: Global Television and Local Empowerment, London: British Film Institute, in association with Channel Four. pp. 176–194.

McGuigan, Jim (1992) *Cultural Populism*, London: Routledge.

McKay, George (1996) *Senseless Acts of Beauty: Cultures of Resistance since the Sixties*, London: Verso.

McKay, George (ed.) (1998) *DiY Culture: Party and Protest in Nineties Britain*, London: Verso.

McQuail, Denis (1987) *Mass Communication Theory: an Introduction*, 2nd edn, London: Sage.

McQuail, Denis (1994) *Mass Communication Theory: an Introduction*, 3rd edn, London: Sage.

McRobbie, Angela (1992) 'Post-Marxism and Cultural Studies: a Post-Script'. In Lawrence Grossberg, Cary Nelson, and Paula A. Treichler (eds), *Cultural Studies*, New York and London: Routledge. pp. 719–730.

McRobbie, Angela (1993/1994) 'Shut Up and Dance: Youth Culture and Changing Modes of Femininity', *Cultural Studies*, 7(3), 1993: 406–426. Reprinted in *Postmodernism and Popular Culture*, London: Routledge, 1994. pp. 155–176.

Malyon, Tim (1995) 'Might not Main', *New Statesman and Society*, 24 March: 24–26.

Malyon, Tim (1998) 'Tossed in the Fire and They Never Got Burned: the Exodus Collective'. In George McKay (ed.), *DiY Culture: Party and Protest in Nineties Britain*, London: Verso. pp. 187–207.

Marliere, Philippe (1998) 'The Rules of the Journalistic Field: Pierre Bourdieu's Contribution to the Sociology of the Media', *European Journal of Communication*, 13(2): 219–234.

Marr, John (1999) 'Zines are Dead', *Bad Subjects*, 46(December). http://eserver. org/bs/46/marr.html.

Mele, Christopher (1999) 'Cyberspace and Disadvantaged Communities: the Internet as a Tool for Collective Action'. In Marc A. Smith and Peter Kollock (eds), *Communities in Cyberspace*, London: Routledge. pp. 290–310.

Melucci, Alberto (1995) 'The New Social Movements Revisited: Reflections on a Sociological Misunderstanding'. In Louis Maheu (ed.), *Social Movements and Social Classes: the Future of Collective Action*, London: Sage. pp. 107–119.

Melucci, Alberto (1996) *Challenging Codes: Collective Action in the Information Age*, Cambridge: Cambridge University Press.

Miller, Daniel and Slater, Don (2000) *The Internet: an Ethnographic Approach*, New York: New York University Press.

Miller, David (1994) *Don't Mention the War: Northern Ireland, Propaganda and the Media*, London: Pluto Press.

Minority Press Group (1980a) *Here Is the Other News: Challenges to the Local Commercial Press* (Minority Press Group Series No. 1), London: Minority Press Group.

Minority Press Group (1980b) *Where Is the Other News: the Newstrade and the Radical Press* (Minority Press Group Series No. 2), London: Minority Press Group.

Molland, Noel (1998) 'The Gandalf Trial', *Arkangel*, 19, unpaginated.

Moritz, Marguerite J. (1992) 'How US News Media Represent Sexual Minorities'. In Peter Dahlgren and Colin Sparks (eds), *Journalism and Popular Culture*, London: Sage. pp. 154–170.

Munson, Chuck (1997) 'Your Friendly Neighborhood Infoshop'. Unpublished second draft of an article for the zine *MAXIMUMROCKNROLL*, forwarded to the author by Chris Dodge of the *Utne Reader*.

Negativland (1995) *Fair Use: the Story of the Letter U and the Numeral 2*, Concord, CA: Seeland.

Negt, Oskar and Kluge, Alexander (1972/1983) 'The Proletarian Public Sphere', translated from the German by Stuart Hood. In Armand Mattelart and Seth Siegelaub (eds), *Communication and Class Struggle, Vol. 2: Liberation, Socialism*, New York: International General. pp. 92–94.

Nelson, Elizabeth (1989) *The British Counter-culture, 1966–73: a Study of the Underground Press*, London: Macmillan.

New Observations (1994) 'Copy Culture'. Themed issue of *New Observations*, 101, May/June.

Nigg, Heinz and Wade, Graham (1980) *Community Media: Community Communication in the UK, Video, Local TV, Film, and Photography*, Zurich: Regenbogen.

Noyce, John L. (1979) *The Directory of British Alternative Periodicals: 1965–1974*, Hassocks: Harvester Press.

O'Sullivan, Tim (1994) 'Alternative Media'. In Tim O'Sullivan, John Hartley, Danny Saunders, Martin Montgomery and Martin Fiske, *Key Concepts in Communication and Cultural Studies*, 2nd edn, London: Routledge. p. 10.

O'Sullivan, Tim, Dutton, Brian and Rayner, Philip (1994) *Studying the Media: an Introduction*, London: Arnold.

Panos (1995) *The Internet and the South: Superhighway or Dirt-track?* (Panos Media Briefing No. 16, October 1995), London: Panos.

Pawson, Mark and Skeet, Jason (1995) 'Narrow Casting in Fibre Space', *Transgressions: a Journal of Urban Exploration*, 1, Summer: 77–78.

Peters, John Durham (1993) 'Distrust of Representation: Habermas on the Public Sphere', *Media, Culture and Society*, 15: 541–571.

Peters, Mike (1996) 'Cyberdrivel', *Here and Now*, 16/17: 24–27.

Quail, John (1978) *The Slow Burning Fuse: the Lost History of the British Anarchists*, London: Paladin.

The Radical Bookseller Directory (1992) edited by Einde O'Callaghan, London: The Radical Bookseller.

Radway, Janice (1984/1991) *Reading the Romance: Women, Patriarchy, and Popular Literature*, Chapel Hill, NC and London: University of North Carolina Press.

Radway, Janice (1999) 'On the Importance of Readers and Reading: Points of Origin in Book History'. Paper delivered at the Society for the History of Authorship, Reading and Publishing's Annual Conference, Madison, Wisconsin, 15–18 July.

Rau, Michelle (1994) 'Towards a History of Fanzine Publishing: from APA to Zines', *Alternative Press Review*, Spring/Summer: 10–13.

Rheingold, Howard (1994) *The Virtual Community: Finding Connection in a Computerized World*, London: Secker & Warburg.

Rimmer, Steve (1995) *Planet Internet*, New York: Windcrest/McGraw-Hill.

Rips, Geoffrey (1981) *The Campaign against the Underground Press (PEN American Center Report)*, San Francisco: City Lights Books.

Robins, Kevin (1995) 'Cyberspace and the World We Live In'. In Mike Featherstone and Roger Burrows (eds), *Cyberspace/Cyberbodies/Cyberpunk: Cultures of Technological Embodiment*, London: Sage. pp. 135–155.

Rose, Gillian (1994) 'The Cultural Politics of Place: Local Representation and Oppositional Discourse in Two Films', *Transactions of the Institute of British Geographers*, 19(1): 46–60.

Royal Commission on the Press (1977) *Periodicals and the Alternative Press*, London: HMSO.

Rushkoff, Douglas (1994) *Cyberia: Life in the Trenches of Hyperspace*, London: Harper/Collins.

Rutherford, Paul (1992) *Fanzine Culture*, Glasgow: Flower Pot Press.

Said, Edward W. (1982/1985) 'Opponents, Audiences, Constituencies and Community', *Critical Inquiry*, 9, September 1982. Reprinted in Hal Foster (ed.), *Postmodern Culture*, London: Pluto, 1985. pp. 135–159.

Said, Edward (1994) *Representations of the Intellectual: the 1993 Reith Lectures*, London: Vintage.

Savage, Jon (1991) *England's Dreaming: Sex Pistols and Punk Rock*, London: Faber & Faber.

Schuman, Patricia Glass (1982) 'Libraries and Alternatives'. In James P. Danky and Elliott Shore (eds), *Alternative Materials in Libraries*, Metuchen, NJ: Scarecrow Press. pp. 1–5.

Scott, Alan (1990) *Ideology and the New Social Movements*, London: Unwin Hyman.

Scott, Keeley (1999) 'Spotlight: TV-12', *Airflash*, July: 12–13.

Searle, Denise (1997) *Gathering Force: DIY Culture, Radical Action for Those Tired of Waiting*, London: The Big Issue Writers.

Shaw, Phil (1989) *Whose Game Is It Anyway? The Book of the Football Fanzines*, Hemel Hempstead: Argus.

Shor, Ira (1980) *Critical Teaching and Everyday Life*, Montreal and New York: Black Rose.

Shore, Albert (1997) 'Managing the Unemployed: Recent Patterns of Resistance to the Government Manipulation of the Jobless', *The Raven*, 9(4), Autumn: 314–317.

Silverstone, Roger (1999) *Why Study the Media?* London: Sage.

Smith, Matthew J. (1999) 'Strands in the Web: Community-Building Strategies in Online Fanzines', *Journal of Popular Culture*, 33(2), Fall: 87–99.

Sparks, Colin (1985) 'The Working-class Press: Radical and Revolutionary Alternatives', *Media, Culture and Society*, 7: 133–146.

Spivak, Gayatri Chakravorty (1988) 'Can the Subaltern Speak?' In Cary Nelson and Lawrence Grossberg (eds), *Marxism and the Interpretation of Culture*, Basingstoke: Macmillan. pp. 271–313.

Spurr, David (1993) *The Rhetoric of Empire: Colonial Discourse in Journalism, Travel Writing and Imperial Administration*, Durham, NC and London: Duke University Press.

Stanfield, Douglas W. and Lemert, James B. (1987) 'Alternative Newspapers and Mobilizing Information', *Journalism Quarterly*, 64(2 and 3), Summer–Autumn: 604–607.

'Sunfrog' (1995) 'A Treatise on Electronic Anarchy and the Net: Arguments for the Elimination of the Information Age', *Fifth Estate*, 29(2) (345), Winter: 3–4, 6, 21.

Swithinbank, Tessa (1996) 'World Exclusive!', *New Internationalist*, February: 28–30.

Tacchi, Jo (2000) 'The Need for Radio Theory in the Digital Age', *International Journal of Cultural Studies*, 3(2), August: 289–298.

Thompson, E.P. (1963/1991) *The Making of the English Working Class*, Harmondsworth: Penguin.

Thompson, John B. (1995) *The Media and Modernity: a Social Theory of the Media*, Cambridge: Polity Press.

Thornton, Sarah (1995) *Club Cultures: Music, Media and Subcultural Capital*, Cambridge: Polity Press.

Tomaselli, Keyan and Louw, P. Eric (1991) *The Alternative Press in South Africa*, Bellville: Anthropos; London: James Currey.

Traber, Michael (1985) *Alternative Journalism, Alternative Media* (Communication Resource, no. 7, October), London: World Association for Christian Communication.

Triggs, Teal (1995) 'Alphabet Soup: Reading British Fanzines', *Visible Language*, 29(1): 72–87.

Turner, Scott M.X. (1995) 'Maximising Rock and Roll: an Interview with Tim Yohannon (18 August 1994)'. In Ron Sakolsky and Fred Wei-han Ho (eds), *Sounding Off! Music as Subversion/Resistance/Revolution*, Brooklyn, NY: Autonomedia. pp. 181–194.

van Dijk, Teun A. (1991) 'The Interdisciplinary Study of News as Discourse'. In Klaus Bruhn Jensen and Nicholas W. Jankowski (eds), *A Handbook of Qualitative Methodologies for Mass Communication Research*, London: Routledge. pp. 108–120.

Wakefield, Stacy and 'Grrrt' [*sic*] (1995) *Not for Rent: Conversations with Creative Activists in the U.K.*, Amsterdam: Evil Twin.

Wehling, Jason (1995) ' "Netwars" and Activists [*sic*] Power on the Internet', *Scottish Anarchist*, 2: 9–12, 15.

Weigert, Andrew J. (1981) *Sociology of Everyday Life*, New York and London: Longman.

Wellman, Barry and Gulia, Milena (1999) 'Virtual Communities as Communities: Net Surfers Don't Ride Alone'. In Marc A. Smith and Peter Kollock (eds), *Communities in Cyberspace*, London: Routledge. pp. 167–194.

Welsh, Ian and McLeish, Phil (1996) 'The European Road to Nowhere: Anarchism and Direct Action against the UK Roads Programme', *Anarchist Studies*, 4(1), March: 27–44.

Whitaker, Brian (1981) *News Limited: Why You Can't Read All About It* (Minority Press Group Series no. 5), London: Minority Press Group.

Williams, Raymond (1963) *Culture and Society: 1780–1950*, Harmondsworth: Penguin.

Williams, Raymond (1970) 'Radical and/or Respectable'. In Richard Boston (ed.), *The Press We Deserve*, London: Routledge & Kegan Paul. pp. 14–26.

Williams, Raymond (1976) *Communications*, 3rd edn, Harmondsworth: Penguin.

Williams, Raymond (1980) 'Means of Communication as Means of Production'. In *Problems in Materialism and Culture: Selected Essays*, London: Verso. pp. 50–63.

Williams, Raymond (1983) *Towards 2000*, London: Chatto & Windus.

Wilson, Tony (1999) 'Conceptualising Cyberspace'. In *Proceedings of the AMCCS Conference, Sheffield, UK, 1998*, edited by Tessa Perkins, Sheffield: Association of Media, Communication and Cultural Studies. pp. 133–141.

Woodworth, Fred (1995) 'How Businesses and Institutions Attempt to Control the Small Press: Part II', *The Match!*, 90, Summer 1995: 46–55. Reprinted in: Sanford Berman and James P. Danky (eds), *Alternative Library Literature: 1994–1995*, Jefferson, NC: McFarland, 1996. pp. 174–183.

Workers' Life (1928/1983) *The Worker Correspondent*. In Armand Mattelart and Seth Siegelaub (eds), *Communication and Class Struggle, Vol. 2: Liberation, Socialism*, New York: International General. pp. 153–157.

Wright, Joanne (1991) *Terrorist Propaganda: the Red Army Faction and the Provisional IRA, 1968–86*, London: Macmillan.

Yorke, Chris (2000) 'Zines are Dead: the Six Deadly Sins that Killed Zinery', *Broken Pencil*, 12, Spring: 18–19.

Zobel, Cheryl (1999) 'Zines in Public Libraries', *Counterpoise*, 3(2), April: 5–10.

index